Purely for Pleasure

SELINA, *Countess of Huntingdon*

Purely for Pleasure

MARGARET LANE

"As for myself, *I love no books but such as
are pleasant & easy, & which tickle me, or
such as comfort & counsel me to
direct my life & death.*"

—MONTAIGNE

New York / ALFRED A. KNOPF

1 9 6 7

THIS IS A BORZOI BOOK
PUBLISHED BY ALFRED A. KNOPF, INC.

First American Edition

© Copyright 1966, 1967 by Margaret Lane

All rights reserved under International and Pan-American Copyright Conventions. Distributed by Random House, Inc. Published in Great Britain by Hamish Hamilton Ltd.

Library of Congress Catalog Card Number: 67–25615

MANUFACTURED IN THE UNITED STATES OF AMERICA

The author wishes to thank the Editors of the following who first published some of the essays in this book: *The Cornhill*, Everyman's Library, John Lehmann, *The Listener*, *New Statesman*, Orion, Panther Books, © 1962, 1963 *Punch, The Sunday Times, The Times Literary Supplement, Transactions of the Jane Austen Society, Wine and Food Quarterly.*

CONTENTS

Contents

INTRODUCTION

THERE IS NO UNIFYING THEME to be found in this handful of essays. They are personal excursions indulged in purely for pleasure—perambulations, so to speak, in chosen company.

The writing of biography is beset with pains and difficulties, but there are also compensating pleasures: one of these is following from time to time those little culs-de-sac of interest that the biographer, keeping his eye on roads that lead to more useful destinations, must regretfully leave behind. No great figure of literature, for instance, has been more magnificently served by his biographers than Dr. Johnson; yet there are details of his life—his domestic arrangements, his eating pleasures, his tender relations with women—which have seemed to me worth considering on their own, as though in extended footnotes. In the same way there are details of Dickens's life, unimportant in themselves, which catch the already engaged imagination, and in the well-worked field of Brontë biography there still appears to be room for a closer look at the problems of that somewhat intractable character Mr. Nicholls.

The aspects that drew me on have often been merely trivial or domestic, the crumbs of evidence of which Browning—'What porridge had John Keats?'—was grandly scornful. The porridge, I suppose, has little to do with the poetry, and yet I would not despise information about a poet's breakfast if I were offered it. Nothing, not even poetry, exists in a vacuum.

The account of Flora Thompson, however, was begun more ambitiously. My first reading of her trilogy, nowadays published in one volume as *Lark Rise to Candleford*, made me eager to have the phenomenon explained—how a cottage child, born to a life of poverty in a bleak Oxfordshire hamlet in the eighteen seventies, could grow into a woman who in old age would produce a prose masterpiece of great strength and beauty, preserving for us, like a pyramid of flowers under glass in a cottage parlour, the humble life of the countryside in a period, not, indeed, remote from us in time, but so far removed by social change as to be almost forgotten. Almost nothing was known of her, and this obscure life, as it was gradually uncovered, appeared to me as a story worth the telling. With the generous help of her daughter, the late Miss Winifred Thompson, who was then living in retirement in Bath, I set to work.

But alas, there are certain conditions essential to biography, and one of these is that people shall not peremptorily destroy letters. The only important correspondence of Flora Thompson's life had fallen into indifferent hands and had been destroyed. She had had only one intellectual friendship of any value, with the Scottish physician and poet Ronald Campbell Macfie. They met only rarely but they corresponded for more than twenty years, and he had kept her letters. These after his death, I discovered, had been destroyed without loss of time by his literary executor. So my account of Flora Thompson is much slighter and less complete than I could have wished. Its best excuse is that there is not likely to be another. That particular road is closed; it leads no further.

At the motive behind this particular act of destruction

Introduction

one can only guess. W. H. Hudson, an even more solitary and reclusive writer than Flora Thompson, erased the evidences of his life with his own hands, determined to make it impossible for anyone after his death to articulate the bones. In his case the motive is one with which I have a certain sympathy—if my theory about that motive is correct.

And Selina Countess of Huntingdon, that intimidating figure of the eighteenth-century Revival, is an attractive subject, surely, for biography? I thought so once, and others from time to time have thought the same, but here I encountered an impediment worse even than the loss of letters or deliberate suppression. No biography of any value is possible without a genuine sympathy between writer and subject. Interest is not enough, nor amusement, nor psychological curiosity, nor even a strong feeling for a particular period. A good rule for biographers would be, perhaps, 'If you can't feel fond of your subject, let it alone.' And the further I went in this last instance the less was I able to feel fond of Lady Huntingdon. I contented myself in the end with accompanying her on her Calvinistic progress only so far as I might with propriety and pleasure.

All of these essays, even one fondly recalling an absurd specimen of juvenile science fiction, even an attempt to appease the prickly shade of Beatrix Potter, are concerned, with one exception, with the pleasures of literature. "*Amitié Amoureuse*," I fear, is not—in spite of its glances at Dickens and Mrs. Gaskell. I include it with some diffidence only because I have often been asked for copies and have been unable to supply them. After its first appearance it was privately printed in a limited edition in America and seems to have given pleasure to a number of people. Since I have no other motive I apologize no further.

MARGARET LANE

Purely for Pleasure

Flora Thompson

LORA THOMPSON DIED IN 1947 AT THE AGE OF
seventy, a writer who had produced a minor
classic in the last years of her life, and about
whom very little else is generally known.
Her work is in a genre of its own not altogether easy
to describe, for it falls into no obvious category. Her three
books, *Lark Rise, Over to Candleford*, and *Candleford
Green*, which first appeared singly and are now published
together as a trilogy under the title *Lark Rise to Candleford*, are not really novels, though fiction plays a part in
them here and there. Nor are they autobiography pure
and simple, for the personal element is evasive and oblique. They are better described, perhaps, as social history; though that, again, is a misleading name to give.
They are more intimate, more personal, more alive than
social history is usually allowed to be, for Flora Thompson dwells on the humble details which social historians
either do not know, or else leave out. They are a simple
yet infinitely detailed record of the life of the poor as it
was lived in an obscure Oxfordshire hamlet in the eighteen eighties and nineties, all remembered from a child's
experience, all faithfully set down, all true. It is precious
as a record of something that has perished, though neither
far away nor long ago, as well as for its literary quality,

and for the fact that Flora Thompson herself was a cottage child, born in poverty, who wrote with a touch of genius of the life she knew.

It was never her intention to write the story of her own life, and though much can be gathered from her work about her childhood and youth, the rest is obscure and has never been recorded. In its way it is a moving and remarkable story, and should perhaps be set down before all the circumstances are forgotten. It is a story which happily illustrates the unquenchable vigour of those strange gifts which are sometimes bestowed in the most unlikely places, and which in her case developed without education or encouragement and blossomed into fulfilment in old age. Flora Thompson wrote her long masterpiece in the last ten years of her life, between the ages of sixty and seventy; in itself an extraordinary achievement. But when her history is known it will be seen that the whole of her life was a preparation, instinctive at first but eventually perfectly conscious and directed, to this one end.

She was born Flora Jane Timms on December 5, 1876, eldest child in the large family of a stonemason who had settled as a young man in the hamlet of Juniper Hill, near Brackley, during the early seventies. Her father, Albert Timms, was not a local man. He had come to Juniper from Oxford, where his father had been first a master builder, then a publican, and finally, come down in the world through 'drinking, gambling and utter recklessness,' a builder's labourer. Albert Timms himself was a man of parts, whose failure in life was due to an unhappy temperament. He had served no apprenticeship to his trade (having grown up, perhaps, during the prosperous public-house period, when the future seemed assured), but he was a skilled craftsman for all that, and in his youth had had ambitions of becoming a sculptor. By the time he settled in Juniper, however, in his middle twenties, he was already soured by lack of opportunity, and made no further effort to escape from the rut in which he found himself. He worked for thirty-five years for a builder in Brackley, travelling the three miles backwards and forwards on foot between work and home and occasionally going farther afield on a building contract. In his youth he was proud of his stone-carving, and liked to remember that he had taken part in the restoration of Bath Abbey. Attempts at sculpture, too, Flora remembered: a stone lion, a child's head, a carved spray of lilies of the valley had stood about the cottage at Juniper as ornaments in the early days, but as time went on had grown dusty and disregarded, and found their way at last to the rubbish heap, where perhaps they still lie crumbling among the nettles.

If he had been content with his lot, as the inhabitants of Juniper were constantly warned from the pulpit it was their duty to be, his life would have been respectable and his home happy. But he was not content. He was a misfit, brooding in resentment on the unfairness of life and clinging to the belief that he came of a 'good' family. There seems to be some ground for the legend that his forebears had once belonged to a different world, for in childhood Flora could remember faded daguerreotypes of ladies in crinolines, magnificent in heavy lockets and gold bracelets, which her father cherished as proofs of former splendour, and which certainly spoke of a way of life unimaginably out of reach of the hamlet people. Poor Albert Timms was embittered by the contrast. He scorned his neighbours and comforted himself with drink, and was not liked in the village. His drinking kept him poorer than he need have been, and this, and the growing moroseness of his temper, cast a shadow and spoiled the happiness of his home. He was the only man in the hamlet, beside the publican, who was not a farm labourer, and he earned something more than the standard farming wage of ten shillings a week; but it was not much; and to the end of her life Flora remembered that it had been her mother's dearest dream to have 'thirty shillings a week, paid regular and to be depended upon.'

Her mother, Emma Timms, though she had none of her husband's pretensions, was in her way remarkable. If it was from her father that Flora inherited her uncommon sensibility, she certainly derived qualities no less valuable from her mother—a love of traditional songs and stories, a down-to-earth common sense and dry humour, upheld by a strong old-fashioned sense of duty. She had been a local girl, daughter of a small-holder who followed the trade of 'eggler' round the farms and villages, collecting with a pony and cart and selling his eggs in the nearby market town. Emma Lapper (as she then was) had gone into service at twelve years old, as they all did, and was nursemaid at Fewcott Rectory when she married. She was small, fair, and pretty, and in her years of service had learned standards of speech and manners a little above those of the cottage women. She was a hard worker, a good cook and an excellent contriver, keeping her children clean, well-mannered, and reasonably well clad against what today would seem insuperable odds. She was also a great repository of country songs and stories, and would sit by the fire of an evening with her two eldest children beside her on little stools and the latest baby on her knee, singing old ballads and songs and making up fairy tales, until their father's uncertain hand was heard on the latch, when they would be sent up the wooden stairs out of the way.

In later years Flora Thompson described her childhood as 'somewhat harsh and restricted,' but she bore no
grudge, for the harshness and restriction were a part of
poverty, and were common to them all. Nor, for all her
sensitiveness, did she resent her mother's rough discipline, or develop emotional complications on account of it,
as a more gently nurtured child or one of a later generation might have done. 'Perhaps,' she wrote in *Lark Rise*,
remembering the childish disgraces of herself and her
brother, 'being of mixed birth with a large proportion of
peasant blood in them, they were tougher in fibre than
some. When their bottoms were soundly smacked, as they
often were, their reaction was to make a mental note not to
repeat the offence which had caused the smacking, rather
than to lay up for themselves complexes to spoil their later
lives.' This practical attitude towards experience, and
total absence of affectation, was to be a constant element
in Flora Thompson's nature. She was, indeed, a down-
to-earth country child, made strange only by the unaccountable poetic streak in her nature, which transmuted
every commonplace experience into something precious.

The hamlet, of which she knew every ditch and stone
in childhood, is still after nearly eighty years almost un-
changed; a nondescript cluster of cottages set down in an
open landscape of flat fields, with nothing about it to
attract the eye. Time seems to have added nothing and to
have taken nothing away. The 'end house,' it is true,
where Flora lived, is no longer the double cottage
thatched with straw which it was in her day; only half of
it remains, roofed with slate, and an unsightly lean-to
annex has been added. But it still stands, as she described
it, 'a little apart, and turning its back on its neighbours as
though about to run away into the fields.' All fields have

local names, though they are seldom written down, and
the big field which in Flora's childhood rippled with corn
almost to the cottage door was known as Lark Rise, from
the great number of larks which nested in it, and from the
fact that it was not quite as flat as the other fields. In
making her slight disguises Flora Thompson stayed as
near as possible to the truth. Flora becomes Laura, Edwin
becomes Edmund, and the hamlet itself hides only behind
the name of its biggest field. She allowed herself, here and
there, to use the real names of actual places, and the
enthusiast who takes the trouble to use a large-scale map
can make many identifications; for such minute clues as
that the beaded footstool which Mrs. Herring offered to
Laura's mother, ' "come out of Tusmore House that time
the fire was," ' are to be found unobtrusively tucked away
in the text, and the classical splendours of Tusmore's
façade are as noble as ever they were when Flora knew it.
'In *Lark Rise*,' she wrote in a letter towards the end of her
life, 'every one of the characters lived at Juniper and were
just as described, with only the names altered'; and as
arguments sometimes arise as to the identity of Flora
Thompson's villages and country towns, it may be as well
to give her own identifications, so far as I have been able
to find them, scattered here and there in a few letters. 'The
real name of the hamlet is Juniper and the mother
village is Cottisford. . . . Candleford is Banbury-
Bicester-Buckingham, mostly Buckingham, as that is
where we went on that first Sunday outing.' 'Candleford
Green . . . is not Fringford, and very few of the characters
are Fringford people, though there is a little of Fringford
in it, with far more of a village in Surrey.' 'In *Over to
Candleford* and *Candleford Green* I wrote more freely
than in *Lark Rise*, and do not think I described any house
or place exactly as it actually existed, excepting "Miss

Lane's" post-office forge, and Shelswell Park, where I
used to carry the letters.'

Cottisford (which is Fordlow, the mother village),
where Flora and the hamlet children walked to school, is
much the same as it was, though perhaps it looks more
cheerful. In *Lark Rise* it is described as 'a little, lost,
lonely place,' and we are told that 'it was a standing joke
in the hamlet that a stranger had once asked the way to
Fordlow after he had walked right through it.' The 'little
squat church, without spire or tower,' has not changed; it
is as small as a chapel-of-ease, and has not lost its solid,
whitewashed simplicity. The pew where the Timms children sat (their parents rarely went to church, apart from
successive baptisms and occasional funerals) is beneath
the modest brass wall-tablet which is Cottisford's
1914–18 war memorial, and Edwin Timms's name, alone
beneath the half-dozen other young men from Juniper and
Cottisford, is last on the list. The village itself is still
much less than a village; the fields come up to the churchyard wall, and beyond the rectory, hidden in trees, the
stone-built manor house and the tiny village school at the
cross-roads, there is nothing but a scattered handful of
cottages. The population is less than half what it was in
Flora's childhood, and the school (small enough, and of a
strangely wooden and impermanent appearance) has
fewer children than in her day. Nowadays the children
come and go by bus, but Flora Thompson and her brothers and sisters (there were ten of them altogether, but
four died young) walked the three miles backwards and
forwards from Juniper, from the age of five until they left
school at twelve years old. She is still remembered as a
thin, dark, long-legged child who was never still, a notable skipper, but in no other way remarkable. Indeed, I
have heard that there was much local incredulity when,

more than fifty years later, her books appeared. It stood to reason, people said, they couldn't have been written by Timms the stonemason's girl.

What made her different from the other children who shared her experiences, but who found nothing in them significant or remarkable, was her marvellously deep focus of observation. The annals of the poor are rarely written; they have no archives. Country churchyards are full of the bones of men and women who have lived her life and found nothing to say about it. To Flora Thompson, even in childhood, every circumstance of the life around her was portentous. Memory stored what eye and ear drank in, and she was haunted by a desire to fashion something, though it took her a lifetime to know what that something was. 'To be born in poverty,' she wrote when she was nearly seventy, 'is a terrible handicap to a writer. I often say to myself that it has taken one lifetime for me to prepare to make a start. If human life lasted two hundred years I might hope to accomplish something.'

What she did achieve was in a genre of its own, since it is rare to find a creative mind of her quality at work on the bedrock level. She was able to write the annals of the poor because she was one of them, and because one of those strange accidents of genius which can never be explained had given her the equipment she needed. The other chronicler of village life who most readily comes to mind when one seeks for a comparison is Mary Russell Mitford, but Miss Mitford wrote, as nearly all other writers on country matters have done, from the genteel standpoint. Miss Mitford lived in a cottage, it is true, but with a difference. She surveyed her village scene with love, and succeeded in making her readers love it, too; but to do this she presented it as a delicious nosegay, the roots and earth concealed or conveniently forgotten. Flora Thompson's work is as different as the country scenes of Stanley Spencer are from one of George Morland's charming cottage interiors, or the primrose-laden fields of Birkett Foster. In hers there is no sentimentality. It was the true and the real that stirred her imagination. Her integrity was absolute, as Miss Mitford's was not, and it is this deep emotional truth which gives her work, in spite of its rigorous plainness, the bloom of poetry, so that even a pig-killing has a gruesome beauty.

When the pig was fattened—and the fatter the better—the date of execution had to be decided upon. It had to take place some time during the first two quarters of the moon; for if the pig was killed when the moon was waning the bacon would shrink in cooking, and they wanted it to 'plimp up'. The next thing was to engage the travelling pork-butcher, or pig-sticker, and, as he was a thatcher by day, he always had to kill after dark, the scene being lighted with lanterns and the fire of burning straw which at a later stage of the proceedings was to singe the bristles off the victim.

The killing was a noisy, bloody business, in the course of which the animal was hoisted to a rough bench that it might bleed thoroughly and so preserve the quality of the meat. The job was often bungled, the pig sometimes getting away and having to be chased; but country people of that day had little sympathy for the sufferings of animals, and men, women and children would gather round to see the sight.

After the carcass had been singed, the pig-sticker would pull off the detachable, gristly, outer coverings of the toes, known locally as 'the shoes', and fling them among the children, who scrambled for, then sucked and gnawed them, straight from the filth of the sty and blackened by fire as they were.

The whole scene, with its mud and blood, flaring

lights and dark shadows, was as savage as anything
to be seen in an African jungle. The children at the end
house would steal out of bed to the window. 'Look!
Look! It's hell, and those are the devils,' Edmund would
whisper, pointing to the men tossing the burning straw
with their pitchforks; but Laura felt sick and would
creep back into bed and cry: she was sorry for the pig.

But, hidden from the children, there was another
aspect of the pig-killing. Months of hard work and self-
denial were brought on that night to a successful conclusion. It was a time to rejoice, and rejoice they did,
with beer flowing freely and the first delicious dish of
pig's fry sizzling in the frying-pan.

That passage comes from the first chapter of *Lark Rise*.
In *Over to Candleford* there is an echo of it, and again the
killing of a pig, so momentous an event in a cottage family, by its depth of observation and truth carries implications of something beyond itself.

A little later in her life came the evening after a pig-
killing when she stood alone in the pantry where the
dead animal hung suspended from a hook in the ceiling.
Her mother was only a few feet away. . . . Out there
in the wash-house they were busy and cheerful, but in
the pantry where Laura stood was a dead, cold silence.

She had known that pig all its life. Her father had
often held her over the door of its sty to scratch its back
and she had pushed lettuce and cabbage stalks through
the bars for it to enjoy. Only that morning it had routed
and grunted and squealed because it had had no breakfast. Her mother had said its noise got on her nerves and
her father had looked uncomfortable, although he had
passed it off by saying: 'No. No breakfast today, piggy.
You're going to have a big operation by and by and
there's no breakfast before operations.'

Now it had had its operation and there it hung, cold

and stiff and so very, very dead. Not funny at all any more, but in some queer way dignified. The butcher had draped a long, lacy piece of fat from its own interior over one of its forelegs, in the manner in which ladies of that day sometimes carried a white lacy shawl, and that last touch seemed to Laura utterly heartless. She stayed there a long time, patting its hard, cold side and wondering that a thing so recently full of life and noise could be so still. Then, hearing her mother call her, she ran out of the door farthest from where she was working lest she should be scolded for crying over a dead pig.

There was fried liver and fat for supper and when Laura said 'No, thank you,' her mother looked at her rather suspiciously, then said, 'Well, perhaps better not, just going to bed and all; but here's a nice bit of sweetbread, I was saving it for Daddy, but you have it. You'll like that.' And Laura ate the sweetbread and dipped her bread in the thick, rich gravy and refused to think any more about the poor pig in the pantry, for, although only five years old, she was learning to live in this world of compromises.

There was no room for sentimentality in the life she was born to; it was too near the bone. Yet in spite of that, and also because of it, it had a value and a saltiness which it would be hard to find in villages today. Life and work were hard, but the work that was done was essential work, and respected, and life was not wasted in a struggle to keep up appearances. In old age Flora Thompson, who like her father was always a bit of a radical, could see clearly that when poverty was abolished it was not the only thing which had been swept away. 'I fear,' she wrote to H. J. Massingham in 1943, 'that much of the salt of the earth will be lost in the process of transforming the old, sturdy, independent type of farm labourer into the proletariat. The only hope is that the countryman's roots are so strong and so well down in the soil that, after this terrible time is over, the country virtues will spring anew.'

When reading *Lark Rise to Candleford*, so rich in detail of sight, sound, and smell that one has the illusion of remembering the very hedgerows for oneself, it is strange to realize that these deep impressions were absorbed by Flora Thompson before she was fourteen, that being the age when she left home to earn her living. It had been supposed that she would go into service at twelve or thirteen, as all the hamlet girls did (some of them, indeed, went out as young as eleven, their mothers frankly declaring, 'I shan't be sorry when our young So-and-so gets her knees under somebody else's table. Five slices for breakfast this mornin', if you please!'); and her mother had planned to get her a place under one of the nurses she knew from her own days in service. But the child's unusual thirst for reading, and the peculiarity of her always wanting scraps of paper to write on, made her mother ambitious, and she decided to place her with another old acquaintance, the postmistress of Fringford, who was willing to take her as junior assistant. So Flora, as she has related in *Candleford Green*, was driven by her father in the innkeeper's cart over the eight miles of country roads to the neighbouring village, and began her adult life as a post-office clerk.

Flora herself has said that Candleford Green is not, strictly speaking, Fringford, but the post office and forge over which Miss Lane presided with so matriarchal an authority can still be seen, though the long, low white cottage has long ceased to fulfil either of its old functions. Miss Lane herself is drawn from a locally celebrated Mrs. Whitton, who had inherited the forge from her father and for many years had carried on the business and that of the village post-office as well.

I knew Mrs Whitton well [Flora Thompson wrote to an acquaintance many years later]. About the time you were born she was teaching me the rudiments of the post-office business and there is a good deal of her in my Miss Lane. That character as it stands in my books is a mixture of her and of another postmistress I served under in Surrey, but the mental attributes are entirely those of Mrs Whitton, and the blacksmith's business of course was hers. She was a wonderful woman. She had the most observant eye and the keenest brain of anyone I have known, and had she been born later must have left her mark on the world. What a psychologist she would have made! She was very good to me, and as I have said in one of my books, had more influence than anyone in shaping the outward course of my life.

That life, in the early Fringford period, she has recorded fairly closely in *Candleford Green*, which gives an unforgettable account of Miss Lane's household, run on traditional lines which were old-fashioned and benevolently strict even for those days. Here Flora learned the post-office business from the bottom, selling stamps, sorting letters, working the sacred telegraph machine (which was kept under a sort of velvet tea-cosy), and for one long and happy spell acting as letter-carrier, covering miles on foot through fields and lanes with her bag. This experience was important, for it deepened the almost mystical love of solitude and nature which was to grow with the years, until it was the dominant strain in her strong character. After Fringford, she tells us no more about her personal life, for although the trilogy was eventually followed by a fourth volume, *Still Glides the Stream*, it is cast in a fictional form and goes back to the old countryside of her youth.

Between *Candleford Green*, however, and *Still Glides*

the Stream she did write another book, *Heatherley*, which carries her own story a little further. She was dissatisfied with it and it was never published, but it is not without interest, since it gives some account of her life from the time that she left Fringford until her marriage. She left Mrs. Whitton, apparently, before she was twenty, and spent some time in various country post offices, taking short holiday-relief engagements in different places, a proceeding which was frowned upon at home.

Her people at home were beginning to speak of her as a rolling stone, and rolling stones were not in favour with country people of that day. The plea that to work, even for a short time, in one of the larger post offices was a valuable gain in experience did not appeal to her parents. They looked upon experience as something to be gathered unconsciously, not a thing to be sought for. They preferred permanence and security.

So in 1897 Flora, at twenty, went to work in the little Surrey village of Grayshott, where she was to remain for three years. She arrived on foot,

dressed in a brown woollen frock with a waist-length cape of the same material and a brown beaver hat decorated with two small ostrich tips, set upright in front, back to back, like a couple of notes of interrogation. . . . The skirt, cut short just to escape contact with the ground, and so needing no holding up except in wet weather, was, her dressmaker had assured her, the latest idea for country wear. The hat she had bought on her way through London that morning. It had cost nine and elevenpence three-farthings of the pound she had saved to meet her expenses until her first month's salary was due in her new post, but she did not regret the extravagance. . . . 'A good first impression is half the battle,' she had been told as a child.

She lived first with the postmaster's family, then independently in lodgings. This latter arrangement was the happier of the two, for the postmaster quarrelled with abnormal violence with his wife and prowled about the house at all hours, a prey to suspicions and delusions, and she had her first taste of independent happiness when she was living alone in a bare little room at ten shillings a week. (Later, the sinister postmaster went out of his mind and murdered his wife and child with a carving-knife, but this was fortunately after Flora had left.) She was able now for the first time to read widely, and embarked on the long haphazard self-education which she afterwards described as having been accomplished on borrowed books, free libraries, and the threepenny and sixpenny boxes of second-hand shops. Here, too, she had her first enthralling glimpse of real writers, for the 'Surrey highlands' had been recently discovered by the intelligentsia, and there being no post office at that time in Hindhead the celebrities who frequented the neighbourhood bought their stamps and sent their telegrams from Grayshott. Conan Doyle, Grant Allen, Richard le Gallienne, and others had taken houses in the neighbourhood, and Bernard Shaw, lately married, had rented a furnished house in Grayshott itself.

I used to listen to the conversation of these [she wrote later], meeting and greeting each other at my counter, myself as unregarded as a piece of furniture, but noting all. Perhaps these 'great examples' encouraged my desire to express myself in writing, but I cannot remember the time when I did not wish and mean to write. My brother and I used to make up verses and write stories and diaries from our earliest years, and I had never left off writing essays for the pleasure of writing. No one saw them; there was no one likely to be interested.

When she was twenty-four, however, this independent single life came to an end, for in the course of the penny readings and village soirées which went on in the neighbourhood she met John Thompson, a young post-office clerk from Aldershot, and as soon as he was transferred to the main post office in Bournemouth they were married.

At the time it must have seemed a sensible step, and at first the marriage was happy enough in a humdrum way, but the world of the white-collar working class was alien to Flora and she was dismayed by its narrowness and prejudice. Her love of reading was now condemned as a waste of time, her attempts at writing sneered at. Everything she did, it seemed, was wrong. A book in one's hand or a handful of garden flowers on the supper table was mocked as a ridiculous pretension, yet she found herself looked down on by her new relations for having been born in a cottage. They considered themselves above the labouring class and spared no pains to make this clear to her.

The Thompsons were very poor. The pay of a post-office clerk allowed no luxuries, and the free library, her one resource, had to be reached on foot after the day's work was done, for there was rarely the penny or twopence to spare for the tram.

With a house to run single-handed and with children being born and nursed my literary dreams faded for a time. But I still read a good deal. For the first time in my life I had access to a good public library, and I slipped in like a duck slipping into water and read almost everything. I had no guidance except my own natural taste. But perhaps I was fortunate in this, as I was able to follow my own bent.

A daughter and son, Winifred * and Basil, were born during the Bournemouth years, and when they were no longer babies and she could contrive a little leisure from children and housework Flora began to write again, as secretly as she could because of her husband's disapproval. Her first attempt was an essay on Jane Austen which she entered for a competition in a women's paper, and which, to her astonishment, was awarded the prize. Encouraged, she sent an article, then a short story to the same paper, and both were accepted. The payment for each was only a few shillings, but the effect of this small success was morally important: if her eccentricities were paid for they would be tolerated. 'I had earned the right to use my scanty leisure as I wished.'

The discovery that she could earn a pound or two by writing delayed for many years her development as a writer, for she determined to earn a good education for her children, and set herself to the manufacture of 'small, sugared love stories,' which, however artificial she knew them to be, were at least easy to sell. She comforted herself by writing verse, for like many writers of pure and musical prose she believed for many years that her gifts were not for prose at all but for poetry, and her unconfessed ambition was to be a poet. This secret hope was never realized, for her verse never rose above modest mag-

* I am indebted to the late Miss Winifred Thompson, who was her mother's literary executor, for much help and information, and for permission to quote from unpublished material. I should also like to thank Sir Arthur Bryant, Mrs. H. J. Massingham, Mr. and Mrs. Arthur Ball, Dr. and Mrs. Max Tyler, Mr. Leonard Clark, Miss Eva Hillsden, the Oxford University Press, and others who were kind enough to lend letters.

azine level, but her love of poetry did at least bring her the one literary friendship of her life, and this proved to be important. In 1912, after the sinking of the *Titanic*, a Scottish physician and poet called Ronald Campbell Macfie wrote an ode on the disaster which was published in *The Literary Monthly*, and readers were invited, as a competition, to send their criticisms. Flora Thompson's admiring review of the ode won the prize, and so pleased Dr. Macfie that he wrote her a grateful and charming letter, and later made a point of coming to see her.

Dr. Macfie is not often remembered today, but at that time, though never a successful man in the worldly sense, he had published a sufficient number of books, and was well enough known and respected as a writer, to seem to Flora Thompson like a glorious messenger from the inaccessible world she longed to enter. He was a poet who had published a considerable body of verse of a traditional sort, and who was at his best when celebrating some public or national event with a classical ode. He was a prolific writer, besides, on popular medicine, having made a special study of tuberculosis and believing passionately in the importance of public education in hygiene. A man of commanding presence and personality, he was quick-tempered, argumentative, and attractive. His life was divided between irreconcilable interests; between poetry, medicine, travel, and a variety of humanitarian causes; and this scattering of his talents kept him poor. His was a restless temperament, and he had never married. He had, he told Flora Thompson, renounced any idea of domestic life 'in order to get a few months here and there to write the poetry and philosophy in me. Without money (in fact with a heavy burden of debt on my shoulders) I have struggled on and have achieved enough leisure here and there to do a little work, which though almost unrecognized I believe to be immortal.' He was never in the same place for long and they met rarely; but from time to time he would descend for a few hours' visit, and from their first meeting until his death twenty years later their friendship was unbroken. From the beginning it was of great importance to Flora Thompson, for apart from his personal fascination Macfie was the only 'beloved friend' she ever had who shared her interests and gave her strenuous encouragement. 'Forty! What is forty?' he wrote to her in 1918. 'I am fifty-one; but if I could yet have ten years of opportunity to write I should be content. Look forward! Rejoice in your great gift and fight for opportunity, even if it be ten years later; and perhaps I who am still fighting may in a few years be able to find some ways and means for you. Who knows?' It was he who, three years later, encouraged her to send a little collection of her verses to a publisher, and accepted her dedication with pride when the paper-bound volume *Bog Myrtle and Peat* eventually appeared. In spite of kindly reviews it was a failure, and the disappointment convinced her at last that she was not a poet. But the achievement, however modest, had its value, and to the end of her life she was grateful for Macfie's faith in her as a writer. When he died in 1931, she wrote his name and the date on the fly-leaf of a book, and then, cryptically, 'The bright day is done, and we are for the dark.'

In 1916 John Thompson was promoted to his first sub-postmastership, and they moved to Liphook in Hampshire. It was a sad year, for Edwin, the brother whom Flora so much resembled and loved, had been killed in action, and her one deeply emotional link with her childhood was broken. She was unable to write, for as well as her work for home and children she had undertaken arduous wartime duties at the post office, sorting the mail at

four o'clock in the morning and doing the work of the
clerk who had been called up. As soon as the war was
over, however, she began again; as she wrote of Laura in
Heatherley, 'the old feeling had revived that in return for
the precious opportunity known as life some further effort
other than those involved in mere living was required of
her'; and on the strength of her small earnings Winifred
and Basil were sent to excellent day schools, one to Peters-
field Grammar School and the other to Haslemere. The
country round Liphook was a renewed pleasure after sub-
urban Bournemouth, and she revived her habit of long
brooding walks, feeding her old hunger for solitude and
nature. These walks bore fruit of a kind, for she began to
write a series of nature essays for a little magazine called
the *Catholic Fireside* (no one now remembers how she
first came across it, for she had no Catholic connections);
and these were so well liked that the series was continued
for nearly twenty years. It was an excellent practice
ground for a writer with her gifts of observation, and this
small success encouraged her to try her hand in a more
general field. The *Daily News* and various women's magazines now printed her occasional essays, and she felt that
at last she had become a professional writer.

She was still, however, a long way from the discovery
of the kind of writing she was best fitted to do, and in the
next ten years incalculable time and energy were wasted
in following false trails. For several years she 'ghosted' for
a big-game hunter who had advertised in the literary press
for an amanuensis, and had the wry satisfaction of seeing
her work appear under his name in *Chambers's Journal*,
The Scottish Field, and various African papers. She also,
in 1924, founded a postal association for literary aspir-
ants, The Peverel Society, and this work, in the value of

which she ardently believed, devoured her leisure and
energy for eighteen years.

It was a modest amateur affair, but it satisfied her
longing for contact with other writers, and since it
brought her a number of distant friends who shared her
interests the time it absorbed was perhaps not altogether
wasted. The members did not meet; each paid a few shillings a year to cover expenses and contributed something
once a month, either prose or verse, to a portfolio which
went the round of the members by post. Each was invited
to criticize and Flora Thompson's criticisms (the few that
survive) are remarkable for their workmanlike approach.
She would have made a good teacher or a good editor; her
advice has nothing amateur about it. Criticizing a short
story or writing a course of instruction for her members
she invariably shows a practical grasp of literary tech-
niques and difficulties. The pity is that she spent so many
years coaching amateurs which might have been given to
the development of her own gifts. There was not time for
both, and as the years went by she began to see that this
work, so earnestly undertaken, was by its very nature
doomed to disappointment. The members fell off or failed
to turn into writers, 'saying that their husband or wife
thought writing was a waste of time, or thought themselves neglected.'

The Peverel Society was begun at Liphook and continued at Dartmouth, where John Thompson was transferred as postmaster in 1928. The Liphook years had not
been unhappy, and she was sorry to go. A third child,
Peter, had been born at the little post office when she was
forty-one and had thought her days of child-bearing were
over, and though she had not welcomed his birth with any
pleasure he became increasingly dear to both parents and

did something to revive the dwindling comfort of their marriage. It was at Liphook, too, that she had first achieved a home she really loved. They had lived for twelve years at the post office and at last had bought a house in the wooded and hilly country outside the village, but no sooner were they settled at Woolmer Gate than her husband in a fit of restlessness which she found hard to forgive, 'put in for promotion,' and was transferred almost immediately to Dartmouth. Flora remained behind to sell the house, an operation quietly prolonged for more than a year; a happy year, spent alone with her children in the sort of countryside she loved, endlessly reading and writing without criticism or reproach.

When at last the move to Dartmouth was accomplished, however, she was pleased with her new surroundings and soon grew fond of the town and harbour and the steep wooded walks behind the house. The house itself, 'The Outlook,' was in that highest part known as Above Town, with a dazzling view over the whole estuary. Here for the next twelve years she lived a secluded life, making few friends and seeming to desire none. With only the youngest child at home she had more leisure, and though the Peverel Society still absorbed the greater part of it, she was beginning at last to write to please herself. She spent much time on the beginnings of several novels, but none of them satisfied her. Her only encouragement still came from Dr. Macfie, and when in 1931 he suddenly died she was slow to recover from the private misery of his loss. At last, however, she began to feel her way towards the theme which had been waiting unrecognized for so long. She began to write sketches about her childhood.

The first of these was *Old Queenie*, a loving remembrance of the bee-keeper and lace-maker of Juniper, whose cottage had stood (and still stands) at the back of

the 'end house' which had been Flora's home. This essay
appeared in 1937 in *The Lady*, and is the kernel of a
much longer chapter which she presently expanded for
Lark Rise. This was the beginning; *May Day*, another
chapter, was accepted by the *Fortnightly Review*, and
with such enthusiasm that she was encouraged to send
these and several other pieces of a like nature to the Oxford University Press, where they came into the hands of
Sir Humphrey Milford, who instantly recognized their
quality and wrote to the unknown author, urging her to
expand them into a book. This was the signal she needed;
the material was rich and copious, and for the first time,
as a writer, she felt at home. She began *Lark Rise* in the
autumn of 1937 and worked on it steadily for eleven
months. It was published in 1939 and was received with
universal praise. The sales were not large at first, but they
were encouraging, and her publishers pressed her to write
more. *Over to Candleford* was written in the following
year and she began to feel the first glow of success; but
failing health and personal sorrow were soon to rob her of
its satisfactions. In 1940 John Thompson had retired
from the Post Office and they had left the house at Dartmouth for a cottage at Brixham. Basil, her elder son, had
gone some years before to farm in Australia; Winifred,
her daughter, was nursing in Bristol, and Peter, the beloved youngest, had left home to join the Merchant Navy.
He was killed within a few months, when his convoy ship
was torpedoed in mid-Atlantic. Flora Thompson never
entirely recovered from this shock. She fell ill, developed
pneumonia, and rallied only at the expense of a damaged
heart and the loss of much of her sturdy vitality. A year
later she forced herself to return to work, and *Candleford
Green* was written in the space of nine months, 'under
difficulties,' as she wrote to a friend, 'several of the pas-

sages to the sound of bombs falling . . . the typescript already looks worn through being taken in and out of the Morrison shelter.' She felt little pleasure in its success, which surprised her by being greater than that of its predecessors. 'I hear that it is the most popular of all my books with the general reader,' she wrote, 'a fact not altogether pleasant to me when I think of *Lark Rise*. I have often thought that I have belittled the latter book by writing these light, gossipy little books around it.' She seems not to have realized that in the three books she had produced a work of art of singular excellence, and even when, in 1945, the three were published together as a trilogy, unequivocally establishing her as a writer, her feeling about it was curiously remote. ('It's got an element of real greatness,' Sir Arthur Bryant had written to H. J. Massingham. 'I put it at least as high as Cranford, and I think higher; for under its quiet artistry and truth there's passion and fire.') 'Most flattering, and astonishing,' she commented, when the reviews began to come in. 'Twenty years ago I should have been beside myself with joy, but I am now too old to care much for the bubble reputation.'

She was nearly seventy. Her small success had come too late, and after too long a struggle, to mean much. Even her husband's surprised pride, now genuinely felt, appealed more to her sense of irony than to anything else.

Words as to the inner emotions do not come readily to me [she wrote to H. J. Massingham, who had written a perceptive introduction to her trilogy], for I have led an isolated life mentally and spiritually. . . . The very few people I know personally . . . are not reading people, and though reviewers have been kind and I have had a few letters of appreciation from readers, no one but you has recognized my aims and intentions in writing of that more excellent way of life of our fore-fathers.

She had still one piece of work to finish, but it was, as she said, like wearily rolling a heavy stone uphill; she felt that she had said what she wanted to say, and would have been glad to write no more if it had not been for the earnest encouragement of her publishers. *Still Glides the Stream* was finished with fatigue and difficulty, a few weeks before her heart finally failed. She died suddenly, alone in her room, in May 1947.

There are very few likenesses of Flora Thompson in existence. All her life she showed a great aversion from being photographed, and even her daughter was able to show me only two faded reproductions—one of a modest studio portrait, with smooth-drawn hair and downcast eyes, the other of a snapshot taken in middle age, when her face had acquired its look of withdrawn stoicism. I am allowed, however, to quote from a letter to Miss Winifred Thompson from Mr. Arthur Ball, a Peverel member of the early days who had visited Flora Thompson a few months before her death. They had corresponded for many years, but had never met, and Mr. Ball's description gives so excellent an impression of her in old age that it tells us, perhaps, more than any photograph.

When we went to Brixham in 1946 [he wrote], and met your mother, my first impression was quite unlike what I expected. Probably because once, in the Peverel days, members' photographs were circulated, and F. T. seemed dark and willowy, the sort of appearance one would expect from her Christian name, very graceful and feminine. I saw a Flora Thompson who was sturdy, resolute, and, with her features chiselled to an expression of remarkable strength, more like the portraits of Marie

Curie than anyone else I can think of. Of course the winning, gentle side was there all right, but she seemed to have attained a remarkable independence in her character, and this struck one immediately. And there was that underlying simplicity which the very best natures usually seem to acquire or have as a matter of birthright. When I think of the terrible time she must have had with her illness I am struck too by her remarkable freedom from absorption in self or self-pity—it was all in the other direction, a vital and eager interest in the people she was talking to.

The few people who remember her dwell on this impression of quiet strength, on a warm and direct simplicity, apparently down-to-earth but not without its humour and quick emotion; also on a hidden, reclusive element in her which held aloof from human contact and led her into mystical sympathy with nature. She once heavily marked a couplet in her copy of Francis Thompson's *To the Dead Cardinal*, and to the end of her life remembered and often returned to it, as though she found in it the poignancy of personal significance.

> Anchorite, who didst dwell
> With all the world for cell.

All this, and more, is to be found in her best work, which for all her reticence is continuously and profoundly self-revealing. Like W. H. Hudson, whom she admired and whom in some ways she resembled, she was secretive about her own life because it afforded little satisfaction. Like his, her essential experience was within.

W. H. Hudson's London

THERE ARE AREAS OF LONDON WHICH, HOW-
ever hopefully planned, however respectably
covered with brick and plaster, adorned with
pediments and porticos, grandiloquently
named in streets and crescents and squares, seem destined
quickly and hopelessly to go down. The prosperous families for whom they were intended do not occupy them
long. The neighbourhood is no sooner built than it deteri-
orates: lean-looking cats abound, weaving their way in
and out the area railings, and the passer-by is made silently aware that it is board-residence, not life, which
mysteriously stirs behind those flaking façades.

This is the fate that long ago laid its hand on Pimlico,
where the river fog rises early and lies late; on long
reaches of Brompton and South Kensington; parts of
Bloomsbury and Bayswater; and the whole sad seedy
world, 'that brick desert' as W. H. Hudson bitterly described it, which lies all about Notting Hill Station, between Kensington and Kensal Green.

Hudson, destined to be a great naturalist and writer of
prose, the poet of the world of birds, a creator of strange
tropical and South American tales, came to London from
the Argentine in 1869 and made his way to Bayswater to
a boarding-house at 11 Leinster Square. He was twenty-

nine years old, immensely tall, already bearded and stoop-
ing, with piercing eyes, an appearance of great strength,
and a diseased heart of which he was told he must soon
die.

He had no parents, no prospects, no money, little hope.
His father had been a New Englander who had emigrated
to the Argentine and had lived by sheep-farming. He
himself had been born at Quilmes, ten miles from Buenos
Aires, and had grown up among gauchos, bad-men, and
hard-bitten farmers on the vast treeless plains of South
America. At fifteen the hardy, sinewy boy, who rode like a
centaur and had spent his whole life on the pampas, contracted rheumatic fever and suffered a long illness which
all but destroyed his heart. There was nothing to be done,
the doctors said; he could never live to be a man. (He
lived, in spite of his heart, to eighty-one, but the doctors
had given him a shock from which he never recovered,
and the fear of death clouded his whole life.)

For the next fourteen years he wandered idly, by the
borders of the Gran Chaco, across the plains of Patagonia,
believing himself doomed, expecting every day to die.
And at twenty-nine, finding himself still alive, though an
orphan and almost penniless, and remembering that his
father's father had been a Devon man and that the dreams
of his youth had always been of England, he packed his
few possessions in a box and made the long voyage from
Buenos Aires to Bayswater.

On the morning after his arrival in London he records:

I went out to explore, and walked at random, never
inquiring my way of any person, and not knowing
whether I was going east or west. After rambling about
for some three or four hours I came to a vast wooded
place where few persons were about. It was a wet, cold

morning in early May, after a night of incessant rain.
. . . As I advanced further into this wooded space the
dull sounds of traffic became fainter, while ahead the
continuous noise of many cawing rooks grew louder
and louder. I was soon under the rookery listening to
and watching the birds as they wrangled with one another, and passed in and out among the trees. . . .

Ten years later that wooded grove in Kensington Gardens, seven hundred splendid trees, was felled, and the
rooks deserted. And Hudson, marooned by poverty, had
married the fifty-year-old landlady of Leinster Square,
Emily Wingrave, a faded soprano who had been kind to
him and for whom he now answered the doorbell and
carved the mutton at the head of the lodgers' table.

They struggled together for eight years against increasing shabbiness and seediness and the steady deterio-
ration of their trade. In a comfortless top room, when he
could be spared, Hudson was beginning to write, though
almost no editor would pay for what he had written. In
his aloof uncommunicative way, too, he was making
friends—Gissing, shabbier and seedier even than himself;
Morley Roberts, ebullient author and journalist; dashing
Cunninghame Graham, courtly as Don Quixote. They
saw him sometimes despondent, sometimes irritable,
jumping up from the supper table to squeeze and drink
undiluted lemon juice at the sideboard; setting off, when
some occasional windfall seemed to justify a break, on
long economical walks 'out of the immense unfriendly
wilderness of London,' through the villages of Hampshire
and over Salisbury Plain, walks on which Emily Hudson,
patient and uncomprehending, sometimes accompanied
him.

In 1884 the boarding-house failed and they moved to a
humbler one in Southwick Crescent, Paddington. Here, in

the two years before this, too, had to be given up as a loss, Hudson wrote his first South American romance, *The Purple Land*, and from the observations and memories of his youth began to construct his *Argentine Ornithology*. The naturalist of genius, awakened in those early years of wandering on the pampas and now conscious and mature, had begun his life's work; and it is a strange reflection that his inspired expression of the beauty of nature, the poetry of birds, the mysteriousness of untrodden and tropical places, was achieved through years of imprisonment in the less lovely areas of London—in Bayswater, in Paddington, in Notting Hill.

Yet it was those very instincts of the naturalist, the detached observer in him, the man passionate for beauty, which enriched his London life and made it rewarding. When he and his wife, after the second boarding-house failure, lived on the edge of starvation for a time at Ravenscourt Park (they subsisted for one empty week on a tin of cocoa) he fed his soul on the park itself in gratitude. 'I lived for a long time beside it in sad days, when the constant sight of such a green and shady wilderness from my windows was a great consolation.' And when he was too hungry for long walks into the country, in that 'wasted and dreary period, when I was often in the parks and open spaces in all parts of London,' he studied the London birds, even the sparrows, 'ever busy at their scavenging in the dusty noisy ways, everywhere finding some organic matter to comfort their little stomachs.'

Fortune smiled, or rather relaxed her frown, on the Hudsons at last. His work, both as naturalist and novelist, began to be known; an influential admirer who recognized his quality and was shocked by the crushing poverty of his condition, persuaded the Prime Minister to award him a Civil List pension of £150 a year; and a sister of Mrs.

Hudson's died, leaving her a tall dark narrow house, number 40 St. Luke's Road, Notting Hill. True, the house was mortgaged for £1,100, almost its whole value; but by letting off the basement and lower floors and themselves living only at the top, they made ends meet, and Hudson was able to take his frugal leisurely summer excursions across the south of England, to Wells-next-the-Sea in Norfolk in November to watch the wild geese, and in the little comfortless top room in St. Luke's Road, where he slept behind a cotton curtain and kept his papers in a trunk under the table, to ripen the splendid fruits of his imaginative life.

Here Hudson lived until he died, spending the last ten years alone. Here he concealed himself, living according to his secretive nature, mixing with his friends when he felt like it, but uncovering himself to none. Here he wrote *Green Mansions*, the moving half-mystical, half-poetic tale of Rima the bird-woman in the forests of the Orinoco; *A Shepherd's Life*, his great calm book of Salisbury Plain; and *Far Away and Long Ago*, the beautiful nostalgic record of his own boyhood.

What he never wrote about, what indeed he concealed, anxiously obliterating all trace as an animal might draw sticks and leaves across the mouth of its hole, was his grey life in London, his fifty years in that 'province covered with houses,' his long living and slow dying in the byways of Notting Hill. Even his nearest friends, even Morley Roberts who knew him for forty years, knew little enough, were allowed to know little of this hidden life. Hudson had a horror of biography, and by destroying all letters and records, and falsifying or suppressing what could not be destroyed, he made certain that nothing approaching a true history of his own life could ever be written.

Why should Hudson have gone to such trouble to blot out his life? The answer perhaps to his fierce concealment lies in the unbearable contrast between his imaginative genius and his life. The mind that fed on beauty in her wildest forms, that had nourished a young spirit in the lovely places of the world, and had beguiled him with a passion for a half-human, half-magical 'daughter of the Didi' in those steaming forests of the Orinoco where he had never been, sickened in dismay at the Bayswater boarding-house, the Paddington lodgings, the 'treeless district, most desolate,' where his maturity was spent. The lover of Rima, the gaucho adventurer, the shepherd of Salisbury Plain, even the rapt bird-watcher of the Norfolk coast, had nothing to do with the old gentleman who came down so carefully from the top room in St. Luke's Road, and on days of special prosperity went to Whiteleys' for lunch, 'flapping along like a great eagle in the old-fashioned tail-coat he always wore,' to meet his friends and hear a little gossip, and complain if there were no suet pudding on the menu.

The disparity was too painful, and Hudson knew it. Only one profile of his life would he turn to the light; the face of beauty and achievement, the poet's, the naturalist's face. Except for their shadowy outline, which he could not quite destroy, the features of his life in London were erased by his own hand, so that what he wished to ignore should remain forgotten.

Dr. Johnson at Home

THE JOHNSON MOST OF US KNOW IS A MAN IN company, dominating the conversation at a friend's dinner-table, holding forth over the tea-cups at Mrs. Thrale's, making the night hours memorable with profundity and wit in a congenial coffee house or tavern. We see him as a man perpetually dining and talking out, as indeed he was. It is not often that we think of him at home.

Yet he had a home; many homes, if the place where a man works and sleeps and passes his private hours can be counted as such; and in three of the London houses that he inhabited he passed a sufficient number of years, in a sufficiently organized domestic way, for us to think of them as homes in every sense. We know something particularly intimate about a man when we have seen him at his own hearth, and for that reason it is illuminating to consider Johnson in his purely domestic character.

During the years that he lived in London—that is to say during the greater part of his life—Johnson changed his address seventeen times. Most of the places he lived in, even when his wife was still alive, were merely lodgings; but three of them were solid middle-class houses in one or other of the little courts off Fleet Street; and it is in these houses, in Gough Square, Johnson's Court, and Bolt

Court that we get our best glimpse of the domestic Johnson. It is an interesting picture.

We know that when Mrs. Johnson was alive—that odd but by no means stupid or unlikeable woman, whom he married when he was twenty-five and she nearly fifty—he suffered to some extent from her excessive cleanliness. She was one of those passionately clean women, he told Mrs. Thrale, 'troublesome to their best friends, slaves to their besoms,' who 'sigh for the hour of sweeping their husbands out of the house as dirt and useless lumber'—and we know that Johnson was an unfastidious and careless man. His famous remarks, that he 'hated immersion' and 'had no passion for clean linen,' suggest what he must have endured under Mrs. Johnson's housekeeping. Besides, there is evidence that she was an indifferent cook, and knowing what a gourmet Johnson was, as well as a greedy man, it says much for the attractiveness of Mrs. Johnson's character that he loved her as much as he undoubtedly did. She, on her side, must have suffered endless exasperation from his untidy habits and late hours, and his disregard for the well-being of the furniture. We know that he made an enemy of Mrs. Boswell by turning the candles upside-down to drip on the carpet when they did not burn to his liking. Still, it was a singularly happy marriage, and if Mrs. Johnson had been younger, and had lived, his life no doubt would have been vastly different. But she died when he was only forty-three.

Johnson was then living in Gough Square, and it was here that he gradually set up the eccentric bachelor household which lasted with few changes almost to his death. It is a solid, well-proportioned eighteenth-century house, as anyone may see today who cares to pay a shilling to go over it. I suspect it is rather cleaner now than it was in Johnson's day; tidier, too, and the furniture better polished; but one would willingly exchange its present perfection for one authentic glimpse into the past, with Johnson drinking tea with Miss Williams in the parlour, his Negro servant running out on errands, the mysterious Levett sneaking in at the back door, and one of the famous rows going on in the kitchen. 'He nursed,' said Mrs. Thrale, 'whole nests of people in his house, where the lame, the blind, the sick and the sorrowful found a sure retreat from all the evils whence his little income could secure them.'

First and most important was Miss Williams, the blind lady who made her home with him for many years, ran his house, entertained his friends, and in many ways helped to fill the lonely gap which had been left by the death of his wife. She was the daughter of a Welsh physician, had been a friend of Mrs. Johnson's, though she was considerably younger, and she first came to stay with the Johnsons in London when she had to undergo a dreadful operation for double cataract. The operation failed, and she became blind, and stayed on in Johnson's house after his wife's death as a more or less permanent inhabitant. She was not penniless, having a tiny income of her own, and as she lived chiefly on bread-and-butter and tea she was not expensive; and she soon made herself indispensable by running the house—as far as she was able, being blind—and by saving Johnson from what he most dreaded, which was being alone. He was a man with a terrible and melancholy horror of solitude, and she performed the invaluable service of being always available, at almost any hour of the day or night, to pour his tea and while away the hours with conversation.

He kept most inconvenient hours, commonly lying in bed till noon, since there was nothing he found more difficult than getting up; going out as a rule about four o'clock, and coming home, sometimes at midnight, more often at two in the morning. No matter how late, Miss Williams always sat up for him and performed the pleasant ritual of the tea-table. Johnson for his part was a supremely diverting companion, so that these nightly tea-drinkings were anything but dull. Indeed, as we know from Boswell, some of his best talking was done in these night sessions, and to be taken in late to drink tea with Miss Williams was an honour which Boswell himself eagerly coveted.

An equally important member of the household was Francis Barber—Frank, Johnson's servant. This young man was a Jamaican Negro who had come into his service very young and who served him so long and so faithfully that Johnson made him the chief heir of what little property he possessed. Frank performed nearly every office for Johnson—dressed him, nursed him when he was ill, ran his errands, cleaned the house and, one supposes, did his share of the cooking. He married a white wife, but of her we know very little save that Frank was jealous when Mrs. Thrale's footman admired her at a dance. There was also a female servant, Betsey, and a certain number of unofficial helpers.

The kitchen was for many years under the command of Mrs. Desmoulins, another indigent lady whom Johnson befriended. She was a widow, the daughter of Dr. Swinfen, his godfather; and one day Boswell found that the bedroom which was usually kept for him when he wanted it had been handed over to Mrs. Desmoulins, her daughter, and another hanger-on called Polly Carmichael. Nor were these all, for Johnson kept in his house for many years a seedy sort of unqualified physician called Levett, whose practice was among the very poor and who was at

times almost destitute. Johnson was much interested in
medicine and he had a regard for Levett, who in return
made himself generally useful. It was his special job to
make Dr. Johnson's breakfast—tea, with milk and sugar,
and rolls, of which Levett ate the crust and Johnson the
crumb. His midday breakfasts were a favourite time for
receiving friends and those who came always found him,
untidily dressed, sitting over his tea and rolls with Levett—always the same breakfast, unless it were Good Friday, when he drank tea without milk or sugar and ate hot
cross buns instead of bread.

Johnson dined out so perpetually and his household
was run on such shifting, haphazard lines that his friends
imagined—quite wrongly—that any meal eaten at home
would be primitive indeed. The first time Boswell dined at
his house he was agreeably surprised. 'I supposed,' he
wrote afterwards, 'we should scarcely have knives and
forks, and only some strange uncouth, ill-drest fish; but I
found everything in very good order.' And when later,
unannounced, he took another gentleman to call on Johnson at breakfast, this being a favoured hour for receiving
friends, he noted that 'His tea and rolls and butter, and
whole breakfast apparatus were all in such decorum, and
his behaviour was so courteous, that Colonel Stopford was
quite surprised, and wondered at his having heard so
much said of Johnson's slovenliness and roughness.' This,
from Boswell, was quite a tribute, since he was inclined to
be nice about his own breakfast. 'I breakfasted with Lord
Eglinton,' he noted on one occasion, 'who keeps the best
breakfast of any man in London—a complete Union of the
good things of Scotland and England: bread and butter
and marmalade of oranges and currant jelly and muffins,
well buttered and comfortably toasted.' Johnson did not

aspire to muffins and jelly, but at least he broke his fast in decent order.

Although the meals in Johnson's house were better than his friends expected there seems to have been a good deal of confusion and bad temper in the kitchen, where Mrs. Desmoulins chiefly reigned and where all the members of Johnson's household—out of his hearing—could give vent to their personal spite against one another. 'Williams hates everybody,' Johnson wrote to Mrs. Thrale, 'Levett hates Desmoulins, and does not love Williams; Desmoulins hates them both; Poll loves none of them. There is as much malignity amongst us as can well subsist, without any thoughts of daggers and poisons.' Amidst all this quarrelling however, the dinners were somehow cooked, and this in an age when kitchens had open fires and usually no oven. Anything that needed an oven was sent out to be baked.

'And pray,' said Mr. Thrale to Johnson one day, 'who is clerk of your kitchen, sir?' 'Why, sir,' said Johnson, 'I am afraid there is none; a general anarchy prevails in my kitchen, as I am told by Mr. Levett, who says it is not now what it used to be!'

'But how do you get your dinners drest?'

'Why,' said Johnson, 'De Mullin has the chief management of the kitchen; but our roasting is not magnificent, for we have no jack.'

'No jack? Why, how do they manage without?'

'Small joints, I believe, they manage with a string, and larger are done at the tavern. I have some thoughts' (with a profound gravity) 'of buying a jack, because I think a jack is some credit to a house.'

'Well, but you'll have a spit, too?'

'No, sir, no; that would be superfluous; for we shall never use it. If a jack is seen, a spit will be presumed!'

Johnson always showed great delicacy in his treatment of his dependants, especially of blind Miss Williams, who, whenever he dined away from home at a tavern was always, Boswell tells us, given her choice of 'a chicken, a sweetbread, or any other little nice thing, which was carefully sent to her from the tavern, ready drest.' In his treatment of servants, too, he showed a sensibility and consideration which surprised those who did not understand the great gentleness that lay at the core of his formidable character. We know from Boswell that when he wished to work undisturbed in the attic, where he kept his books and chemical experiments in a state of dust and disorder, he used to steal upstairs without telling anyone, so that Frank, supposing him to have gone out, would not have to tell a lie in saying he was not at home. And when Hodge, his cat, was ill, and would eat nothing but oysters (a cheap enough delicacy in those days) Dr. Johnson himself went out to buy them, lest Frank's feelings should be hurt by being asked to run errands for an animal.

It is with Hodge, the only one of his various cats of which we know anything, that we get one of our most endearing glimpses of Johnson. For Hodge threaded his way silently about the house, and caught the mice in Mrs. Desmoulins' kitchen, and had a saucer of milk by Miss Williams's fire during the late tea-drinkings, and stood up hopefully at Dr. Johnson's knee when he entertained his friends to oysters and porter in the parlour.

I recollect him one day [says Boswell], scrambling up Dr Johnson's breast, apparently with much satisfaction, while my friend, smiling and half-whistling, rubbed down his back and pulled him by the tail; and when I observed he was a fine cat, saying, 'Why, yes, sir; but I have had cats whom I liked better than this'; and then, as if perceiving Hodge to be out of countenance, adding, 'but he is a very fine cat, a very fine cat indeed.'

And again, having told some little anecdote about a harum-scarum young man who had been last seen running about town shooting cats, 'then,' says Boswell, 'he bethought himself of his own favourite cat, and said, "But Hodge shan't be shot: no, no, Hodge shall not be shot."'

It is in these little glimpses—trivial, perhaps, but revealing—that we add a surprising depth to our knowledge of character. We should know a great deal less of the gentle and lovable side of Johnson's nature if it were nowhere possible to see him thus, sitting by the fire with Hodge, at ease and at home.

Dr. Johnson at the Table

N IRISH DIVINE WHO KNEW HIM WELL SAID OF Dr. Johnson, 'The very minutiae of such a character must be interesting, and may be compared to the filings of diamonds.' We know something of a man's character if we know his pleasures, and Dr. Johnson, prey to tremendous melancholy though he was, was a great lover of pleasure, believing it to be a good in itself, provided it hurt no one. There is no doubt in his case that the pleasures of the table were among the best solaces of a life 'radically wretched.'

Johnson's appetites were in proportion to his bulk, and demanded huge satisfactions which were a source of enjoyment, but which led him to repeated self-examination and reproach. He was a man incapable of moderation. He could fast, or he could overeat. He could abstain from wine, or else get hugely drunk. The control of a sober temperament was beyond him, and this extravagance was a quality which ran through his whole character like a grain. He could sit up all night convivially with his friends, until, 'about five,' his 'face shone with meridian splendour, though his drink had been only lemonade'; or he could spend nights wretchedly awake in that black pit of melancholy into which his prayers, his journal, and his meditations give terrifying glimpses. Like many whose imaginations are darkened by a sense of guilt and the fear of death, he was childishly eager for convivial pleasures, his best protection from the frightful reflections which haunted him when alone. This horror of solitude must have driven him ever further into conviviality, developing him from pure sage and scholar into the man of wit, humour, and good company whom 'everybody thought they had a right to visit and consult.' 'He made his company exceedingly entertaining,' Mrs. Thrale admitted, 'when he had once forced one, by his vehement lamentations and piercing reproofs, not to quit the room, but to sit quietly and make tea for him, as I often did in London till four o'clock in the morning.'

But whatever the cause of his extravagant love of company, he was undeniably a greedy man. 'He told me,' said Boswell, '. . . that he had never been hungry but once,' but added, 'They who beheld with wonder how much he eat upon all occasions, when his dinner was to his taste, could not easily conceive what he must have meant by hunger.' Even as a boy, as Johnson himself recorded in his *Annals*, his prodigious feats at the table were long remembered. 'At my aunt Ford's I eat so much of a boiled leg of mutton that she used to talk of it. My mother, who had lived in a narrow sphere, and was then affected by little things, told me seriously that it would hardly ever be forgotten.'

I never knew any man [again it is Boswell speaking] who relished good eating more than he did. When at table, he was totally absorbed in the business of the moment; his looks seemed rivetted to his plate; nor would he, unless when in very high company, say one word, or even pay the least attention to what was said by others, till he had satisfied his appetite: which was so fierce, and indulged with such intenseness, that while in the act of eating, the veins of his forehead swelled, and generally a strong perspiration was visible.

Yet for all the grossness of this picture he was not merely a pig; he was also a gourmet. (The two go together more often than is commonly supposed.) Mrs. Thrale, whose husband could afford to keep a luxurious table both at Streatham and in the Borough, made it her care to study Johnson's tastes for twenty years, and found him greedy indeed, but also knowledgeable.

Johnson loved his dinner exceedingly [she wrote in her *Anecdotes*] and has often said in my hearing, perhaps for my edification, 'that wherever the dinner is ill got there is poverty, or there is avarice, or there is stupidity; in short, the family is somehow grossly wrong: for (continued he) a man seldom thinks with more earnestness of anything than he does of his dinner; and if he cannot get that well dressed, he should be suspected of inaccuracy in other things.' One day [Mrs. Thrale continues], when he was speaking upon the subject I asked him if he ever huffed his wife upon his dinner? 'So often (replied he), that at last she called to me, and said, Nay, hold Mr Johnson, and do not make a farce of thanking God for a dinner which in a few minutes you will protest not eatable.'

Johnson loved the niceties of a good table. He had been painfully poor in youth, and had known what it was to eat for eightpence a day at the City ordinaries ('I had a cut of meat for sixpence, and bread for a penny, and gave the waiter a penny; so that I was quite well served, nay, better than the rest, for they gave the waiter nothing'); and never had any patience with sentimental humbug about poverty. He was particularly irritated by a much-admired line in one of David Garrick's songs—'I'd smile with the simple, and feed with the poor.' 'Nay, my dear lady,' he said to Mrs. Thrale, who had quoted it with approval, 'this will never do. . . . Smile with the simple—what folly is that? And who would feed with the poor that can help it? No, no; let me smile with the wise, and feed with the rich.' 'To be merely satisfied,' he observed to Boswell on another occasion, 'is not enough. It is in refinement and elegance that the civilized man differs from the savage. . . . Sir, a hungry man has not the same pleasure in eating a plain dinner that a hungry man has in eating a luxurious dinner.'

'His invitations to dinners abroad,' Sir John Hawkins tells us, 'were numerous, and he seldom balked them.' He was a critical and expectant guest, offering his comments unsolicited on the dinner, much as the late A. J. A. Symons used to do; sometimes causing consternation, sometimes, by his approval, conferring a sort of gastronomic blessing.

When invited to dine, even with an intimate friend, he was not pleased if something better than a plain dinner was not prepared for him. I have heard him say on such an occasion, 'This was a good dinner enough, to be sure: but it was not a dinner to *ask* a man to.' On the other hand, he was wont to express, with great glee, his satisfaction when he had been entertained quite to his mind.

Johnson, then, was a greedy man and a gourmet, 'a man of very nice discernment in the science of cookery,' who 'used to descant critically on the dishes which had been at table where he had dined or supped, and to recollect very minutely what he had liked.' What did he like? Johnson's own notions of a good dinner, says Mrs. Thrale, were

nothing less than delicate; a leg of pork boiled till it drops from the bone, a veal-pye with plums and sugar, or the outside cut of a salt buttock of beef, are his favourite dainties, though he loves made dishes, soups etc.; sowces his Plumb Pudden with melted butter, and pours sauce enough into every plate to drown all taste of the victuals. With regard to drink [she goes on], his liking is for the strongest, as it is not the flavour but the effect of wine which he professes to desire; and he used often to pour capillaire into his glass of port.

For the last twelve years of his life, after a serious illness, Johnson abstained from wine, but

to make himself some amends for this concession [Mrs. Thrale observed], he drinks chocolate liberally, and puts in large quantities of butter or of cream. He loves fruit exceedingly, and though I have seen him eat of it immensely, he says he never had his bellyful of fruit but twice—once at our house and once at Ombersley, the seat of my Lord Sandys.

At Johnson's own house in Bolt Court, where he had 'supposed we should scarcely have knives and forks,' Boswell was agreeably surprised to sit down to 'a very good soup, a boiled leg of lamb and spinach, a veal pye, and a rice pudding.' When they went out to dine together at the Mitre there was always 'a little circumstance of kind attention to Mrs Williams,' the old ill-tempered lady in poor circumstances who lived at Johnson's expense. Before leaving the house he never omitted to see that whatever dish she fancied should be sent in, hot and ready, from a nearby tavern.

The great man's table manners, it must be confessed, were gross, though he was a stickler for good manners in others and sincerely believed his own to be scrupulous to the point of foppery. He could be, and sometimes was, elaborately courteous at table; his disconcerting aspect showed itself as a result of deep abstraction, when he would eat in total silence, his eyes 'rivetted to his plate,' or be terrifyingly abrupt, as at a gentleman's seat in Devonshire, 'when the lady of the house was pressing him to eat something,' and 'he rose up with his knife in his hand, and loudly exclaim'd, "I vow to God I cannot eat a bite more," to the great terror, it is said, of all the company.'

Johnson's attitude to wine, which he loved, was not that of a connoisseur. He drank wine for its effect upon him—'to get rid of myself, to send myself away'—and left it off for the same reason because, haunted always by his melancholy fear of madness, he suspected that effect.

The dread of so great a calamity [says Sir John Hawkins], was an inducement with him to abstain from wine at certain periods of his life, when his fears in this respect were greatest, but it was not without some reluctance that he did it, for he has often been heard to declare, that wine was to him so great a cordial, that it required all his resolution to resist the temptation to ebriety.

Mrs. Thrale believed that he gave up wine for religious reasons, but it seems clear enough that what he feared were the effects of possible drunkenness on the brain. 'I did not leave off wine,' he told Boswell, 'because I could not bear it; I have drunk three bottles of port without being the worse for it. University College has witnessed this.' The reason, he said, was that 'it is so much better for a man to be sure that he is never to be intoxicated, never to lose the power over himself.' He advised Boswell, who was fast becoming a drunkard, not to attempt moderation but to drink water only: 'For [said he] you are then sure not to get drunk; whereas, if you drink wine, you are never sure.' It was the only course for a man who could not trust himself. 'Many a day did he fast, many a year did he abstain from wine; but when he did eat, it was voraciously; when he did drink wine, it was copiously. He could practise abstinence, but not temperance.' He had found that resolving to drink moderately was useless, for by the time he had drunk moderately, he no longer cared. Total abstinence, which admitted of no doubt or hesitation, was the only safe course. 'When one doubts as to pleasure,' he told Boswell, 'we know what will be the conclusion. I now no more think of drinking wine, than a horse does. The wine upon the table is no more for me, than for the dog that is under the table.'

Wine, he considered, 'makes a man better pleased with himself,' but denied that it could ever illuminate the mind. 'It neither gives him knowledge or wit; it only animates a man, and enables him to bring out what a dread of the company has repressed.' And when Boswell insisted, 'You must allow me, Sir, at least that it produces truth; *in vino veritas*, you know, Sir'—'That [replied Mr. Johnson] would be useless to a man who knew he was not a liar when he was sober.'

In his last years Johnson drank wine again from time to time, 'but not socially.' His social life, his convivial nights in taverns, his late sitting up with friends at home or at the Thrales', was refreshed by chocolate, lemonade or tea. Tea, indeed, with its agreeable paraphernalia, the elegant cups and tray, the necessity to be made afresh as the night advanced and as often as Mrs. Thrale could be persuaded, was his favourite social beverage. He drank it with milk and sugar, except on Good Fridays, when he took it plain. 'I suppose,' says Boswell, 'no person ever enjoyed with more relish the infusion of that fragrant leaf than Johnson. The quantities which he drank of it at all hours were so great, that his nerves must have been uncommonly strong, not to have been extremely relaxed by such an intemperate use of it. He assured me, that he never felt the least inconvenience from it.'

If he denied himself wine, he must make an 'intemperate use' of tea. In tea-drinking, as in any other pleasure enjoyed, there was no middle way. Yet he did not philosophically accept this weakness in himself, but all his life long fought the battle against intemperance and sloth of which we find constant traces in his *Prayers and Meditations*. On Good Friday, 1764, he made the entry, 'I have made no reformation; I have lived totally useless, more sensual in thought, and more addicted to wine and meat'; and at the same season of reflection, many years later, 'Whether I have not lived resolving till the possibility of performance is past, I know not. God help me, I will yet try.'

A powerful mind and strenuous conscience, allied to powerful appetites (as in Johnson or Tolstoy), produce conflicts, pleasures, revulsions, and torturing self-denials such as more temperate natures never know. In both Johnson and Tolstoy the moralist, after scathing struggles, was triumphant; but as the Puritanism of Johnson was less extreme and more rational than Tolstoy's, so it did not embitter or pervert his genius. At one period he stands out as a sober giant in that drunken age, at another we see him through a haze of wine and smoke; and it was Mr. Dempster, a friend of Boswell's, who made perhaps the perfect pronouncement on Johnson's drinking days: 'When I complained,' said Boswell, 'that drinking port and sitting up late with him, affected my nerves for some time after, he said, "One had better be palsied at eighteen than not keep company with such a man." '

Dr. Johnson in His
Relations with Women

DOCTOR JOHNSON WAS FOND OF WOMEN, AS
they were of him, fonder than most men of
strict morals can generally be bothered to be;
and his relations with them, traceable in a
series of bold flourishes running from birth to death, is
undoubtedly the happiest element in a life that had more
than its share of waking nightmares. He seems to be a
particularly apt illustration of the simple proposition that
the boy who has a satisfying relationship with his mother
will be well disposed, as a man, to women in general; for
it is clear that Mrs. Johnson, for all her limitations, was
the right sort of mother.

Sarah Johnson was a woman of naturally vigorous
though uncultivated mind. Boswell called her a 'woman of
distinguished understanding,' but this seems to have been
a touch of biographical flattery, since, though she evidently had good capabilities, she had had little education
and next to no experience of the world. 'My father and
mother had not much happiness from each other. They
seldom conversed; for my father could not bear to talk of
his affairs; and my mother, being unacquainted with
books, cared not to talk of anything else. Had my mother
been more literate they had been better companions.'

Poor woman, she had little but her own domestic cares

to occupy her mind, for Johnson's father, morose and melancholy and absorbed in his ill-run business as a book-seller, frowned on her little excursions among the Lich-field neighbours. 'My father considered tea as very expensive, and discouraged my mother from keeping company with the neighbours, and from paying visits or receiving them. She lived to say, many years after, that, if the time were to pass again, she would not comply with such unsocial injunctions.'

She had married late, and was forty years old when, after a difficult and dangerous labour, her first child, Samuel, was born. At his father's wish he was sent to a wet-nurse in the town, and from her contracted the glandular disease which gradually disfigured him. 'My mother visited me every day, and used to go different ways, that her assiduity might not expose her to ridicule; and often left her fan or glove behind her, that she might have a pretence to come back unexpected; but she never discovered any token of neglect. . . . In ten weeks I was taken home, a poor diseased infant, almost blind.'

One gets the feeling, reading his all too brief and fragmentary *Annals*, of an alliance between Johnson and his mother, tender, reassuring, yet curiously equal, in which the father had no part, as though child and woman secretly supported one another. When she took him to London to be touched for the King's Evil by Queen Anne, she bought him a little silver cup and spoon, and had them marked SAM I.—'lest if they had been marked S.I. which was her name, they should, upon her death, have been taken from me.' She told him, as he lay in bed with her early one morning, about a future life, to be spent either in a 'fine place filled with happiness called Heaven,' or, according as one behaved, in 'a *sad* place, called Hell'; and, though she had no learning herself, she was proud of him when he came to an age to be forming verbs at school, and encouraged him when he dreaded the next day's lesson. ' "We often," said she, dear mother! "come off best, when we are most afraid." '

Her fond indulgence in the face of poverty touched Johnson's heart even in boyhood, and made him, as Mrs. Thrale recorded after his death, 'exceedingly disposed to the general indulgence of children,' being 'strongly persuaded himself of the difficulty people always find to erase early impressions either of kindness or resentment.' He should never, he told her, 'have so loved his mother when a man, had she not given him coffee she could ill afford, to gratify his appetite when a boy.' And love her he did, though not on quite the reverential terms that Mrs. Thrale thought proper between child and parent. 'Poor people's children, dear Lady [said he], never respect them: I did not respect my own mother, though I loved her: and one day, when in anger she called me a puppy, I asked her if she knew what they called a puppy's mother.'

Once Johnson had married and gone with Garrick to seek his fortune in London, his mother, of whom we never learn quite enough, fades into the Lichfield distance, where she lived to the great age of ninety, proudly contemplating the fame he had reached in his middle forties as 'Dictionary Johnson.' Mr. Hector, a Birmingham surgeon and one of Johnson's old schoolfellows, told Boswell, 'She had too much good sense to be vain, but she knew her son's value.' He had already proved it against formidable odds in the literary world, and she, it seems, had shed some of her innocent narrowness and was subtly changed. In his boyhood she 'had lived in a narrow sphere, and was then affected by little things. . . . Her mind, I think was afterwards much enlarged, or greater evils wore out the care of less.'

She died in the possession of a handful of brief letters from her son, letters sent from London to Lichfield when he was not aware (until too late) that she was dying. Like all Johnson's letters written in emotion, they have lost none of their power, and move us still with the strength of their love and sorrow.

DEAR HONOURED MOTHER

Your weakness afflicts me beyond what I am willing to communicate to you. I do not think you unfit to face death, but I know not how to bear the thought of losing you. . . .

Neither your condition nor your character make it fit for me to say much. You have been the best mother, and I believe the best woman in the world. I thank you for your indulgence to me, and beg forgiveness of all that I have done ill, and all that I have omitted to do well. God grant you His Holy Spirit, and receive you to ever-lasting happiness, for Jesus Christ's sake. Amen. Lord Jesus receive your spirit. Amen.

I am, dear, dear Mother,
Your dutiful Son,
SAM. JOHNSON

This, then, is the beginning of the pattern which Johnson's heart—a strong heart, capable of many and deep affections, and of singular ardour—was to follow; a great *affectionateness*, a sense of kindness and comfort and reassurance where women were concerned, an expectation of indulgence and encouragement. All these he learned from his mother, and from her, too, the elements of a religious faith which his own melancholy changed into something terrible and uncomforting. It was this inherited melancholy, this 'disease,' this 'kind of madness,' as he defined it, which drove him in self-defence, and far more than is usual with men of his moral strictness, into the society of women. He was only nineteen, as Boswell records, when 'he felt himself overwhelmed with an horrible hypochondria, with perpetual irritation, fretfulness and impatience; and with a dejection, gloom and despair, which made existence misery.'

It is a common effect of low spirits or melancholy [Boswell proceeds]—and it is well to check unseemly surprise at the acuteness of his observation, for the human heart was an object of study long before we were handed the crib of psycho-analysis—to make those who are afflicted with it imagine that they are actually suffering those evils which happen to be most strongly presented to their minds. Some have fancied themselves to be deprived of the use of their limbs, some to labour under acute diseases, others to be in acute poverty; when, in truth, there was not the least reality in any of the suppositions; so that when the vapours were dispelled, they were convinced of the delusion. To Johnson, whose supreme enjoyment was the exercise of his reason, the disturbance or obscuration of that faculty was the evil most to be dreaded. Insanity, therefore, was the object of his most dismal apprehension.

Johnson's fears for the health of his mind were not groundless, though it was not madness in the Bedlam sense of which he stood in danger. He was aware, constantly and uneasily, of illness in himself, of the kind which nowadays we should call neurotic. There is also evidence in his behaviour of obsessive neurosis of which we cannot know the origin, and of which Johnson himself, naturally enough, never suspected the significance. His peculiar unconscious rituals at doorways and stairs, his horror of solitude, his sense of guilt and conviction of personal damnation, are more interesting, because more significant, to us than they were to the contemporaries of

Boswell and Mrs. Thrale. But however we may assess the dark hints in *Thraliana*, we cannot with certainty interpret Johnson's oddities of behaviour. We know something about them, but we can never know enough. We can safely assert only that he was a man of powerful instincts, whose conscience (to give it an old-fashioned and somewhat misleading name) had imposed on him equally powerful prohibitions; and that his fear of temptation had driven him unconsciously to fortify himself with all manner of strange rituals, and to avoid at all costs the dangers of being alone. It was this conflict, we can suppose, which had given rise to the frightful melancholia from which he suffered, and which only obsessions of guilt married to convictions of eternal punishment can produce in quite the evil perfection in which Johnson knew it.

Johnson, then, was a man neurotically ill, and it is important to remember this in considering his relations with women, for it was in their society, and in the emotional comfort and gaiety that he derived from it, that he found one of the best defences against his malady. His greatest pleasure, as we know, was conversation with worldly and intelligent companions, and these, on a mental level most nearly approaching his own, were naturally men; but he found happiness of a less stimulating and more reassuring sort in the company of attractive, intelligent, and 'complacent'[1] women, even an instinctive comfort in the society of women of almost any sort.

Why women liked Johnson, as they undoubtedly did, is another matter. At first glance his attraction for them is difficult to understand, for he was massive, uncouth, and unfastidious, and his conversation held such ferocious possibilities that he was more or less debarred from good society. Even Mrs. Thrale, admiringly partial, could

[1] 'Civil; affable; soft; complaisant.' *Johnson's Dictionary*.

think of no stronger physical recommendation than that
his leg and foot were 'eminently handsome; his hand
handsome too, in spite of dirt, and of such deformity as
perpetual picking his fingers necessarily produced.' But to
think of him only in these terms is to be content with a
very superficial judgement, and to leave out of account all
that was most valuable and endearing in the man. He had
a fund of gaiety, playfulness, and irresistible humour
which is too readily forgotten by those later biographers
who prefer to dwell on his melancholy and his ferocity:
one has only to turn over the pages of Fanny Burney's
diary to realize how affectionate and entrancing he could
be as a companion, how pre-eminently he was, to use an
expression of our own day, 'good value.' 'Johnson has more
fun, and comical humour, and love of nonsense about him,
than almost anybody I ever saw. . . .' 'In the evening he
was as lively and as full of wit and sport as I have ever
seen him. . . .' 'Dr Johnson was in the utmost good humour. . . .' 'At tea we all met again, and Dr Johnson was
gaily sociable.' 'Dr Johnson, as usual, came last into the
library; he was in high spirits, and full of mirth and sport.'
'Dr Johnson was charming, both in spirits and humour. I
really think he grows gayer and gayer daily, and more
ductile and pleasant. . . .' And it was not only Fanny
Burney who found him loving and playful, for even Anna
Seward, the somewhat jealous and censorious Swan of
Lichfield, admitted (though with a qualification) that 'no
man's manners are more affectionate.' There has never
elsewhere, as Robert Lynd has justly written, 'been so
great and magnanimous a man in whose life there was
such a current vein of comedy.'

He had, indeed, that fertile and brilliant gaiety which
is not uncommon among melancholics and which is developed to its full perfection as self-defence, an insurance

against solitude. His comic genius was especially sensitive
to the light and frequent occasions of domestic laughter,
the trivial affectionate jokes that women enjoy. Who but
Johnson, seeing Queeney Thrale in her best clothes on her
way to dine with the tremendous Mrs. Montagu, would
have expressed in verse, without a moment's pause, his
delight and sympathy?

> Wear the gown and wear the hat,
> Snatch the pleasures while they last,
> Hadst thou nine lives like a cat
> Soon those nine lives would be past.

His humour, said Hawkins (who could appreciate
that quality in others although it was not conspicuous in
himself), was 'ever of that arch and dry kind, which lies
concealed under the appearance of gravity'; and it is difficult to resist the impression, both in Boswell and elsewhere, that even much of his ferocity was intentionally
comical, and that some of his bitter sayings become so
only when the warm tide of his personality has receded,
leaving them stranded in print. Fanny Burney has a good
example of this which is worth quoting, since it brings out
Boswell's contention that 'many of his pointed sayings
. . . rather show a playfulness of fancy than any settled
malignity.' Mrs. Thrale, in a brisk exchange with Johnson about Garrick and Hawkins, had accused him of allowing no one to abuse either of them, except himself.

'Why, madam,' answered he, 'they don't know when to
abuse him and when to praise him; I will allow no man
to speak ill of David that he does not deserve; and as to
Sir John, why really I believe him to be an honest man
at the bottom: but to be sure he is penurious, and he is
mean, and it must be owned he has a degree of brutality,

and a tendency to savageness, that cannot easily be defended.' We all laughed, *as he meant we should*. . . .

Besides this playfulness, there was a delicate gallantry in his address to women which flattered their self-esteem, and which coming from a man of Johnson's intellectual stature, was more telling, perhaps, than even physical attraction. Sir Joshua Reynolds's sister observed that he 'set a higher value upon female friendship than, perhaps, most men'; and Sir John Hawkins analysed his undoubted charm for women with some acuteness.

In his conversation with women he had such a felicity as would put vulgar gallantry out of countenance. Of the female mind, he conceived a higher opinion than many men, and though he was never suspected of a blameable intimacy with any individual of them, had a great esteem for the sex. The defects in his powers of sight rendered him totally insensible to the charms of beauty; but he knew that beauty was the attribute of the sex, and treated all women with such an equable complacency, as flattered every one into a belief that she had her share of that or some more valuable endowment. In his discourses with them, his compliments had ever a neat and elegant turn: they were never direct, but always implied the merit they were intended to attest.

Though very short-sighted he would peer, when interested, into every detail of a lady's dress and ornament, and though his criticisms were sometimes a little too harshly expressed, there always remained that important element of flattery, implicit in the great man's interest. These charms of manner, this very complete and ingratiating technique of being agreeable to women, were undoubtedly important in his relations with them; but we may, perhaps, look a little more deeply without risk of making facile interpretations.

Johnson was a highly moral man, and by the time he reached middle age had become, in morals as well as in literature, considerably larger than life. We see him, then, massive with accretions of authority, as an ideal father figure, trustworthy, a little terrifying, an authority whose praise was desirable and whose censure chastening, and with whom a lightly amorous playfulness could be enjoyed without fear. Johnson's strict sexual morality, in fact, is a crucial element in the situation, imposed as it was on a temperament of more than common ardour. (There has naturally been no lack of commentators eager to point out that because he never gave cause for scandal he must have been incapable, but there is no evidence whatever to support such an idea, and no grounds for disbelieving Boswell when he tells us that 'it was well known that his amorous inclinations were uncommonly strong and impetuous.') Johnson, so far as we know, allowed himself no sexual indulgence outside marriage, and he was widowed at forty-three. He seems to have comforted both his masculine and his melancholic nature by affectionate social intimacies with women of some attraction and mental calibre (Mrs. Thrale, Fanny Burney, Hannah Moore, Molly Aston, Hill Boothby, and Charlotte Lenox, not by any means to name them all) and to have demanded a high standard, an 'endearing elegance' in his female friendships, to compensate for the denial of more straightforward gratifications.

His moral strictness (which seems to have had much to do with his neuroses) goes far to explain, if explanation be needed, his somewhat curious marriage. His wife, Tetty, has been much laughed at. The boys at Johnson's short-lived 'academy' started the joke, Garrick improved and perpetuated it; and it is unlikely that she will ever acquire much dignity in the eyes of posterity, having to overcome, poor creature, the irresistible jests of female middle-age, fatness, a large bosom, and a fondness for cordials and cosmetics. Yet we know that Johnson thought her beautiful, and there is much to account for his genuine passion, however grotesque the pair of them may have appeared to schoolboys (never the most delicate of observers) and to David Garrick. It is not uncommon for a man of strong instincts and strict principles to be very uxorious; it is his happiest solution; and for the eighteen years of his married life Johnson, who was affectionate as well as passionate, seems to have concentrated all his love of the sexual and companiable sort on Elizabeth Johnson, his Tetty. (On this psychological point, again, Boswell shows himself shrewdly observant. 'In a man whom religious education has secured from licentious indulgencies, the passion of love, when once it has seized him, is exceedingly strong; being unimpaired by dissipation, and totally concentrated in one object. This was experienced by Johnson, when he became the fervent admirer of Mrs. Porter, after her first husband's death.') And Tetty herself is not to be despised, though she married a man of twenty-five when she was nearly fifty (in itself something of an achievement) and was in some ways absurd. She recognized Johnson's quality when he was poor and unknown, and his appearance so unprepossessing that one cannot suppose her to have been much beguiled by it. It seems, indeed, to have been a sense of his intellectual grandeur which drew her to him, for she was 'so much engaged by his conversation' that she overlooked his poor appearance and odd behaviour, and told her daughter, 'this is the most sensible man that I ever saw in my life.'

Anna Seward has an anecdote of Mrs. Porter's reply to Johnson's proposal which leaves the faint but unmistakable imprint of a salty wit. 'You are not twenty-five,' his mother said to him when he asked for her consent to the marriage, 'and she is turned fifty. If she had any prudence, this request had never been made to me. Where are your means of subsistence? Porter has died poor, in consequence of his wife's expensive habits. You have great talents, but, as yet, have turned them into no profitable channel.' 'Mother,' said Johnson, 'I have not deceived Mrs. Porter: I have told her the worst of me; that I am of mean extraction; that I have no money, and that I have had an uncle hanged. She replied, that she valued no one more or less for his descent; that she had no more money than myself; and that, though she had not had a relation hanged, she had fifty who deserved hanging.'

The married life of the Johnsons seems, then, to have been seasoned with a touch of acerbity on both sides, which, since there was also the ingredient of good humour in their disputes, led to no bitterness. They disputed, Johnson told Mrs. Thrale, 'perpetually,' but about nothing very serious. Mrs. Desmoulins told Boswell that Tetty 'by no means treated him with that complacency which is the most engaging quality in a wife.' Still, she was no fool, and she admired her husband and seems to have returned his 'tumultuous and awkward fondness,' so that, as Boswell recognized, her faults were 'perfectly compatible with his fondness for her, especially when it is remembered that he had a high opinion of her understanding, and that the impressions which her beauty, real or imaginary, had originally made upon his fancy, being continued by habit, had not been effaced, though she herself was doubtless much altered for the worse.' Mrs. Johnson, with her love of rouge and cordials and her celebrated bosom, seems to have had the attraction of an intelligent middle-aged barmaid, playfully girlish on occasion, but at the same time to be relied upon for considerable good sense. Their mutual

fondness has never been in doubt; its very excesses provoked unfeeling laughter, and Sir John Hawkins (who
never saw Tetty) was assured by Johnson's friends that
'there was somewhat crazy in the behaviour of them both.'

When Mrs. Thrale, years after Mrs. Johnson's death,
questioned Levett about her, she could learn only of 'perpetual illness and perpetual opium.' (What Levett had
acutally said, according to Mrs. Thrale's private notes,
was that 'She was always drunk and reading romances in
her bed, where she killed herself by taking opium'; but, as
Mrs. Thrale sensibly adds, 'I rather think she must have
been in most respects a woman quite like her neighbours,
but that her second choice made her a person to enquire
about.') Did Mrs. Johnson, we wonder, die of cancer?
The echoes that reach us from her deathbed are, though
faint, still terrible: her death shook Johnson to his foundations and left him 'a childless widower, abandoned to
sorrow, and incapable of consolation.'

Consolation, fortunately, came in the course of time,
after thirteen comfortless years; and it is with a satisfaction scarcely equalled in the whole literature of biography
that we come each time to the fifty-sixth year in Boswell,
and find it marked as the memorable year in which Johnson was first taken to the Thrales. How we enjoy, for
Johnson's sake, the buttered muffins and the pineapples!
How we approve, our solicitousness in every detail grati-
fied, the budding and growth, the perfect, the almost
exotic flowering of his long *amitié amoureuse!* For Mrs.
Thrale, in return for the literary celebrity which his presence shed, was able to enfold him in just that virtuously
luxurious and sprightly atmosphere which his imagination demanded in his ideal intercourse with women. Why
have so many people been angry with him for enjoying
Streatham? 'He loved her,' said Anna Seward, 'for her

wit, her beauty, her luxurious table, her coach and her library.' Indeed, we may think that no woman could have a more dazzling constellation of attractions; and in Johnson's frank enjoyment of the delights of Streatham we, being less puritanical in outlook than the Lichfield Swan, see only the candid appreciation of the pleasure-loving man. For the Thrales were really very rich indeed, and nobody but a political prig would pretend nowadays that there is not something wonderfully pleasant about a cultivated life solidly supported by wealth, which is what Mrs. Thrale, fortunate woman, was able to offer; and Johnson made a fair return of all her hospitality by fertilizing the intellectual soil of Streatham until Mrs. Thrale was garlanded for posterity.

But the relation between them was not a mere calculation of benefits exchanged. There was a more private, sombre, even terrifying link between them which American scholars have only comparatively recently (and with some misgiving) examined. The first signals from something hidden beneath the surface were picked up in 1942, when *Thraliana* was first published. Miss Katherine Balderston, editing Mrs. Thrale's vast compendium of notes, anecdotes, and reflections with a scrupulousness which no other Johnsonian scholar has surpassed, had been puzzled by an item in the sale of Mrs. Thrale's effects in 1823: a padlock, attached to a label on which was written, 'Johnson's padlock, committed to my care in 1768.' By itself this suggested nothing much, but there was a possible clue in Johnson's diary for 1771, six words in Latin, *De pedicis et manicis insana cogitatio*—'insane thoughts of footfetters and manacles.' This, too, seemed more or less inexplicable, but in 1932 there had been published some hitherto unseen letters, among them an extremely curious communication from Johnson to Mrs. Thrale in French,

and part of Mrs. Thrale's diary, written in English. Johnson's letter was evidently written under abnormal mental
stress, while he was staying in the Thrales' house at
Streatham; also, apparently, under some kind of voluntary
physical restraint. Its tone is loaded with morbid self-
abasement; he implores her authority to decide whether or
not he is to remain a prisoner, even what he may eat
and drink. He supplicates her protection and discipline,
'*comme auparavant.*' in piercing tones reproaching her
with neglect.

Mrs. Thrale's answer is equally extraordinary, though
couched in terms of tenderness and respect. 'Let not your
fancy dwell,' she advises, 'on confinement and severity. If
it be possible, shake off these uneasy weights, heavier to
the mind by far than fetters to the body.' He must no
longer remain alone, but must seek company. 'Dissipation
is to you a glorious medicine, and I believe Mr Boswell
will be at last your best physician. For the rest you are
really well enough now if you will keep so,' and concludes—whether metaphorically or not we can never
know—'Farewell and be good; and do not quarrel with
your governess for not using the rod enough.'

Clearly there was an uncomfortable secret here, which
Mrs. Thrale, even in her diary, was solicitous to keep.
There are hints on various pages that Johnson has confided a momentous secret to her, for which she pities and
respects him, wearied and appalled though she is by his
strangely perverse method of dealing with it. 'Poor Johnson!' she wrote in *Thraliana* after his death, 'I see they
will leave *nothing untold* that I laboured so long to keep
secret; and I was so very delicate in trying to conceal his
fancied insanity, that I retained no proofs of it—or hardly
any'; and later, when the supposed secret was found to be
known to others, 'How many times has this great, this

formidable Doctor Johnson kissed my hand, ay and my foot too, upon his knees! . . . but the fetters and padlocks will tell posterity the truth.'

This then, with other privately noted hints on the same subject, is the evidence that one of Johnson's most unmanageable neuroses (he may well have suffered from several, as Lord Brain in his essay on Johnson as *The Great Convulsionary* [2] has pointed out) grew out of an irresistible conviction of guilt, almost certainly sexual in origin, which he could relieve only by masochistic self-abasement and physical suffering. Johnson's own pronouncements on madness, on the sensuality of madmen and their desire for subjection and pain, are profound and revealing, since they refer always to this one type of mania, as though drawn from personal experience. Miss Balderston's conclusion, which she is at pains to insist is not that of a psychiatrist but of a layman, is that after the death of Tetty, and increasingly as he grew older, Johnson's most powerful temptation was to erotic day-dreams, and that these compulsive fantasies, which his strenuous moral nature obliged him to condemn, established such a hold on his imagination as to carry him sometimes out of touch with reality to a point where he found himself on the brink of madness.

In this pitiful dilemma his own nature, and also that of his malady, drove him to turn for emotional relief to a woman, and Mrs. Thrale, intelligent, affectionate, and discreet (up to a point) was mercifully at hand. It is impossible from the evidence to conclude otherwise than that she was wholly unaware of the erotic implications of their relationship. She saw him as a great man possessed by dangerous delusions and herself as the loyal if sorely

[2] Russell Brain: *Some Reflections on Genius* (1960).

tried confidante in whose power (her vanity was touched by this) he unconditionally placed himself. 'Johnson,' she privately wrote in this connection, 'is more a hero to me than to anyone—and I have been more to him for intimacy than ever was any man's valet-de-chambre.' But the tremendous secret, awful and largely inexplicable to them both, had imposed private obligations which the world could neither recognize nor understand. This, as only Miss Balderston has stressed, is surely the explanation of his violent repudiation of Mrs. Thrale when she finally married Piozzi. Nothing else, she writes,[3] 'Neither the loss of his creature comforts, nor the disruption of the only domestic happiness he had ever known, nor his doubtless sincere conviction of her rash imprudence and failure in her duty to her children, not even the wound she inflicted on that half-paternal, half-romantic love of her which his biographers have recognized, quite explains his irrational and unjust behaviour at that juncture.'

It is a measure of the vitality of personality of both Johnson and Mrs. Thrale that few people are able to write about the situation, even today, without violently supporting the one and accusing the other. We still take sides and dispute about their parting as though we were of the Streatham circle, and at least one writer has been so carried away by his hatred of Mrs. Thrale in the affair that one feels he would welcome any new fact, however sordid or trivial, which would help to blacken her. This is in the fashion set by Macaulay, who censured Mrs. Thrale's middle-aged falling in love as a 'degrading passion,' and described Johnson, at the time of her marriage to Piozzi, 'leaving for ever that beloved home for the gloomy and desolate house behind Fleet Street, where the few and evil

[3] In *Johnson's Vile Melancholy* (*The Age of Johnson*) (New Haven: Yale University Press; 1949).

days which still remained to him were to run out.' Mrs.
Thrale, however, has had her champions, so that the
breach becomes again the very thing it must have been
when Mrs. Thrale's determination to marry Piozzi after
her first husband's death produced such a turmoil—the
sort of crisis, in fact, in which all one's friends take sides,
supporting and blaming and gossiping and giving advice.
It is Anna Seward's comment, after all, which most nearly
fits our own conclusions about the quarrel between Mrs.
Thrale and Johnson—'I do not approve of either but I
think it unfair that one should be considered a saint, the
other a demon.'

It is now possible to understand, though not to excuse,
Johnson's behaviour, for the affectionate man (which he
supremely was) is fully as possessive as the passionate
man (which he was also) and just as easy to wound; and
for nearly twenty years Johnson had been growing into
the Streatham household until he had roots in every part
of it, like an old ivy in a wall; and the shock of uprooting
him produced cries of rage and pain which are still
mournfully echoing. And Mrs. Thrale, too—surely she
had a right to fall in love, though she was over forty?
Only those who have no knowledge of the heart at all will
be surprised at her behaviour. For Mrs. Thrale was simply blinded by her desire for Piozzi. Though she had been
married at twenty-two and had borne Thrale twelve children, she seems, in this headlong passion, to have experienced the full tide of sexual emotion for the first time.
(Indeed, though she wrote down Thrale as 'a man exceedingly comfortable to live with' there are faint hints here
and there of increasing physical dislike.) Nothing mattered for the time being but that she should have this
unsensational, well-behaved Italian gentleman, who felt,

apparently, no comparable ardour for Mrs. Thrale, but who, after some hesitation, mildly and decorously consented to be caught; and everything else—children, friends, even reputation—temporarily lost hold. And Johnson, we must remember, had not the importance in the affair for Mrs. Thrale that she had for him. He was getting old, he was a burden, a secret embarrassment, an incubus, and she longed for a life of her own. It is an interesting situation—the passionate woman and the deeply affectionate man; one which inevitably leads to some betrayal.

Inevitably? It might, perhaps, have been better managed, and have ended amicably; but each, driven by temperament, made a fatal mistake. Mrs. Thrale, by concealing from Johnson what everyone else knew about her feeling for Piozzi; Johnson, by greeting the revelation when it came with a bellow of rage. If Mrs. Thrale, who confided in him so affectionately about everything else, had not withheld the only confidence that mattered . . . if Johnson, exquisitely tender as he could be to those he loved, had been generous on this occasion . . . then they might each have been spared the pain of a bitter parting; and we, instead of those sombre and appalling last hours which Hawkins recorded, might have dwelt without pain on a death made easy by every tender support, in a soft bed in a great room with a fire, amid the comforts of Streatham.

But each made the cardinal mistake, and the intimacy of twenty years was instantly shattered, with a sound like the splitting of rock. We see only too well the cowardice, the understandable cowardice, with which Mrs. Thrale turned a smiling ambiguous face to Johnson, and told him nothing; we see, too, how Johnson's unconscious fear of the impending catastrophe drove him to ignore or disbelieve what was obvious to all. 'I should beg your pardon,' Mrs. Thrale wrote to him, in the admirable letter which finally broke the news, 'for concealing from you a connection which you must have heard of by many people, but I suppose never believed. Indeed, my dear Sir, it was concealed only to spare us both needless pain; I could not have borne to reject that counsel it would have killed me to take.' Johnson's bitter and violent answer, a mere dozen lines, has sealed and preserved for us, as in a fragment of amber, his humiliation and shock; a letter we may regret, yet should not, since it tells us so much about the Johnson whom Fanny Burney described as 'this great, but *mortal* man.'

Mrs. Thrale appears at her best in the just reply which she made to this cudgel blow, and Johnson himself, in his next letter, in which he breathes out 'one sigh more of tenderness,' has recovered his balance and is himself again. It is the last act of a long play, and we watch in a gathering twilight. Mrs. Thrale rattles cheerfully away to Italy and Wales with her Piozzi, and we are glad to know that she will be justified in her noisy struggle for the heart's freedom, and that Piozzi will make her a good husband, and that she will live to dance on her eightieth birthday in the Assembly Rooms at Bath. For Johnson, bereaved by her going and so deprived of his best defence, there remains only the recognition of the approach of death, the final acceptance of that last experience, that single certainty which had darkened his life.

We see, then, completed (in this one aspect at least) the pattern traced by Johnson's emotional relationships, and against this shadowy background, dominated by the three fine arabesques described by his mother, his wife, and Mrs. Thrale, he emerges with even more than his customary strength as a supremely *affectionate* man. This character, perilously balanced and accentuated by neurosis, repeated over and over again in delicate variation, is the basic motif, the clue to his relations with the many women for whom he showed a fondness. It appears in his playful love for Fanny Burney, and the showers of witty nonsense which were thrown off by his affectionate (but essentially fear-ridden) desire to keep her by him. It appears in his long, quiet, and curious domestic intimacy with Anna Williams; in his stringently innocent but appreciative contacts with those cheerful creatures of the *demi-monde* (led by the unforgettable Bet Flint) who inhabited their special eighteenth-century element, half-way between the theatre and the street; in the compassion which led him to carry home a sick prostitute from the gutter, and in the love which comforted the deathbed of Catherine Chambers, his mother's old servant, with kisses and prayers. It appears with special charm in his long friendship with Queeney Thrale, Mrs. Thrale's eldest daughter, which began (or rather, attained the dignity of a correspondence) when she was seven years old, and ended only with his death; a friendship which gives Queeney a little fame of her own as the recipient of a long series of entrancing letters which almost persuade us that she herself had charm. This suggested charm is nowhere else apparent; she seems, indeed, to have been a stodgy girl, and her bad relations with her mother, while casting a suggestive shadow on Mrs. Thrale, do not make Queeney interesting. But as the girl whom Johnson's letters greet as 'My dearest,' 'My dear Sweeting,' 'My dear Charmer,' 'Dearest Love,' 'Dearest Miss,' the child with whom Johnson shared a birthday for

which the summer-house was 'filled with food and fiddles,'
she presents a fleeting apparition of eighteenth-century
girlhood, muslin-gowned, curly-haired, learning Latin
with Johnson, collecting objects of interest for her cabi-
net, taking tea in a shady hat in a Zoffany landscape and
vanishing between the clipped hedges of Streatham.

The Queen of the Methodists

HY DO THE APOSTLES OF GREAT movements rarely appear singly? They are first observed, as a rule, in twos and threes, like early mushrooms, and before there is time to digest them the field is white, and a movement or revolution has begun.

The rise of Methodism in the eighteenth century we associate with the name of Wesley, and are apt to think of him as setting off the huge convulsion single-handed; whereas, if we could look back on it, we should see the scene dotted all over with the intently purposeful forms of 'awakened' clergymen, threading their way hither and thither as busily as starlings. We should see Whitefield as well as the Wesleys; Venn, Romaine, Fletcher, Augustus Toplady, even (the strangeness of their names!) the Reverend Neptune Blood; and a remarkable throng of reverend gentlemen preaching in the fields, the streets, in prisons, in churchyards, and in the drawing-rooms of the mighty. We should see, in a London already rich with the personalities of Johnson and Chesterfield and Garrick, that unexpected, unsmiling Cassandra of society, the Countess of Huntingdon.

She is not much remembered today, though there are still a few churches bearing her name over their doorways

and a handful of her letters was raked out of paper sal-
vage during the last war. She would be dismayed if she
could see how Wesley's connection has flourished and her
own been forgotten. But in her own time she was as
conspicuous a torch-bearer for the revival as Wesley himself and in some ways more sensational, for the wave of
Puritanism which threw up Wesley and Whitefield and a
host of others sent at least one powerful ripple among the
rich and great, awakening this singular lady to her arduous mission of bringing the upper classes to salvation.

In making this bold attempt she was facing a task
almost as difficult as she would find it today, and con-
sciously making herself a target for ridicule. The polite
world was orthodox, and largely indifferent; atheism was
openly fashionable among the wits, and sexual morals in
high places were extremely free. Gaming and drinking
had reached a pitch of general profligacy that has never
since been equalled, and there was, besides, such a conviction of natural privilege among people of rank that the
spiritual self-abasement demanded by the Methodists was
particularly offensive.

> Their doctrines (wrote the Duchess of Buckingham to
> Lady Huntingdon) are most repulsive, and strongly
> tinctured with impertinence and disrespect towards
> their superiors, in perpetually endeavouring to level all
> ranks, and do away with all distinctions. It is monstrous
> to be told, that you have a heart as sinful as the common
> wretches that crawl on the earth. This is highly offensive
> and insulting; and I cannot but wonder that your Lady-
> ship should relish any sentiments so much at variance
> with high rank and good breeding.

Such indignation provokes a smile today, but it was serious then. Rank and riches still enjoyed their divine rights
of privilege, never dreaming of such a thing as the French

Revolution; and that wonderful sense of power which the aristocracy still enjoyed made Lady Huntingdon's missionary effort among her own class a formidable undertaking. But there was one factor on her side which she would be startled to find missing in the twentieth century. Nearly everyone believed, some as a matter of course and some uneasily, in their immortal soul; and where there is belief in eternal life the possibility of hell, forcefully presented with sorrowful Puritan relish, can be marvellously unsettling.

It is the fear at the back of Puritanism that gives it its drama, its powerful and intimate attraction. Mr. V. S. Pritchett once summed up its pleasures with much shrewdness.

Extreme puritanism gives purpose, drama and intensity to private life. One of the greatest mistakes which the genial critics of puritanism make is to suppose that puritanism seen from the outside is the same as puritanism seen from the inside. Outwardly the extreme puritan appears narrow, crabbed, fanatical, gloomy and dull; but from the inside—what a series of dramatic climaxes his life is. . . . He lives like a soldier, now in the flash of battle, now in the wangling of camp and billet. However much he may bore others, he never suffers from boredom himself.

Methodism was discovered in the eighteenth century as a fierce draught to be swallowed by passionate natures, inducing a changed life in which the lights and shadows were intensified to the pitch of hallucination, alternately ravishing and terrible. It was, naturally, unfashionable. It implied 'enthusiasm,' which in its eighteenth-century sense was sheer bad form, regarded askance in the polite world as ardent and avowed spiritualism is today. Enthusiasm, as Dr. Johnson disapprovingly defined it, meant 'a vain belief of private revelation.' An enthusiast was 'one who has a vain confidence of his intercourse with God.' Correct intercourse took place in one's parish church, according to the Thirty-nine Articles. If individuals were to claim direct guidance from on high, where might this not lead? Besides, that sort of thing was extraordinarily ill-bred, and made one look absurd. The wits were openly amused by Lady Huntingdon, whom they mentioned flippantly in their letters to one another as Pope Joan Huntingdon, or the Queen of the Methodists.

This remarkable woman was born Lady Selina Shirley, second daughter of the second Earl Ferrers, and dated her own conversion from the age of nine, when she chanced to see the funeral of a little girl of her own age and was impelled to follow the coffin to the grave. Certainly she seems to have been a pious and morbid child, but her real conversion in the Methodist sense did not come until she was married, and, emotionally ripe as she was for this very experience, came under the influence of her husband's sisters. Repelled by the frivolity of the fashionable world, Selina Shirley had often prayed that God would allow her to marry into a serious family, and in marrying the ninth Earl of Huntingdon it seemed that her petition had been answered. Her husband, though no ascetic, was conspicuous in that profligate age for the most unmodish decency of behaviour, and his two sisters, the Ladies Margaret and Elizabeth Hastings, were celebrated for their benevolent piety. Elizabeth Hastings, indeed, is one of those figures of a vanished age who still, faintly and across the separating centuries, seem to be making us a perceptible signal, as though she had something of importance to communicate. Steele bestowed on her one unfading laurel with his famous epigram, 'To love her is a liberal education,' and everything (it is not much) that we can learn about her is attractive. Handsome, rich, sweet-natured, she seems indeed to have been one of the natural saints, one of those rare *dévotes* who wore the early Methodism not as a hair shirt but as a halo. Her life is a long placid poem of sensible benevolence, and her terrible heroism in death (from cancer, after the amputation of both breasts with the aid of no stronger opiate than prayer) leaves us with the appalled conviction that human endurance has after all no limits.

Her sister, Margaret Hastings, equally pious though perhaps in other respects not quite her equal, had her own sort of courage, for she took the unthinkable step (for a woman of her rank) of marrying a travelling Methodist clergyman and throwing in her lot with his life of hand-to-mouth preaching and good works. It was this lady who took the young Selina's spiritual education in hand and brought her to the point where she could herself experience the strange and violent inner crisis of salvation.

From this point the young wife's life at Donington Park, her husband's seat in Leicestershire, takes on a kind of sombre splendour, in which wealth, privilege, and piety combine to produce a Goya-like chiaroscuro. In the flickering shadows we glimpse great comings and goings of servants and clergymen, almost indistinguishable; of women of fashion, amused, indignant, or uneasy, according to their natures; great cynics of the polite world like Chesterfield and Bolingbroke, scoffing behind their hands but attending her religious séances because of her position; and always present but never in the foreground, the plump, benevolent, faintly puzzled features of the Earl of Huntingdon. What privately he thought of it all we shall never know. The impression he makes is of a man pleasant and pliable and exquisitely diplomatic, who, being fond of his wife (there seems no doubt of this), was

content, to please her, to do such unfashionable things as
accompany her to hear Wesley in Fetter Lane and to have
his house infested with obsequious clergymen. It is certain
that he was never converted to Methodism, never 'saved,'
though he attended his wife's 'spiritual routs' and was
never rude to any of the visiting clergy. He even excited
surprise among his own class by never forbidding his
wife's Methodist practices, by permitting the sacred
goings-on with an almost culpable tolerance. He had, it is
true, while his wife was still convalescent from her spiritual rebirth, called in the Bishop of Gloucester, who had
been his tutor at Oxford, to reason with her, for he was
man of the world enough to see that a case of 'enthusiasm'
in the family was going to be socially embarrassing. But
Selina had a greater appetite for religious argument than
the Bishop had, and a great deal more vitality, so that the
interview ended in a triumph for the lady and extreme
annoyance (which his regard for rank prevented him
from expressing) for Bishop Benson. After that Lord
Huntingdon interfered no further but allowed his town
house and his country house to become hotbeds of revival,
himself remaining neutral, occupying himself inoffen-
sively with the pleasures of a well-kept table, a choice
library, and the care of his estate. He seems to have been a
man without ambition, since he took no part in politics or
public life and preferred the stay-at-home middle-class
virtues to cutting any sort of figure. One respects him for
the moral stamina which enabled him to endure, under his
sisters' and his wife's eyes and in his own house, all the
most persuasive Methodist preachers of his day without
ever exhibiting the smallest symptom of salvation; but one
also suspects, studying that shrewd, self-indulgent, faintly
amused face that the secret both of his tolerance and of his
orthodoxy was—just conceivably—that he was lazy.

Lady Huntingdon's conversion, and her self-imposed mission to the rich and great while Wesley and White-field laboured among the humble, provoked amusement and some resentment in society. The spectacle of a count-ess penitent and openly proclaiming herself a sinner was nothing less than sensational. She was regarded by people like the Duchess of Buckingham as a traitor to her class, and the Duchess persisted in her resentment to the grave, administering a last magnificent snub from its very brink when Lady Huntingdon, much concerned with deathbeds and attending as many as she could, begged to be allowed to see the Duchess in her extremity.

The Duchess of Buckingham presents her compliments to the Countess of Huntingdon, is extremely obliged by her kind offer and attentions, but regrets exceedingly her entire inability to undergo the fatigue of conversa-tion.

The Duchess of Marlborough received similar over-tures with a more generous warmth, though we feel sure that that explosive character was never one of Lady Hunt-ingdon's successes.

Your concern for my improvement in religious knowl-edge is very obliging. . . . God knows we all need mending, and none more than myself. . . . Your Lady-ship must direct me. You are all goodness and kindness, and I often wish I had a portion of it. Women of wit, beauty and quality cannot hear too many humiliating truths—they shock our pride. But we must die—we must converse with earth and worms.

The astonishing thing was that a woman so fortunate, in every worldly sense, as Lady Huntingdon should have been willing to bend her mind to these graveyard con-cerns, and the incredulous surprise of her contemporaries is nowhere more artlessly expressed than in the Rev. John Fletcher's innocent exclamations in a letter to Charles Wesley. He has just, he says, breathlessly underlining, 'passed three hours with a modern prodigy—*a pious and humble Countess!* I went with trembling, and in obedience to your orders; but I soon perceived a little of what the disciples felt, when Christ said to them, *It is I, be not afraid*.' But to Selina herself, that unsmiling, passionate, and power-loving woman, there was nothing strange in her devotion to the Methodist cause. On the contrary, she had exchanged the boredom of conventional society for a life of the greatest drama and excitement—for who could fail to be intoxicated by intercourse with God? Besides, every detail of the revival was as full of emotional meat as a Greek tragedy. At nearly every preaching, when men like Wesley and Whitefield ascended the pulpit, there were the dramas of conversion—groans, convictions of sin, pleadings and wrestlings, the mounting crisis and detumescence of salvation. Once, in Yorkshire, when Whitefield, supported by Lady Huntingdon, preached on the text *It is appointed unto men once to die, and after death the judgement*, two members of the congregation died of terror, and the great preacher, who understood the manipulation of mass emotion and from whom no secrets of eloquence were hidden, proceeded in a deathly silence and with the bodies before him to warn the stricken gathering of the wrath to come. Again and again scoffers, egged on by frivolous companions to jeer at the preachers, stayed listening until their hair rose on their heads and they found themselves on their knees at last, weeping and groaning. Sinners, hypnotized by the fury of Methodist eloquence, saw their first convincing glimpse of hell and their first hope of heaven; and each man heard the accusations and the pleadings as though they were being aimed at him alone. 'As soon as he got upon his stand,' wrote John Nelson, himself afterwards a famous preacher, of his conversion by Wesley, 'he stroked back his hair, and turned his face towards where I stood, and I thought fixed his eyes upon me. His countenance struck such an awful dread upon me, before I heard him speak, that it made my heart beat like the pendulum of a clock.' Then there were those lacerating private occasions, those exhausting death-beds when the Evil One was almost physically present like a vulture, and the suspense of the struggle, the fight against time to bring the dying penitent into a state of grace before the soul quitted the body, was almost suffocating. And as though all those sensations were not enough there was even an exquisite possibility of martyrdom, for the Methodists at first were sufficiently unpopular and often enough roughly handled by the crowd. Preachers were daubed all over with paint, pelted with egg-shells filled with blood, held under water until they were all but drowned. 'The gentlemen,' wrote Howell Harris from Wales, 'in part of Brecknockshire and Carmarthenshire hunt us like partridges; but still the work prospers,' and Lady Huntingdon herself was abused in the streets and her windows at Ashby broken. For these unmistakable marks of divine regard she was passionately grateful, gathering up humiliations like precious crumbs, yet with a touch of pride, as of one conscious of her favour with Jehovah.

Our affronts [she wrote to one of her clergymen] and persecutions here, for the word's sake, are hardly to be described. But, alas, these are among those honours that should not be mentioned by me: that so unworthy a mortal should thus be favoured by so loving a Father, ought to make me bow down with confusion of face, that he should regard me. . . . They called out in the open streets for me, saying, if they had me, they would tear me to pieces, etc., but, alas, this does but prove that it is the Lord that offends them.

The Lord was soon to visit her with such distinguishing attentions that a weaker spirit might have failed under them. Her two younger sons, George and Ferdinando Hastings, who were thirteen and eleven, died almost at the same time of smallpox, and not long afterwards her husband, after an unnerving dream, died of apoplexy.

His Lordship [we are told by her anonymous early Victorian biographer], who it was remarkable had hardly ever dreamt in his life before, dreamed one night that death, in the semblance of a skeleton, appeared at the bed's foot and after standing awhile, untucked the bedclothes at the bottom and crept up to the top of the bed (under the clothes) and lay between him and his lady. His Lordship told his dream in the morning to the Countess, who affected to make light of it; but the Earl died of a fit of apoplexy in about a fortnight after.

At the time of this Gothic apparition and treble bereavement Lady Huntingdon was thirty-nine years old.

From this time, deprived of her husband and two of her children (she had seven, and was fated to outlive all but one of them), Lady Huntingdon gave herself up—house, fortune, her indestructible energy—to what she so largely described as the glory of God. 'Early in the month of January,' says her biographer simply, '. . . Lady Huntingdon arrived in London full of plans for the glory of God and the immortal happiness of her fellow creatures.' There is no doubt that her sincerity was absolute, and she marshalled her forces with the deliberation of a general and a full sense of responsibility to God and history. The contemporary religious scene, as she surveyed

it, seemed almost a desert. Passionate piety like Dr. Johnson's, within the limits of orthodoxy, was comparatively
rare, and the clergy were for the most part conventional,
sluggish, apathetic, even cynical. Yet the inner crisis
which Lady Huntingdon had experienced was one which
was happening spontaneously all over the country, both
within the Church and without; the gathering of a wave of
reaction against rational materialism. The movement so
generated based its appeal on the mercies of redemption,
and though in innumerable ways it brought comfort and
improvement to the neglected, it is too often the chastising
God of the Old Testament who seems to have been behind
it, a God whose paradise was reserved for the elect, whose
hell was real, whose punishment eternal.

There is no doubt that Lady Huntingdon, opening her
spiritual treasure to the poor in her kitchen (where they
gathered to hear her preachers) and to the rich and great
in her drawing-rooms in London and Leicestershire,
frightened a great many of them out of their wits. In her
intercourse with the poor, her biographer tells us, she
always zealously impressed on them 'the sinfulness and
misery of their state by nature; the desperate depravity of
their own hearts; the entire pollution of their natures; the
heavy guilt they were under, and their liability to everlast-
ing punishment.' And there is a description of a successful
deathbed which can be taken as a fair sample of many
others. Lady Huntingdon, who had been attending the
sick-bed of one of her sons at Brighton, visited a soldier's
wife who lay dying in great poverty after the birth of
twins, and so forcefully described to her 'her awful state,
by nature and by practice, and the imminent danger of her
soul if she died unpardoned, unrenewed, unwashed in the
Saviour's blood, that the poor soldier's wife burst into a
flood of tears under a sense of her guilt and misery, and

began to call on the Lord with all the earnestness of which her dying frame was capable.' This edifying scene was overheard through a crack in the wall of the bakehouse next door, and the result was not, as one might suppose, a deputation of protest from the baker and his customers, but the formation of a small congregation who begged to be allowed to meet there in order to hear more. Clearly the Methodist revival did not so much awaken a new appetite as feed one already ravenous.

In her campaign among her equals, however, Lady Huntingdon was more circumspect, and managed matters so well, in tune with the times, that after a while her religious parties became positively fashionable. The occasion of them was always to hear some celebrated preacher, for in affording the Methodists a favourable and protected place to preach in she performed one of her most valuable services to the movement. Many of them, as time went on, were lay preachers, but at the beginning they were all ordained clergymen of the Church of England who had caught the contagion of 'enthusiasm' and were inspired to preach in the new manner, as channels of divine communication. Many, through these 'irregularities,' lost their churches, for (as one observes today in related political parties) nobody hated the Methodists so much as the Establishment; and they were debarred from preaching in other parishes except with the incumbent's permission. This permission was usually refused (at least in the beginning; later on, as Methodism became fashionable, vicars of churches whose funds were low became more broad-minded as they discovered the marvellous effect a Whitefield, a Romaine, or a Venn had on the collection) and they were therefore driven to preach in the open country and in the streets. By appointing these homeless clergymen her chaplains (which by her right as a peeress

allowed them to preach in her house or private chapel)
and providing a smart audience, Lady Huntingdon
launched many of them on their apostolic careers, and
even carried them still further, when the number of her
domestic chaplains became embarrassing, by providing
money to build them special chapels.

This practice, as time went on, was to lead her into
controversy and difficulties, but in the middle years of the
century it is in her crowded drawing-rooms that we feel
the strongest pulse of life and come upon a scene so bizarre, so rich in suggestive contrasts, that it would be
hard to match in any other period of social history. We see
her, then, at Donington Park (before it was rebuilt in the
Byronic style with pinnacles and plaster), the solid, imposing Augustan pile set in a fine rolling parkland among
venerable oaks. The Donington oaks are said to have been
planted before the Conquest, and it may well be so, since
they are nearly all dead now and stand derelict among
nettles like the house, putting forth here and there, as
though from the grave, little plumes of foliage. Donington
Park was no derelict in the eighteenth century. Deer
grazed under the still leafy oaks, there were no nettles, the
house hummed with various self-supporting activities in
kitchen and dairy and farm, in garden and stable, and the
big doors with the brass bulls' heads, ducally gorged,
swung open under the strength of fresh-faced Leicestershire footmen, who often had (perhaps without valuing it
as they should) the privilege of opening the door to Lord
Chesterfield himself and seeing with their own eyes how a
man of the most perfect breeding in the world handed
over his hat and malacca.

For people of the first rank and fashion attended these
sacred receptions, as well as an endless train of eager
clergymen who were perpetually arriving on horseback

and staying for a week, and holding councils of holy strategy with their hostess.

Good Lady Huntingdon [wrote Whitefield] goes on acting the part of a mother in Israel more and more. For a day or two she has had five clergymen under her roof, which makes her Ladyship look like a *good archbishop*, with his chaplains around him. Her house is a Bethel: to us in the ministry it looks like a college. We have the sacrament every morning, heavenly conversation all day, and preach at night. This is to *live at Court* indeed!

It was to hear such virtuosos of the pulpit as White-field, as well as to enjoy an odd experience and make sure of missing nothing, that such notorious atheists as Boling-broke and Chesterfield, both lovers of good oratory, at-tended her parties and sat on the crimson velvet chairs of the front row with the grave and judicious air of connois-seurs. Both Wesley and Whitefield were magnificent preachers with a fine emotional range, and Madan, Venn, Romaine, Fletcher, and Toplady all had their different attractions, so that men of taste, however little attention they paid to the subject of the discourse, found plenty to interest them at these séances. 'Wesley,' wrote Horace Walpole in one of his letters, 'is a clean elderly man, fresh coloured, his hair smoothly combed, but with a little soup-çon of curl at the ends. Wondrous clever, but as evidently an actor as Garrick.' Garrick himself was interested in the Methodist preachers and gave at least one of them valu-able advice on manner and timing. But Whitefield, Lady Huntingdon's special protégé, was far and away the most brilliant of them all, with his fascinating voice, dramatic gestures, and a power of acting which even Garrick might have envied. On one occasion, when in the pulpit he was portraying a blind beggar tottering on the brink of a precipice, Lord Chesterfield—of all people—was so carried away that he sprang from his seat, exclaiming, 'Good God, he's gone!' This effect was all the more remarkable because, as we know from his own letters, Chesterfield was by then almost totally deaf, and so must have been rapt out of himself by sheer miming. (Or does something stealthily remind us that Lord Chesterfield was the politest man of his time?)

Lady Huntingdon, at all events, was encouraged by his appearance at her parties, and also by Lord Bolingbroke's, to hope that she might be God's instrument for the conversion of those celebrated infidels. She spent much prayer and effort on the project, but was disappointed, for Bolingbroke, as great in public life as he was disgraceful in private, was too hard a nut for her to crack, and Chesterfield, waving aside all pious exhortation even at the end and proclaiming death to be what he had always thought it, 'a leap in the dark,' was, at the very time when he was so politely attending her religious drawing-rooms, writing letters to her eldest son which would have made her shudder.

Chesterfield had a great regard for the young Lord Huntingdon, who seems to have been a well-bred and charming boy, but of no special distinction. The old courtier, who for long had been trying to form his own natural son into a model of polite breeding, was fascinated by the advantages which Huntingdon possessed; he seemed the perfect material for the perfect courtier; and Chesterfield, with his passion for moulding aristocratic youth, could not leave him alone. Accordingly he appointed himself a sort of guardian or adoptive father, and while the young man was making the Grand Tour plied him with letters full of exquisitely worldly advice; letters only less valuable and amusing than those to his own son because,

[87]

writing to another peer, he was inhibited by respect for a social equal.

How bland they are, those letters, how sensibly witty, and how the young man's mother would have hated them! His love affairs, as he progresses splendidly across Europe, are often and often the subject of delighted comment. 'Let dulness, age or bigotry say what they will about it; but for my part I have met with no one body absurd enough to suppose that you left England a spotless virgin, or to expect, if you had, that you would have returned such to it. Desires are natural to youth and warm blood, and the gratification of them is neither disgraceful nor criminal, unless procured by crimes.' What would Lady Huntingdon have said to that? Or again, what would she have made of this mocking titbit about that same Lord Bolingbroke who had been sitting in the front row, with such apparent decency, listening to her preachers?—'They write me word from London that Lord Coventry will be ill-natured enough to send his wife to perpetual exile, in his Mansion seat in Worchestershire; and all this only for lying with Lord Bolingbroke. What a brute must he be?'

But to tell the truth Lady Huntingdon, with one exception, was not fortunate in her children. The two sons who survived the smallpox showed, she had wretchedly to admit, a dislike for religion; they were neither better nor worse than other fashionable young noblemen, but bored with their mother's clergymen and slightly ashamed of them. They both died young. Of her daughters, one, her first Selina, had died in infancy; her second girl, Elizabeth, who married Lord Moira, had little in common with her mother; and the third daughter, another Selina, the only one of her children with whom she was in sympathy, died of a sudden fever at twenty-six. The loss of this beloved child came near to making her mother wail and beat her breast like the Old Testament matriarch she was at heart, and she touches our feelings at this moment as at no other. Only one cry escapes her as she records with anguish in her journal that God has been pleased to take from her 'at three quarters after four in the morning, my dearest, my altogether lovely child and daughter Lady Selina Hastings, the desire of my eyes and continual pleasure of my heart.' But she is soon smacked down into an attitude of resignation by bracing letters of condolence from her clergymen. 'I received your letter from Brighthelmstone,' wrote the Rev. Mr. Berridge, the spirited apostle who had taken her to task before for 'threatening him like a Pope'—'and hope you will soon learn to bless your Redeemer for snatching away your daughter so speedily. Methinks I see great mercy in the suddenness of her removal, and when your bowels have done yearning for her you will see it too. O! what is she snatched from? Why, truly, from the plague of an evil heart, a wicked world, and a crafty devil.' And Fletcher of Madeley wrote in his turn with a sort of spiritual *bonhomie* that makes one's flesh creep: 'Blessed be God for giving us the unspeakable satisfaction to see Lady Selina safely landed, and out of the reach of vanity. . . . This is an earnest of what the Lord will do for my Lady in his time.' It was the same pungent medicine that she herself had pressed on parents and children beside innumerable deathbeds, and, to her credit, she swallowed it with no more than a brief shudder. Indeed, the whole logic of her religious position was at stake, for if what she believed were true it was absurd to do otherwise than rejoice at death. It was a mercy, a divine favour, a glorious promotion; and as this world was nothing but a haunt and prowling ground of Satan it was an escape, too, and matter for congratulation.

Even Mrs. Thrale, who enjoyed this world as much as any woman alive, was frank enough to admit the Methodists' logic, for (as she wrote to Fanny Burney) 'they certainly reconcile one to death, by rendering all temporal enjoyments obtuse, or representing them as illicit. Whoever considers this world as a place of constant mortification and incessant torment will be well enough contented to leave it.'

So the old Selina, who at the time of her daughter's death had been selling her jewellery to build a chapel at Brighton, bowed her head and acquiesced, being now stripped by God of almost all human ties and all claims on her earthly affections, and rose up more than ever like a resolute soldier, laying her plans, deploying her forces, rallying and whipping up her ministers into fresh battles. But now, somehow, when so much seemed won, when her chapels were established in London and Bath and Brighton and Tunbridge Wells and in almost every place where the polite world congregated, when she had made numerous converts even among her own class and had established a flourishing college for the training of her ministers, something, slightly but irrevocably, was beginning to go wrong. Whitefield and the Wesleys had quarrelled; but it was not only that. Schisms, arguments, and doctrinal hair-splittings were sweeping through the ranks like an epidemic; but it was not that either, at least not altogether. The trouble was that she was beginning to see the direction in which her life's work was taking her—and it was not at all the one she had intended.

Her whole aim, she would have said, had been to infuse new life into the established Church. To this end she had encouraged and protected those clergymen who had been of a similar mind and who had seemed to her to be vessels of salvation. When they were deprived of their churches she made them her chaplains, and built them chapels to preach in. With the authority of wealth and position she had admonished and disciplined them, and had never hesitated to tilt against the bishops for their sake. What she had not perceived, as she laboured and prayed for the Church, was that she was working herself into a position where she could no longer stay in it. The Methodists, and she with them, were growing daily more foreign to the Establishment in manner, thought, doctrine and even speech. Steadily, almost against their will, they were becoming dissenters.

This had not been Lady Huntingdon's intention. She had wished, by remaining in the Church and behaving according to its rules or not, as she saw fit, to have her cake and eat it; but the time came when this was no longer possible. A choice was forced on her in 1779, when to her amazement she was strenuously opposed by a Church of England clergyman, the Rev. William Sellon, curate of the parish of St. James's, Clerkenwell. In this parish stood a large, empty, circular building, the Spa Fields Pantheon, which had been built for purposes of public amusement (chiefly, one is startled to learn, on the Lord's Day) and which now stood deservedly derelict. Busy manning her garrisons right and left, Lady Huntingdon had considered buying the Pantheon and converting it into a chapel but had been dissuaded by the Rev. Augustus ('Rock of Ages') Toplady, with whom she was intimate; and instead, it had been bought by a group of other Methodists who lost no time in altering it for religious use and supplying it with preachers.

Immediately Mr. Sellon, who was extremely hostile to the Methodists, made it known that since the Pantheon stood within the boundaries of Clerkenwell he considered he had the right to appoint its preachers, preach there himself whenever he liked, and appropriate the collections. A serious contest developed, with threats, missives, and ultimatums flying almost hourly backwards and forwards across the parish; and at last Mr. Sellon (who, one suspects, had looked it all up beforehand) instituted a suit in the Bishop of London's Consistorial Court, and exultingly won it. The Pantheon's preachers were convicted of irregularity in preaching in a building not episcopally consecrated, and of carrying on divine worship contrary to the wish of the minister of the parish. They were suspended from preaching. The congregation was dispersed and the Pantheon closed. It was at this point that Lady Huntingdon entered the battle.

Throughout her long and active religious life (she was now close on seventy) she had been in the habit of appointing as her chaplains any promising Methodist clergymen who appeared in difficulties. No sooner was one deprived of his licence to preach than she drew him under her wing, where he preached in comfort; and she had already, in building and endowing chapels to accommodate them, spent upwards of a hundred thousand pounds of her personal fortune. She now, seeing the battle of the Pantheon ignominiously lost, bought it at once from its defeated owners, changed its name to Spa Fields Chapel, and had it reopened by one of her best chaplains. To her indignation Mr. Sellon immediately returned to the attack, making it plain that he intended to take the same proceedings against every clergyman who preached there. What is more, he did so, and to the disgust of many people besides the Methodists was again successful. A peeress's protection, now first clearly defined in the ecclesiastical courts, was found to be less far-reaching than had been supposed. The term 'domestic chapel' could no longer be stretched to include any building used for religious purposes by a peer or peeress; it must be actually inside a nobleman's house, and must not be open to the public. The Pantheon, then, and indeed all Lady Hunting-don's chapels, were held to be subject to the rules of the Establishment so long as they remained in it, which gave unequivocal victory to Mr. Sellon. This being so, the only alternative to acquiescence (which to one of her tempera-ment was unthinkable) was to secede from the Church—her chapels, under the Toleration Act, being registered as dissenting places of worship and her chap-lains taking the oath as dissenting ministers. It was in some ways a painful step, but in others, she saw, it left her a freer hand. She instantly took it. Her numerous chapels, her congregations, and those of her students and ministers who followed her saw themselves at last with a separate identity. They had shaken off the dust of the Church of England and had gone over to the endlessly subdividing Nonconformist sects as the Countess of Huntingdon's Connexion.

We wonder, as we see the venerable figure living on into her eighties, transfigured already to a kind of ascetic transparency, so that the fine hands emerge like the hands of a delicate skeleton and the draperies have something about them suggesting a shroud, with what emotion she looked back on the course of her long life, whether she looked with pleasure or disappointment. For so many things were gone—husband, children, the great house at Donington, the town houses in Park Street and Chelsea, most of her personal fortune—all, all had been laid down in the Lord's service, and now she was alone. For the last twenty years she had lived in the greatest simplicity in Clerkenwell, in a house next door to Spa Fields Chapel and in the detestable Mr. Sellon's very parish; a district which then had a quiet elegance and from which she could gaze, on clear days, across open country to the villages of Highgate and Hampstead. Yet there was nothing about her life which suggested retirement. As always, it was as rich in incident as a campaigning general's, and the thin white hand, framed at the wrist in lace, had for twenty years been moving rapidly over sheet after sheet of paper, planning, commanding, exhorting her ministers and magnifying the Lord in that extraordinary style, encrusted with bathos and mixed metaphor, of which the early Methodists were masters. She had organized the life of her chapels, appointed their ministers, maintained students for the ministry at her own expense in her college at Trevecca, published her own hymn book, sent out lay preachers and made long personal excursions in heavy coaches with a retinue of clergy into nearly every county in the kingdom. She had made her converts among her own class and she had had her failures.

The most stubborn infidel, perhaps, with whom she had wrestled had been her own first cousin and her father's heir, Lord Ferrers, whose trial for murder and subsequent hanging at Tyburn had been one of the most intensely pleasurable experiences of a public addicted to both lords and executions, and the witty contempt of his rebuffs may still have rankled. She had visited him in the Tower, where he lay condemned, and had wrestled daily for his soul until he refused to see her. (She had not here the advantage of her chaplain, Mr. Venn, whom she sent to visit another condemned criminal and who reported with satisfaction, 'The man is chained to the floor whilst I am preaching to him.')

An adventure more gratifying to look back upon had been her celebrated rebuking of the Archbishop of Canterbury, an undertaking which must have called for unusual courage even from Lady Huntingdon. The Archbishop,

Dr. Cornwallis, had given several large balls and routs at Lambeth Palace which had been the subject of gossip, and Mrs. Cornwallis was more noticeably fashionable than was usual with the wives of prelates. Jealous of the reputation of the Church, from which she had not yet seceded, Selina went privately to Lambeth Palace to remonstrate with the Archbishop. She was accompanied by the Marquis of Townsend and is said to have put her case with the greatest delicacy; nevertheless the Archbishop took offence, and Mrs. Cornwallis lost no time in openly ridiculing the Queen of the Methodists. Undismayed, or at least undeterred, Selina then desired a private audience of the King and was received by George III and Queen Charlotte at Kew. The King listened attentively to what she had to say, confessed he had been curious to meet her because he had been 'told so many odd stories,' agreed with her disapproval of the Archbishop's goings-on, and promised to do what he could towards 'reforming such indecent practices.' And so he did, for a few days after this interview the Archbishop received an admonitory letter and was sharply taken to task for his 'improprieties'; while the King at the same time confided to Lord Dartmouth (who repeated it, naturally, to Lady Huntingdon) that he had been very agreeably surprised by his pious visitor. She was not, he said, freakish at all, as he had supposed, but very clever and well informed, with 'all the ease and politeness belonging to a woman of rank.'

Such triumphs were burnt-offerings before the Lord, but what, when one summed it up, did it all amount to? There had been for so long such a fabulous output of energy, such a driving and striving and building and planning, such a spending of money, such a fury of missionary zeal, that the mark it had all made should surely have been bigger than it was. Something was lacking in herself, perhaps—the essential spark of genius that shone in Wesley. And even if it were not, events themselves had somehow perversely betrayed her. The religious revival had begun with such a pure up-welling; hearts had been quickened and souls refreshed as with dew: she herself had experienced it in ecstasy. But doctrinal controversy had drifted in, even in the early days, like gritty dust. Wesley and Whitefield had quarrelled, been reconciled, then twenty years later had quarrelled more terribly again, until the whole Methodist world had been split in two, minister reviling minister, Arminian ranged against Calvinist, the whole movement in civil war over the difference between election and free grace and what God had, or had not, originally intended. There had been such an uproar, such a flow of biblical abuse from opposing pulpits, such appeals to heaven, such admonitory pointings down below, that the controversy, as Selina's pious biographer sadly admits, took on 'a sort of infernal tone,' and left a lingering odour of pitch and sulphur.

And then, Whitefield had died in the very heat of battle, worn out with gigantic labours, with distant American missions and buffetings backwards and forwards across the Atlantic; and Lady Huntingdon, who had always tended to back him up against Wesley, and at the great divide had sided with Whitefield and Calvinism, found herself strangely at a loss without the man who for so many years had been both protégé and leader. Nor was this all. Wesley was becoming estranged. He had none of Whitefield's ecstatic veneration for rank and had referred to her following with some asperity as 'the genteel Methodists.' Soon after this, and naturally without diffidence, she had voiced her disapproval of Wesley's famous *Minutes of the Methodist Conference*, and since Wesley refused to be publicly rapped over the knuckles there had been some candid exchanges. After that, it seems, there was a Christian coolness, and for all her humble resignation to the will of God she cannot have failed to perceive that the main stream of Methodism was flowing not her way but Wesley's.

Perhaps, though, there is a mercy in human near-sightedness, which prevents us from seeing our own times in historical perspective, even in old age; and it is very likely, as she sat at her desk in the drawing-room at Spa Fields in her eighty-fourth year, writing, writing those innumerable letters about innumerable projects, planning to convert the Jews, to equip a Calvinist mission for Otaheite, to improve the American properties which Whitefield had left her, to make a special purchase of a female slave and christen her Selina . . . it is more likely than not that she saw her work as a great foundation which would endlessly prosper. And why not? Her college was growing, her chapels were crowded, she had put the affairs of the Connexion in order and appointed her successor. She had lived through almost the whole of her splendid century. She had seen the birth of a movement which was to change England for ever, had scooped out and hollowed her particular course, preparing a bed for the waters of salvation to flow in, had seen the level rise and the flow increase.

The spring of 1791, she would have said, had been a season of fulfilment. She was ill, had broken a blood-vessel and suffered as well from 'complicated disorders,' but her mind was as clear as ever and her spirit triumphant. 'My work is done,' she told the ministers around her bed, 'I have nothing to do but to go to my Father,' and a little before she died, 'Can he forget to be gracious? Is there any end of his loving-kindness?' On the seventeenth of June she rallied sufficiently to make further plans for a mission to the South Seas, 'in the pious hope,' wrote Dr. Lettsom, who attended her, 'of introducing Christianity among that mild but uninformed race of people,' and shortly afterwards sank into sudden silence.

What she could not foresee in that final hour was the steady, inexorable dwindling of what she had begun; the draining away to other streams; the climatic changes; nor, in our own time, that stretch of featureless country near the sea where the stream that took its course from her hand is petering out at last among marsh and grasses.

The Singular Conduct
of Lord Ferrers

I N 1760, THE YEAR IN WHICH MONTREAL SUR-
rendered to Amherst and Sterne wrote *Tristram
Shandy*, London was enlivened by a sensational
murder trial which filled the newspapers and came
to a grand climax at Tyburn with the hanging of an earl.
Tradition has it that Lord Ferrers was the last English nobleman to insist on his peer's privilege of being
hanged with a silken rope, though whether he actually
availed himself of this comfort is by no means certain.
One can only say that such emphasis on dramatic if useless privilege would have been well in character, for he
was one of the most arrogant and bizarre eccentrics which
that rich age of aristocratic oddity produced.

Laurence Earl Ferrers was arraigned and tried by his
peers in full Parliament for the murder of his steward,
John Johnson, and conducted himself throughout with an
inspired sense of fitness as a murderer, a lunatic, and a
gentleman. In his death, said Horace Walpole (who took
time off from the building of Strawberry Hill to enjoy the
trial), 'he shamed heroes,' and this in spite of the fact that
there was no possible excuse for the murder he had committed and precious little to be said in his defence.

Lord Ferrers in private life was rakish and *farouche*,
though not, it seems, without an inherited sense of good

manners and a certain attraction. He had married a young lady of no fortune and somewhat below him in rank, and had behaved to her with such ferocity that her family had procured an Act of Parliament granting her a separation. Lord Ferrers was bound over to keep the peace and to maintain her in a manner befitting her style and rank. Her chief complaint against him had been that she went in fear of her life; he never went to bed without two or three pistols and frequently offered to strangle her before morning. Added to this he had publicly taunted her with having met him when he was drunk (which was very likely) and of having kept him so until after the marriage ceremony. He also took back his mistress, Mrs. Clifford, into his house, and the four young children he had had by her, openly preferring their company to that of his wife.

The settlement having been drawn up in the face of much authoritative rage on the part of Lord Ferrers, a trustee was appointed to see that his wife's income was regularly paid. Lord Ferrers himself appointed this trustee, and chose a certain Mr. Johnson, steward of his own estate, believing that he could rely on a man who had been in the employment of the Ferrers family all his life to share his own resentment in the affair. To his amazed annoyance, however, Johnson proved honest, carrying out his trusteeship with plodding thoroughness and ignoring threats and bribes. He even went so far as to send the poor lady an overdue fifty pounds without permission, a piece of impertinence which turned all Lord Ferrers's smouldering fury against him, on the grounds that Johnson was the instigator of a family conspiracy to rob him.

His first step was to order Johnson to leave the farm which he occupied, but failing on legal grounds to evict him, he decided to extort a confession and then kill him.

He laid his plans with a certain crazy precaution. Stanton Hall, his Leicestershire home, had long been a scene of disorder, kept up in drunkard's style with a mixture of affluence and squalor. Cellar and stables were well stocked but the house itself was dirty and untidy; there were only five servants. On the afternoon of the eighteenth of January the two menservants were dispatched on a long errand, the three maidservants ordered to stay in the kitchen. Meek Mrs. Clifford and her four children were sent out for a walk and told on no account to return before five o'clock. Ferrers then sent a village boy with a summons to Johnson and sat cleaning his numerous pistols in the parlour.

Johnson came, and was admitted by his master, who appeared perfectly sober, but who somewhat alarmed him by locking the parlour door. He was then, in very peremptory terms, ordered to sign a paper confessing his villainy. The poor man, having nothing to confess, refused, and one of the maidservants crept to the kitchen door to listen to the quarrel. 'Down upon your knees!' she heard. 'Your time is come, you must die!' and prudently retired to another part of the house, since, as she admitted in evidence, she 'did not care to venture into his lordship's presence.'

In the locked parlour meanwhile the terrified Johnson, not seeing what else he could do, knelt down upon the carpet, whereupon Lord Ferrers shot him in the stomach.

The wound, though mortal, did not prevent the steward from rising to his feet and staggering a few steps, groaning piteously; and Ferrers, touched as he afterwards confessed by momentary compassion, unlocked the door, allowed the maids to lead Johnson upstairs and put him to bed, and himself poured a bottle of arquebusade over the wound and covered it with a rag. He then sent for a Dr. Kirkland who lived in the neighbourhood, and settled down in the stillroom to drink porter.

When Dr. Kirkland arrived some two hours later he saw at once that the wounded man was dying; also that Lord Ferrers was tolerably drunk and in great anxiety of mind for his own safety. Knowing the crazy eccentric he had to deal with (for Ferrers was boasting that the deed had been premeditated and that he gloried in it), the doctor had the wit to pretend that Johnson was in little danger. He afterwards told the Court that he believed that if he had told the truth Lord Ferrers would have put a bullet into him as well.

'Kirkland,' said he, 'I believe Johnson is more frightened than hurt. My intention was to have shot him dead, but finding that he did not fall at the first shot I intended to have shot him again, but the pain he complained of made me forbear. . . . I desire you will take care of him for it would be cruel not to give him ease now I have spared his life.'

Ferrers now pressed the wretched doctor to join him in a drinking bout, which, though it lasted until past midnight, 'only contributed to raise his spirits without disordering his understanding.' He asked Kirkland to take an oath that Johnson would not die, and when the doctor had prudently done so, expressed surprise that the bullet should have remained in the body, 'For,' said he, 'I have made a trial with this pistol, and it pierced through a board an inch and a half thick.'

Frightened and confident by turns, he allowed Johnson's daughter to be sent for, assuring her that he was her friend, and that if her father died he would provide for her and her family on condition she did not prosecute. Occasionally his resentment against Johnson would get the better of him and he would rush upstairs, brandishing his pistols, to abuse the dying man to his face and drag the bedclothes off him. Neither Kirkland, Miss Johnson, nor Mrs. Clifford dared oppose him, and since he refused to have Johnson removed to his own house, saying he wished to keep the villain under his own roof in order to plague him, the night wore on in this terrifying fashion until Ferrers at length, lulled into a false security by the doctor, went off to bed.

As soon as he was out of the way Kirkland and Mrs. Clifford between them got the groaning steward into a chair, and with the help of the servants carried him half a mile through the winter darkness to his own house, where after several hours of miserable suffering he died. Dr. Kirkland then collected a handful of armed men and returned to seize the murderer.

They found horses saddled and everything ready for flight and Ferrers, half dressed, crossing the stable yard with his garters in his hand. On seeing them he darted back into the house, where he locked himself in and stood a determined siege of five hours, occasionally appearing with a blunderbuss at a garret window to bargain angrily, in a most peremptory fashion, for his freedom. At last he made a dash through the garden and was caught by a local collier named Cutler, ' a bold man and determined to take him,' who succeeded—in spite or perhaps because of his lordship's being armed with a blunderbuss, three pistols, and a dagger, his arms being so numerous as to prevent his making effective use of any of them.

He was removed to Leicester Gaol and from there, a fortnight later, to the Tower of London. By this time he had decided that his best hope lay in behaving in as lordly a manner as possible, and the extraordinary circus of his trial and execution began with this journey, which he made in his private landau drawn by six horses, himself being dressed for some obscure reason in the costume of a jockey.

The trial was the social and criminal sensation of the season. 'It is a happiness,' the Lord High Steward (the Earl of Nottingham) told him, 'resulting from your lordship's birth and the constitution of this country, that your lordship is now to be tried by your peers in full parliament,' and a court for this purpose was erected in Westminster Hall. Fifteen dukes, one marquess, fifty-six earls (Ferrers being one of themselves the earls turned out loyally in great numbers), five viscounts, and thirty-nine barons attended the trial in the full solemnity of robes and coronets. The peeresses' seats, perhaps out of delicacy, were less crowded. The trial lasted three days, and every one of the peers voted him Guilty.

In the matter of his defence Lord Ferrers found himself in something of a difficulty. Strictly speaking he had none to offer, but his anxious family had insisted on his pleading insanity, citing his uncle and various aunts who had died mad; his two brothers personally testified that they had long thought him out of his mind. 'Never,' wrote Horace Walpole appreciatively, 'was a criminal more literally tried by his peers, for the three persons who interested themselves most in his examination were at least as mad as he—Lord Ravenscroft, Lord Talbot and Lord Fortescue. Indeed, the first was almost frantic.' Lord Ferrers, however, was unable to conceal his distaste for this defence, and when it failed addressed the House with something like relief. 'My lords,' said he in his concluding speech, 'the kind of defence I mentioned to your lordships before, I really don't know how myself to enter upon; it is what my family have considered for me, and they have engaged all the evidence.' And again, before sentence was passed, 'I am extremely sorry that I have troubled your lordships with a defence that I was always much averse to, and which has given me the greatest uneasiness, but was prevailed on by my family to attempt.'

Certainly he was more than a little mad, but in that age and in his exalted sphere eccentricity and the aristocrat's sense of privilege ran closer to madness than ever they could again. The defence he would have preferred to offer, apparently, was that Johnson deserved death; he was convinced of the man's villainy and felt that he had acted within his rights both as a peer and an employer. His family had conspired against him to the last by refusing to submit this direct if old-fashioned excuse.

He was sentenced to be hanged, the body afterwards to be dissected and anatomized at Surgeons' Hall, following the customary procedure with the bodies of felons. He received the sentence calmly, asking only for a short stay of execution, 'that I may have an opportunity of preparing myself for the great event.'

For the next three weeks he prepared himself in the Tower by drinking, playing picquet, and composing verses expressing religious doubt. His celebrated cousin, Selina Countess of Huntingdon, visited him in prison, but was unable to make any impression upon his conscience. He tolerated her visits, he said, for the sake of company, but would not listen to her sermons. Discouraged but not defeated, she gave him what spiritual succour she could by having his wine ration reduced and his playing-cards taken away, and by advising Lord Cornwallis, Governor of the Tower, against granting his request for a last interview with Mrs. Clifford. 'Oh, by no means,' said Lady Huntingdon, genuinely horrified; 'it would be letting him die in adultery.'

On the night before his execution Lord Ferrers cor-

rected the infidel verses which he thought the most promising, paid all his bills as coolly as if leaving an inn, and
made one of the gaolers read *Hamlet* aloud to him in bed.
He had prepared a scurrilous attack on his wife's family
which he much looked forward to reading aloud on the
scaffold, but at the last minute was persuaded by Lady
Huntingdon to abandon this idea, which he did with evi-
dent reluctance.

At nine o'clock in the morning on the second of May
the Sheriffs of London and Middlesex arrived in procession at the Tower and formally intimated to the Governor
that they were ready to receive the body of Laurence Earl
Ferrers, Viscount Tamworth. To their surprise he appeared in his wedding clothes, a light-coloured satin suit
embroidered with silver. 'You may, perhaps, Sir,' he said
to one of the Sheriffs, 'think it strange to see me in this
dress, but I have my particular reasons for it,' and explained that he thought this at least as good an occasion of
putting it on as that for which it was made.

He declined to enter the mourning coach provided by
his family for the ride to Tyburn, having obtained permission to go in his landau and six. One of the Sheriffs and the
Chaplain of the Tower rode with him; the mourning coach
and the hearse (this last being also provided by his family) followed empty.

The procession included four parties of horse and foot
grenadiers, a large body of constables for the County of
Middlesex and various City dignitaries in their coaches,
and was so long and so much impeded by the crowd that it
took three hours to get from the Tower to Tyburn (now
Marble Arch)—a distance of rather less than three and
a half miles.

At first Lord Ferrers seemed to find some satisfaction
in the greatness of the crowd. He asked the Sheriff

whether he had ever seen so great a concourse of people before, and being told No, he hadn't, 'I suppose,' said he, 'it is because they never saw a lord hanged before, nor are likely to see one again.' His bearing was so decent and composed that the crowd hurled at him none of the insults usually offered to criminals on the way to execution, and even from time to time wished him God's mercy and a good deliverance.

Conversation in the landau was strained but courteous. Mr. Sheriff Vaillant told his lordship that 'it gave him the highest concern to wait upon him upon so melancholy an occasion, but that he would do everything in his power to render his situation as easy as possible.' 'Sir,' said Lord Ferrers, 'I am very much obliged to you. I take it very kindly that you are pleased to accompany me.'

Not to be outdone, the Chaplain, Mr. Humphries, begged to know his lordship's spiritual views, since, said he, the world would naturally be inquisitive to know what religion he professed. But here this last-minute interviewer drew a blank, for Lord Ferrers replied that he did not think himself at all accountable to the world for his views on religion.

The morning was hot and progress insufferably slow; the condemned man complained that the apparatus of death, and the passing through such crowds of people, was ten times worse even than death itself. To the Sheriff's compliments on his calm demeanour he answered, 'I thank you, Sir, I hope I shall continue so to the last.'

By the time they reached Drury Lane Lord Ferrers was thirsty and said he would be glad of some wine and water, but the Sheriff advised against halting the procession, as it was already late. 'That's true,' said Ferrers. 'I say no more. Let us by no means stop.'

Near Tyburn, very courteously, he again asked that

the procession might be halted, as 'a person for whom he had a very sincere regard' was waiting in a coach to say farewell. This can have been none other than poor Mrs. Clifford, from whom he had been prevented from taking leave by Lady Huntingdon, and the Sheriff, guessing as much, again advised him to give up the idea, as 'the sight of a person for whom he had such a regard might unman him, and disarm him of the fortitude he possessed.' 'Sir,' said Lord Ferrers, 'if you think I am wrong, I submit.' The Sheriff then offered to deliver any message or token to the person, and was given a pocket-book containing a bank-note, a gold ring, and a purse filled with guineas.

They were now arrived at the scaffold, which his embarrassed family had had draped in black baize at their own cost. Lord Ferrers made a motion of distaste at the sight of these funeral trimmings, but ascended the scaffold with a firm step and gazed calmly at the crowd. The Rev. Mr. Humphries, a little distracted by the ill success of his office, suggested that the time had come for his lordship to say his prayers, but this Lord Ferrers firmly declined to do. The Chaplain then asked if he might repeat the Lord's Prayer on his behalf, and was told that he had always thought it a very good sort of prayer, and that he might use it if he pleased. Mr. Humphries did so, kneeling at the gallows' foot on a black baize cushion.

Lord Ferrers meanwhile presented his watch to the Sheriff and attempted to give five guineas to the executioner, but unfortunately handed it by mistake to the executioner's assistant, with the result that the Chaplain's voice was drowned by an ugly tussle between the two men, who were finally silenced by menaces from the Sheriff.

Order restored on the scaffold, the condemned man's neck-cloth was removed, a white cap which he had brought in his pocket put on his head, his arms pinioned by a black sash, and the rope put round his neck. He then mounted by three steps on to an eighteen-inch elevation under the gallows, and asked the executioner, 'Am I right?' He himself declined to give the signal to the hangman, although he was civilly offered this last privilege. The Sheriff therefore, when the white cap had been pulled down over his eyes, raised a hand, and the elevation was pushed down under the floor of the scaffold, leaving Lord Ferrers's feet dangling only a few inches above the platform.

The crowd watched in fascinated silence as he twisted and struggled, which he did for four minutes, at the end of which the executioner did him the customary service of swinging on his legs. The body was allowed to hang in the public view for an hour and then was removed in the hearse to Surgeons' Hall where the second part of the sentence was carried out.

The remains were delivered six days later to his relations and privately buried in St. Pancras Church, under the belfry—a concession possibly obtained by Lady Huntingdon. What he himself would have thought of this last squeezing of pious privilege one can only guess. The last letter he wrote before his death had been to the Governor of the Tower begging him not to mind the requests of his family on his behalf, as he himself considered them extremely absurd.

Jane Austen's Sleight-of-Hand

S EVERAL YEARS AGO I HAD OCCASION TO SPEND some time in a fairly remote bush village of East Africa. I was to live in the wilds for a good many weeks, cut off from the distractions and annoyances of normal life, and the thought of taking with me my shabby pocket editions of Jane Austen and rereading them at leisure in the bush was so attractive that I was unable to resist it. It turned out very differently. I found myself plunged into fresh difficulties, with no leisure or solitude by day and no light but a feeble hurricane-lamp by night; but even so, I reread four of them; and the experience of taking that highly civilized world with me into the long grass, and the strange preoccupations, and the heat, was one that I would on no account have missed. What I was not prepared for, however, was that it completely upset the theory I set out with.

I have in my possession a charming book of engravings, published in 1779, called *The Seats of the Nobility and Gentry*, engraved by W. Watts 'from Drawings by the most eminent Artists, with descriptions of each View'; and it is one of my favourite books for a long evening, because it enables me to identify, to admire, and study the details of many of the houses known to me from Jane Austen. It does not, of course, contain the Prices' house at Portsmouth, or anything low; it doesn't even contain a decent and commodious parsonage; but it does afford a fine choice of Pemberleys, a nice range of Abbeys for either Donwell or Northanger, some convenient great houses, parks, and halls which will do for Kellynch, Norland, Mansfield, and Uppercross, and a few charming cottages and lodges which, if a little on the ambitious side, with weeping willows and deer, and ladies in hats and veils walking beside ornamental waters, will do for some of the less grandiose establishments. We know well enough, from Mr. Robert Ferrars, what a cottage can be made to contain. 'My dear Lady Elliott,' said he, 'do not be uneasy. The dining-parlour will admit eighteen couple with ease; card-tables may be placed in the drawing-room; the library may be open for tea and other refreshments; and let supper be set out in the saloon.'

The Seats of the Nobility and Gentry shows only the exteriors of these houses, but we all know what the interiors are like. We all have a lively vision of the grandeurs of Pemberley—the long gallery with its portraits, the windows opening down to the ground, with yellow satin curtains, in the saloon. (Miss Elizabeth Jenkins has recently traced to its source a legend, enshrined in a notice on the wall of the Rutland Arms, Bakewell, that Jane Austen stayed there in 1811 while revising *Pride and Prejudice*, and there, it says, conceived a scene between Darcy and Elizabeth as taking place in a particular room, and took Chatsworth as her model for Pemberley. Visitors are apparently shown 'her bookcase, still on the wall, and her desk by the window,' when there is not a shred of evidence that she was ever north of the Trent; and Pemberley, for all its splendour, is a handsome country house, while Chatsworth is a palace.) We could sketch a plan of the drawing-room at Hartfield, marking the exact site of Mr. Woodhouse's armchair and the table where Emma and Harriet do needlework and draw; we know exactly how the supper-table (presumably in the dining-room) is moved forward to the fire, with dishes of minced chicken and scalloped oysters on it, with soft-boiled eggs and gruel for the cautious, and a fruit tart and a dish of custard which the host does *not* advise. We know that at Donwell, where the drawing-room contains plenty to amuse one—'books of engravings, drawers of medals, cameos, corals, shells'—the service in the dining-room leaves something to be desired, since Mrs. Elton tells us that anything is 'very likely to happen with the Donwell servants, who are all, I have often observed, extremely awkward and remiss. I am sure I would not have such a creature as his Harry stand at our sideboard for any consideration.' We know, to come to humbler and more intimate apartments, exactly what the East Room at Mansfield Park is like, a 'nest of comforts' in spite of its wanting a fire, where Fanny shivered in privacy in the winter, and we have an excellent idea of the compact comforts of Captain Harville's lodgings at Lyme, and that other and very different naval officer's home, the Prices' at Portsmouth, where the rooms were too small and everybody slammed the doors and shouted.

So vivid, indeed, is the private vision of every domestic interior in Jane Austen's novels that I turn with a particular eagerness, and some distrust, to any illustrated edition that comes my way, to see whether the artist has got it right or not. Only in Miss Joan Hassall's engravings in the Folio Society edition do I find what I am looking for—a perfect response, in period, elegance, and feeling, to Jane Austen's magical evocations of proportion and space, of comfort and refinement or the want of them, of furniture, sofas, tables, work-baskets, albums, harps, pianofortes.

So with this lively impression in my mind of the domestic interiors of Jane Austen's novels, and the moving and comical scenes that they enclose, I thought what a pleasure it would be to reread the novels with the specific purpose of paying them special attention, of trying to analyze her method of setting her interior scenes, with that feeling for good furniture and arrangement, for dress and muslins and finery, which she reveals so unselfconsciously in her letters. I set off, as I thought, with this interesting prospect before me; but to my dismay and eventual bewilderment found that all those interiors of great house and cottage and parsonage which we know so well have been conjured up, so to speak, out of thin air, and very nearly without the aid of description.

Now, this is a very curious thing, and surprised me more than I can say, for though I am one of those who derive an extreme pleasure from the visual world I am not particularly imaginative about it, and therefore do not suppose that I have a clearer impression of these familiar interiors than anyone else who enjoys and has made a habit of reading the novels. I began with *Mansfield Park*, of which I believed I had a particularly clear impression, and was amazed to discover that there is hardly a word of interior description in it from beginning to end. Jane Austen tells us so little, in fact, about that well-ordered house that it is hard to guess how we form so sharp an impression. It is almost as though she feels it unnecessary to describe a large, quiet, orderly, and dignified dwelling because everyone surely knows what it must be like and any word of description will be superfluous. The servants, for instance, are anything but obtrusive; the house runs on oiled wheels and apparently by magic. We know there are footmen, since Mrs. Norris 'insults them with injunctions to despatch'; we know that Lady Bertram's maid is called Chapman, and that there must be several housemaids, when one of them interrupts Fanny's conversation with Edmund on the stairs, and on the night of the ball Chapman rather than the head housemaid is sent, rather late, to help her to dress. But beyond these passing references they remain invisible. The only object in the drawing-room which is mentioned is the sofa, which is almost a physical extension of Lady Bertram, like the fringe which she is always knotting and which gives her so much trouble; and indeed the only room described at all is the East Room, which had been the schoolroom and which we know so well because (this is a rare exception in Jane Austen) she lovingly mentions some of the objects in it.

The aspect was so favourable [she tells us] that even without a fire it was inhabitable in many an early spring and late autumn morning, to such a willing mind as Fanny's; and while there was a gleam of sunshine, she hoped not to be driven from it entirely, even when winter came. The comfort of it in her hours of leisure was extreme. . . . Her plants, her books—of which she had been a collector from her first hour of commanding a shilling—her writing desk, and her works of charity and ingenuity, were all within her reach. . . . The room was most dear to her, and she would not have changed its furniture for the handsomest in the house, though what had been originally plain, had suffered all the ill-usage of children; and its greatest elegancies and ornaments were a faded footstool of Julia's work, too ill-done for the drawing-room, three transparencies, done in a rage for transparencies, for the three lower panes of one window, where Tintern Abbey held its station between a cave in Italy and a moonlight lake in Cumberland, a collection of family profiles, thought unworthy of being anywhere else, over the mantelpiece, and by their side, and pinned against the wall, a small sketch of a ship sent four years ago from the Mediterranean by William, with H.M.S. Antwerp at the bottom, in letters as tall as the mainmast.

So detailed a description is so rare in Jane Austen's work as to be almost unique; and if one supposes that the Prices' squalid house at Portsmouth is surely described in equal if not greater detail I confess I thought so, too, and turned to it eagerly for a second set-piece at least in *Mansfield Park*. But I was totally wrong. Except that we are told that the parlour into which Fanny is shown was so small that her first conviction was of its being only a passage-room to something better, so that she stood for a moment expecting to be invited on, the whole appearance and atmosphere of the house are built up, not by visual impressions, but in terms of discomfort and noise. Doors bang; grubby little boys crash about and wrestle on the stairs; the bell is out of order, and everybody shouts for what they want; Mr. Price kicks things out of his way and calls loudly for a candle, which takes a long time in coming; the parlour door is slammed until Fanny's head aches; there are quarrels on the landing; there is a wrangle about a pocket-knife; somebody's shirt-sleeves are mislaid and finally run to earth in the kitchen dresser. It is all noise and movement, sound and discomfort which produce the visual impression. Only the cramped quarters are insisted on, and that subjectively: 'The smallness of the rooms above and below, indeed, and the narrowness of the passage and staircase, struck her beyond her imagination. She soon learned to think with respect of her own little attic at Mansfield Park, in *that* house reckoned too small for anybody's comfort.'

By the time we turn to *Pride and Prejudice* we are aware that interior description is a thing that Jane Austen pared to an absolute minimum. In the whole of that great and almost perfect novel, whether we are at the Bennets', or at Netherfield, or Pemberley, or Rosings, or Mr. Collins's parsonage, we are made to see them without the aid of description. It is perhaps the most extraordinary sleight-of-hand in the whole of fiction. Think for a moment of the work of a great contemporary and admirer of Jane Austen, and consider the descriptive force—almost too overpowering for modern taste—being deployed at this very time by Sir Walter Scott. Take a look at another great woman writer, born in the year before Jane Austen died, and see how totally opposite, how inconceivably different, is her method of setting out an important interior. One can *see* how Charlotte Brontë does it: she does it like a painter, working in colours, masses, and light; using everything, in fact, from which Jane Austen deliberately abstains. Consider that short passage in *Jane Eyre*, the description of the red room, in which Jane as a child is locked in disgrace by her aunt.

The red room was a spare chamber, very seldom slept in; I might say never . . . yet it was one of the largest and stateliest chambers in the mansion. A bed supported on massive pillars of mahogany, hung with curtains of deep red damask, stood out like a tabernacle in the centre; the two large windows, with their blinds always drawn down, were half shrouded in festoons and falls of similar drapery; the carpet was red; the table at the foot of the bed was covered with a crimson cloth; the walls were a soft fawn colour, with a blush of pink in it; the wardrobe, the toilet-table, the chairs were of darkly polished old mahogany. Out of these deep surrounding shades rose high, and glared white, the piled-up mattresses and pillows of the bed, spread with a snowy Marseilles counterpane. Scarcely less prominent was an ample, cushioned easy-chair near the head of the bed, also white, with a footstool before it; and looking, as I thought, like a pale throne.

And to that fine set-piece, so skilfully prepared for the onset of childish terror, can be added one remarkable sentence from *The Professor* in which Charlotte Brontë, working again like a painter, like Goya, in black and white, conjures up the breakfast-room of the little Brussels hotel in which the narrator receives his first foreign impressions of Belgium:

> I repaired to the public room; that, too, was very large and very lofty, and warmed by a stove; the floor was black, and the stove was black, and most of the furniture was black; yet I never experienced a freer sense of exhilaration than when I sat down at a very long, black table (covered, however, in part by a white cloth) and, having ordered breakfast, began to pour out my coffee from a little black coffee-pot.

These are both very telling passages of interior description, based almost wholly on masses of light and shade with exclamations of colour. Nothing could be further removed from the oblique and abstemious methods of Jane Austen, who, though she will go so far with the outside of a house as to tell us that it was 'a spacious, modern-built house, situated on a sloping lawn,' that it had, or had not, a park, a plantation, or a shrubbery, although she is prepared to admire a private demesne or recommend a landscape, no sooner are we inside the door

than she falls mysteriously silent; and we are left, solely
from our knowledge of the people she is concerned with
and from a few apparently trivial hints that she lets fall by
the way, to construct the interiors out of our own fancy.
And this is exactly what we do, with peculiar success,
making remarkably serviceable bricks without straw, and
wondering afterwards, if we ever pause to take the bricks
to pieces, how we managed to do it.

The puzzle was partly solved by Virginia Woolf, who
in a memorable essay on Jane Austen wrote, 'She stimulates us to supply what is not there.' That is certainly part
of her famous sleight-of-hand; she takes such an immediate grasp of our attention, so firmly trains our imagination
on to her characters and the exact social milieu in which
they have their being, that our inner eye obediently supplies everything that she has economically left out, which
her classic feeling for simplicity tells her is unnecessary,
and which she knows the reader will invent for himself if
she gives him a sly suggestion here and there.

These hints, which our imagination picks up and enlarges visually, are almost always conveyed through the
behaviour of her characters, for her first concern is with
the human heart, and her second with the manners of
society. She never allows us a word of description unless it
is certain to increase our understanding of the one or the
other. 'My preference,' she once wrote in a letter to her
sister Cassandra, 'for Men and Women, always inclines
me to attend more to the company than the sight.' A case
in point is Lady Bertram's sofa: that sofa is more often
mentioned than any other piece of furniture, with the
possible exception of Marianne Dashwood's instrument,
and they are both mentioned only as they contribute to our
understanding of indolence or romanticism. Description
for description's sake, however fine, is something that one

suspects Jane Austen would have found vulgar. In *Northanger Abbey*, the only novel in which she slightly indulges in it, it is done purely for purposes of mockery—for laughter at precisely the kind of atmosphere that Charlotte Brontë and innumerable other novelists would have found stirring. (This is clearly why Miss Brontë found Miss Austen's work so disappointing.) The drawing-room at Northanger, for instance, when Catherine Morland first steps into it, is very far indeed from her fearful imaginings, and to give us a glimpse into Catherine's mind description of the room and furniture is unavoidable.

An Abbey! Yes, it was delightful to be really in an Abbey! But she doubted, as she looked round the room, whether anything within her observation would have given her the consciousness. The furniture was in all the profusion and elegance of modern taste. The fireplace where she had expected the ample and ponderous carving of former times, was contracted to a Rumford, with slabs of plain, though handsome, marble, and ornaments over it of the prettiest English china. The windows, to which she looked with peculiar dependence, from having heard the General talk of his preserving them in their Gothic form with reverential care, were yet less what her fancy had portrayed. To be sure the pointed arch was preserved, the form of them was Gothic, they might be even casements, but every pane was so large, so clear, so light! To an imagination which had hoped for the smallest divisions and the heaviest stone work, for painted glass, dirt, and cobwebs, the difference was very distressing.

And when she cautiously enters her bedroom she is at first reassured to find that 'it was by no means unreasonably large, and contained neither tapestry nor velvet'—negatives which give us an opportunity of smiling at both our heroine and Mrs. Radcliffe.

In the other novels there is nothing to compare with these deliberate set-pieces, which are done strictly for a purpose, to display the novel-fed romanticism which caused Catherine to care for no 'furniture of more modern date than the fifteenth century.' Where other interior descriptive passages occur, much more briefly and obliquely introduced, they serve solely to contribute to a character, and it is by knowledge of the character that we in turn are able to conjure up the room. We are given some clues to the interior of Captain Harville's lodgings at Lyme because the effect he has had on the lodgings will give us the man. We need to know

all the ingenious contrivances and nice arrangements of Captain Harville, to turn the actual space to the best possible account, to supply the deficiencies of lodging-house furniture, and defend the windows and doors against the winter storms to be expected. . . . His lameness prevented him from taking much exercise; but a mind of usefulness and ingenuity seemed to furnish him with constant employment within. He drew, he varnished, he carpentered, he glued; he made toys for the children; he fashioned new netting-needles and pins with improvements; and if everything else was done, sat down to his large fishing-net at one corner of the room.

Jane Austen loved the practical abilities of sailors, and even spared us a glimpse of domestic comfort aboard a man-of-war, in the interest of showing us that Admiral Croft's wife was every bit as alert and practical as her husband.

'Women,' said Mrs Croft, 'may be as comfortable on board as in the best house in England. I believe I have lived as much on board as most women, and I know nothing superior to the accommodations of a man-of-war. . . . I speak, you know, of the higher rates. When you come to a frigate, of course, you are more confined; though any reasonable woman may be perfectly happy in one of them; and I can safely say, that the happiest part of my life has been spent on board a ship. While we were together, you know, there was nothing to be feared.'

Once one has become aware of this remarkable conjuring trick in Jane Austen's work, the discrepancy between the extreme spareness of her descriptions and the lively picture we have of the scenes which she has *not* described, it becomes a habit to pause over the few concrete objects which she consents to mention. Being so few, they are striking. They are always deliberately placed, and never wasted; they tell us much and are sometimes also puzzling. Consider for instance the court-plaster which both Emma and Harriet apparently keep in their pockets. It serves its purpose, of course, since nothing could be more ludicrous than a bit of old sticking-plaster when preserved as a romantic memento of Mr. Elton, and it displays the idiot innocence of poor Harriet to perfection. But it also sets one wondering. For what purpose did young ladies carry sticking-plaster in their apron pockets? Can it be to do with needlework? Did they prick their fingers with needles, cut them with scissors, to such an extent that plaster was part of their equipment, like bobbins or thimbles? Did they constantly cut their fingers with pen-knives, as Mr. Elton once did to require the constant provision of court-plaster? Was this a normal hazard involved in the mending of pens? It is evidently one of the things which Jane Austen takes for granted, this carrying of sticking-plaster in young ladies' pockets, as being too universal to require comment; and perhaps after all, considering the amount of needlework done, the cutting out of paper flowers and transparencies, the pencils to be sharpened for sketching a fine landscape or taking a portrait, cut fingers were more to be reckoned with then than they are today. Half a century later another romantic young person, Marie Bashkirtseff, was recording in her journal that as she was leaving by train for Geneva an admirer made her an offering of court-plaster, in case she cut her finger on the journey. It was evidently one of the daily hazards of the nineteenth century.

And then again, how do you revive a young lady with lavender water? When we read of Elinor doing this for Marianne, after her shattering encounter with Willoughby at a London party, we imagine her dabbing forehead and temples with a moistened handkerchief; but a few pages further on, when Marianne has become hysterical with grief, we find that 'some lavender drops, which she was at length persuaded to take, were of use'—and we are all at sea again, since clearly one swallows the stuff, a medication rather hard to believe in.

But these minutiae are of no importance; they are marginal details which catch and amuse the eye, like the cut of a flounce or the pattern of a footstool in a nineteenth-century painting. The alphabet letters which the little Knightleys play with, cut out of stiff paper and lettered by their aunt's hand; Lady Bertram's fringe and Mrs. Jennings's carpet-work; the 'rage for transparencies' and the painting of fire-screens—these are some of the few details which do not contribute to any knowledge of character, but which touch in the detailed background of intimate life. Jane Austen is economical to the point of parsimony with her descriptions, and it still remains one of the mysteries of her genius that we have so fine and firm an impression of her domestic scenes. It is true indeed that she stimulates us to supply what is not there. She is prodigal in telling us always what her principal characters think, more prodigal still in telling us what they feel; and this being so, it is curious that she should be so consistently underrated as a novelist of *feeling*. We are more immediately moved by the secret history of Anne Elliott's heart, by the undisciplined woe of Marianne Dashwood's—and how could Sir Harold Nicolson ever have called Marianne 'insufferable'?—than by the far more romantic treatment of more fervid novelists. It seems that for all her classical perfection, her wit, her irony, and for that sprightly heartlessness of which some critics complain, she knew as much as can possibly be known about certain types of female heart in the vicissitudes of love. And she very well knew, without ever glancing at the faintest indelicacy, the whole range of sexual attractions as displayed by handsome young men. This is particularly clear in her artful presentation of those young men of whom her moral sense insists that we shall disapprove. Ah, those young men! Willoughby, Wickham, and of course the entrancing, and surely less heartless and dangerous, Henry Crawford! There is no spinsterish primness in her approach to them; she knew what she was writing about; there is ardour under the surface of her civilized prose, and it is surprising that she is still not always given credit for it.

But this is a digression; all I intended to do was to set out a puzzle, hoping for a solution. What people think, what they say, how they feel and what they do, Jane Austen is scrupulous to tell us; the background of all this activity she leaves generally to the reader. Her descriptive set-pieces are remembered because they are so rare; when they occur they are brief, only a few lines; and the warm and lively Christmas scene at Uppercross, which immediately springs to mind as an exception, is memorable chiefly because it stands alone:

> Immediately surrounding Mrs Musgrove were the little Harvilles, whom she was sedulously guarding from the tyranny of the two children from the Cottage, expressly arrived to amuse them. On one side was a table occupied by some chattering girls, cutting up silk and gold paper; and on the other were tressels and trays, bending under the weight of brawn and cold pies, where riotous boys were holding high revel; the whole completed by a roaring Christmas fire, which seemed determined to be heard in spite of all the noise of the others. Charles and Mary also came in, of course, during their visit, and Mr Musgrove made a point of paying his respects to Lady Russell, and sat down close to her for ten minutes, talking with a very raised voice, but from the clamour of the children on his knees, generally in vain. It was a fine family piece.

And so it is, almost in the manner of Dickens, and we have a very clear picture of it. But where we get the others from, which we carry about with us as part of our enjoyment of Jane Austen, but which she has never, when we come to look for them, given us, is one of the elusive puzzles of her genius.

Mr. Nicholls

I N 1838 THE REV. PATRICK BRONTË, INCUMBENT OF
Haworth in Yorkshire, applied to the Pastoral Aid
Society for a grant to enable him to keep a curate.
He needed help in the parish; he was a widower,
with no wife to shoulder the teaching and visiting which
was commonly her share, and he suffered to a wretched
degree from nervous dyspepsia. 'My own health is generally but *very* delicate,' he wrote to a friend, '. . . indeed
I have never been very well since I left Thornton.' Haworth
as a parish he found bleak, laborious, unsympathetic. 'In
this place,' he wrote sadly, 'I have received civilities, and
have, I trust, been civil to all, but I have not tried to make
any friends, nor have I met with any whose mind was
congenial with my own.' What he needed was a curate.
His own daughters (of whom Charlotte, the eldest, was
now twenty-two) taught in the Sunday school when they
were at home, but Charlotte and Anne were about to go
out as governesses and Emily was occupied in the house.
As for Branwell, the only boy, on whom the dearest hopes
of the family rested, it was becoming disappointingly plain
that he was not a likely candidate for holy orders. So
Mr. Brontë wrote to the Bishop and to his clerical acquaintance, begging them to find him a suitable assistant, a
man 'active as well as zealous,' free from any Evangelical

taint which might lead him to 'deem it his duty to preach
the appalling doctrines of personal Election and Reproba-
tion.'

In spite of a youthful flirtation with the Methodists
Mr. Brontë had always been a plain Church of England
man, and on the niceties of dogma his mind was clear.
Evangelicalism, alive with dissent and heresy, was all
around; scarcely a parish in Yorkshire but had the infec-
tion. All the more important, then, to make sure that his
own curate should be above suspicion, since 'inconvenience might arise from a collision with my future Assistant in our preaching and exhortation.' It was not until
several years later, after a succession of curates who had
been neither good nor bad, and of whom only one (and
that one had died) had at all touched the affections of the
Brontë family, that a happy chance sent Mr. Brontë a
thoroughly satisfactory answer to his requirements.

Arthur Bell Nicholls was twenty-six when he came to
Haworth, his first and only curacy. He was ordained
priest the following year. Born at Crumlin, County An-
trim, of Scottish parents who had died when he was seven
years old, he had been brought up by an uncle and aunt at
Banagher on the Shannon, in the very heart of Ireland. He
was educated at the Royal High School, Banagher, of
which his uncle, Dr. Alan Bell, was headmaster, and at
Trinity College, Dublin, where he achieved a second class
in Divinity and took his degree the year before coming to
Haworth. He seemed solid, safe, sensible, and not at all
brilliant. 'Papa has got a new curate lately,' Charlotte
Brontë wrote to a friend a few days after he arrived, 'a
Mr. Nicholls from Ireland—he did duty for the first time
on Sunday—he appears a respectable young man, reads
well, and I hope will give satisfaction.' His appearance
was not arresting, but it was by no means disagreeable.

Of middle height, with a pale serious face framed in a long oval by thick dark hair and whiskers, he made an impression of rather dull sobriety with his straight eyebrows, long upper lip and sensitively chiselled mouth. He was unprepossessingly reserved in manner, but anyone who took his calm demeanour for passivity would have been mistaken. His level gaze could have a startling intensity.

It was not surprising that Charlotte scarcely noticed him. He had come into the Brontë household at a time of emotional self-absorption, when both Charlotte and Branwell were experiencing the miseries of thankless love, and Charlotte, on whose heart both the hopelessness and the secrecy of her passion must have lain like lead, was wearily engrossed in her own suffering. It was a year since she had returned from Brussels, equipped by her period of pupillage at the Pensionnat Héger for the scheme which the sisters had cherished for opening a school at the parsonage. She had also, unwillingly and painfully, fallen in love. There was no hope, ever, in her feeling for M. Héger, the Brussels professor who had taught her and Emily so well; he was a correct and comfortably married man with a family. There was even an extraordinary innocence in Charlotte's attitude towards him. Faced with the complete hopelessness of the situation she had yet managed to convince herself that she, an unmarried woman, could with propriety claim from M. Héger, as from teacher to pupil, a continuance of special interest and tenderness. It was useless, and she knew it; but she could not endure the pain without making piteous, unobtrusive efforts to relieve it. At the very moment when Mr. Nicholls arrived in Haworth and took up his lodging at the sexton's house across the lane, Charlotte was engrossed in an agonized and long-drawn-out correspondence with M.

Héger, sending him at painfully disciplined intervals letters of appeal which, for all their control, are so bursting
with anguish that one cannot read them even now without
wincing.

Monsieur, the poor have not need of much to sustain
them—they ask only for the crumbs that fall from the
rich man's table. But if they are refused the crumbs they
die of hunger. Nor do I, either, need much affection from
those I love. . . . Forgive me then, Monsieur, if I adopt
the course of writing to you again. How can I endure
life if I make no effort to ease its sufferings?

She had written this letter, one apparently of many,
shortly before Mr. Nicholls came to Haworth. When he
had served six months curate to her father she was
writing even more desperately to Brussels.

I tell you frankly that I have tried meanwhile to forget
you . . . I have done everything; I have sought occupations; I have denied myself absolutely the pleasure of
speaking about you—even to Emily; but I have been able
to conquer neither my regrets nor my impatience. That,
indeed, is humiliating—to be unable to control one's own
thoughts, to be the slave of a regret, of a memory, the
slave of a fixed and dominant idea which lords it over
the mind. Why cannot I have just as much friendship
for you, as you for me—neither more nor less? Then I
should be so tranquil, so free—I could keep silence then
for ten years without an effort.

Haunted day and night by her own misery, how could she
even notice Mr. Nicholls?

There were other things, too, which made it an unhappy period at the parsonage. The plans for the school
had fallen as flat as it is possible for plans to fall. Not a
single inquiry had been made in response to the circular

which the sisters had had printed to advertise 'The Misses Brontë's Establishment for the Board and Education of a Limited Number of Young Ladies.' The expense, the time and the pain of the Brussels experiment had borne not the smallest profitable fruit. Branwell had been sent home in disgrace from his post as tutor, and was drinking himself into a state of despair in his *'utter wreck'* over the wife of the Rev. Edmund Robinson. Less controlled than Charlotte, without either her reticence or her pride, he seems to have suffered to the limit of his capacity. 'What I shall *do* I know not—I am too hard to die and too wretched to live . . . my appetite is lost, my nights are dreadful, and having nothing to do makes me dwell on past scenes—on her own self, her voice, her person, her thoughts, till I could be glad if God would take me. In the next world I could not be worse than I am in this.' Anne, too, had left her situation as governess in the same household, where she had looked after the children of the woman with whom her brother was—whether 'guiltily' or not we shall never know—in love; and the moral discomfort of the position was probably what had decided her to come home.

Mr. Brontë himself was close on seventy and nearly blind; he was considering, and necessarily dreading, the possibility of an operation for cataract. It must have been an immense relief to him to have a satisfactory curate who could take over most of the burdens of his office, who could attend every morning at the village school for religious instruction, and who could visit the sick and take a good many of the services; and we may picture Mr. Nicholls rising early and donning his surplice with sober regularity, tramping about Haworth in his stout clerical boots, and spending his evenings alone in his upstairs room at the sexton's, where he ate in solitude, read religious works of a Puseyite flavour, and presumably went to bed early. We may also, perhaps, suppose that that level gaze and serious impassive face were turned more often than was absolutely necessary towards Charlotte; often enough, at least, for some lively gossiping glance to intercept it.

Who [inquired Charlotte, rather sharply, of her bosom friend Ellen Nussey] gravely asked you whether Miss Brontë was not going to be married to her Papa's curate? I scarcely need say that never was rumour more unfounded. It puzzles me to think how it could possibly have originated. A cold far-away sort of civility are the only terms on which I have ever been with Mr Nicholls. I could by no means think of mentioning such a rumour to him even as a joke. It would make me the laughing-stock of himself and his fellow curates for half a year to come. They regard me as an old maid, and I regard them, one and all, as highly uninteresting, narrow and unattractive specimens of the coarser sex.

Charlotte's initial indifference, then, was now coloured by dislike. She had already refused offers of marriage from two clergymen, one of whom (the Rev. Henry Nussey, brother of Ellen) was by no means ineligible, and it clearly nettled her that she could be supposed likely to marry her father's commonplace Irish curate. Charlotte's views of marriage were romantic, and strenuously opposed to the overwhelming social pressure of her time, which was towards marriage at all costs. It is easy to forget how strong that pressure was, how much to be dreaded the obloquy of the spinster. Yet Charlotte had without hesitation rejected Henry Nussey, and this in spite of the fact that she dearly loved Ellen and 'esteemed' and 'had a kindly leaning towards' himself. 'Yet I had not,' she told Ellen, 'and could not have, that intense attachment which would make me willing to die for him; and, if ever I marry, it must be in that light of adoration that I will regard my husband.' (Charlotte's instinct in this case was sound, since everything we now know of Henry Nussey suggests a frigid and sententious prig. His diary, whose secrets, of course, were never known to Charlotte, betrays the fact that, having made up his mind to marry, he had drawn up a list of prospects, with Charlotte Brontë occupying second place. 'On Tuesday last received a decisive reply from M.A.L.'s papa; a loss, but I trust a providential one. . . . God knows best what is good for us, for His church, and for his own glory. Write to a Yorkshire friend, C.B.' And a little later, 'Received an unfavourable reply from C.B. The will of the Lord be done.' It is perhaps not surprising that when Mr. Nussey did eventually find a wife, and one, moreover, with 'a handsome fortune,' the marriage proved unhappy.)

The dislike Charlotte felt for Mr. Nicholls apparently deepened, perhaps as a result of Ellen's unflattering rumour. When, after a long period of duty lasting many months (during which Mr. Brontë had had his operation for cataract and then a prolonged convalescence), Mr. Nicholls 'begged a holiday' and went home to Ireland, Charlotte uncharitably suggested that it would be just as well if he did not 'trouble himself to re-cross the channel'; and when Ellen mildly offered some consideration in his favour she quickly retorted, 'I cannot for my life see those interesting germs of goodness in him you discovered; his narrowness of mind strikes me chiefly. I fear he is indebted to your imagination for his hidden treasure.'

Clearly there was little hope for Mr. Nicholls, should he ever be so presumptuous as to wish to marry Miss Brontë; and there is evidence that he did already, but hopelessly, desire her. She disliked him, she despised the general run of curates, and his stipend was a hundred pounds a year. Worse—since it placed an impalpable but even more formidable barrier between them—in the two years since Mr. Nicholls had come to Haworth Charlotte had changed from an obscure parson's daughter into a successful author. Mr. Nicholls did not at first know this: like the rest of the world, he was deceived by the pseudonym of Currer Bell into believing that nothing of particular note went on at the parsonage. If he had seen a review of *Jane Eyre* in the newspaper he would have passed it over; he was not a man to trouble himself with novels. True, he must have been aware that the three sisters (and even the brother, though he was by now far gone in his illusory rake's progress, and must often have shocked Mr. Nicholls by his disordered air and drunken breath) spent much time quietly writing together in the parlour. Whenever he called in the evening to discuss some parish matter with Mr. Brontë he was likely to find, as he came and went, the parlour door indifferently closed against him, and to hear the withdrawn murmur of women's voices. He did not know that the sisters had published a volume of poems together, which had been a sad little failure and had sold only two copies. He did not know that Charlotte had made her first attempt to give the Brussels experience a bearable form, and had written a novel so disciplined and subdued that even Mr. Nicholls could have approved of it; a novel, however, which had not found a publisher. Still less did he imagine that she had written one of the great romantic novels of her time, so beautifully clear in its note of authentic passion that the reading world had been thrilled and a little shocked. (Queen Victoria, noting her appreciation of it in her diary, had felt bound to add that it was 'very peculiar in parts.') The only difference that Mr. Nicholls can have noticed was that Miss Brontë was more remote from him than ever; that she received many letters and watched for the postman with marked eagerness. He must have suspected that she had interests of which he could guess nothing: on one occasion, accompanied by Anne, she had even gone at a moment's notice to London.

During 1848 the atmosphere was full of secret excitement and even much undivulged happiness. *Wuthering Heights*, *Agnes Grey*, and *Wildfell Hall* had quietly followed *Jane Eyre* into the world, and though they had been so quietly received as to disappoint their authors, still, they *were* authors now, and Charlotte's success and the fertility of their own imaginations suggested that the future was full of promise. Alas, for two out of the three, and for unhappy Branwell, the thread was almost spun: all that remained were the few and dreadful months which ended in their deaths.

Branwell was the first to go, after a collapse of shocking suddenness. Almost before they knew that he was seriously ill, 'the last agony came on,' and Mr. Brontë found himself on his knees beside the deathbed of his only son and of all his dearest hopes. At the very crisis Charlotte herself fell ill, and was too sick and weak to be able to support her father, so that it may well have been Mr. Nicholls who was left with the hopeless task of trying to comfort him. 'My poor father naturally thought more of his *only* son than of his daughters,' wrote Charlotte after the funeral, 'and, much and long as he had suffered on his account, he cried out for his loss like David for that of Absalom—my son! my son!—and refused at first to be comforted.'

In another three months Emily, too, was dead, after a stoical refusal of all aid which wrought her sisters to the last pitch of helpless sorrow.

Some sad comfort I take [wrote Charlotte] as I hear the wind blow and feel the cutting keenness of the frost, in knowing that the elements bring her no more suffering —their severity cannot reach her grave—her fever is quieted, her restlessness soothed, her deep, hollow cough is hushed for ever; we do not hear it in the night nor listen for it in the morning; we have not the conflict of the strangely strong spirit and the fragile frame before us—relentless conflict—once seen, never to be forgotten. A dreary calm reigns around us, in the midst of which we seek resignation.

Anne began to droop and fail after Emily's death, and died in May. Charlotte and her father were alone.

During these dreadful months Mr. Nicholls's love for Charlotte deepened in sympathy; he suffered for her, though he could not help her; and it may well have been at this gloomy time that he became aware of the possibility of hope. At the beginning of her brother's and sisters' illnesses Charlotte had been at work on a new novel; it had been laid aside and returned to in anguish and solitude after their death. Now it was finished; now it was published; and Mr. Nicholls learned from a piece of gossip the astounding truth about Miss Brontë's habitual seclusion. There was, apparently, a famous novelist called Currer Bell, and Currer Bell was no other than Miss Brontë. Nor was this all. Her new novel, Mr. Nicholls was told, contained recognizable portraits of her father's curates, including himself. Incredulous, and none too well pleased (since, portraits apart, his cherished image of Charlotte had nothing to do with cleverness or fame) he rushed out and procured *Jane Eyre*, and was 'now crying out for the "other book" . . . Much good may it do him,' wrote Charlotte cruelly to Ellen. According to Mrs. Gaskell, who wrote to John Forster at the time of Charlotte's engagement, 'Mr. N. never knew till long after *Shirley* was published that she wrote books, and came in cold and disapproving one day to ask her if the report he had heard at Keighley was true, etc. Fancy him, an Irish curate, loving her even then, reading that beginning of *Shirley!*'

The poor man, however, was so little used to Charlotte's good opinion that when he opened the book and found himself represented in terms not wholly contemptuous, he was pathetically pleased, and went about in high feather for some time after. It was, no doubt, a gratifying surprise to find himself, in the character of Mr. Macarthey, described as 'decent, decorous and conscientious,' to learn that Miss Brontë had noticed that 'he laboured faithfully in the parish,' and that 'the schools, both Sunday and day schools, flourished under his sway like green bay trees.' Even the rest of the character, which might conceivably to another man have given offence, delighted Mr. Nicholls, because it proved conclusively that she had noticed him, and was not entirely hostile to what she saw.

Being human, of course, he had his faults; these, however, were proper, steady-going, clerical faults: the circumstance of finding himself invited to tea with a dissenter would unhinge him for a week; the spectacle of a Quaker wearing his hat in the church, the thought of an unbaptised fellow-creature being interred with Christian rites—these things could make sad havoc in Mr Macarthey's mental and physical economy: otherwise he was sane and rational, diligent and charitable.

'Mr Nicholls,' wrote Charlotte to Ellen, 'has finished reading *Shirley*, he is delighted with it. John Brown's wife seriously thought he had gone wrong in the head as she heard him giving vent to roars of laughter as he sat alone, clapping his hands and stamping on the floor. He would read all the scenes about the curates aloud to papa, he triumphed in his own character.' He could not resist, one suspects, the exquisite opportunity of rubbing it into Mr. Brontë that he, almost alone of all the curates, had been satisfactory; even satisfactory enough, perhaps, if nothing better offered and if he dared suggest it . . . ?

From this point we can follow the slow, painful, discouraged progress of Mr. Nicholls's love, and the gradual, unbearably gradual, melting of Charlotte's indifference. During the next three years Miss Brontë was—for her—a good deal away. She paid three visits to London, staying at the home of George Smith, her young and handsome publisher. She met Thackeray and Harriet Martineau, had her portrait painted by a fashionable artist, visited Miss Martineau twice in the Lakes, went to Scotland with the Smiths and to the Great Exhibition with Sir David Brewster, met Mrs. Gaskell and visited her in Manchester, and in short had her first taste of literary fame. All this Mr. Nicholls must have observed from afar, awaiting her return each time with apprehension. Supposing she came back engaged to the eligible Mr. Smith, or to some other suitor? But she did not. Whether, given the chance, she would have married George Smith, we cannot tell. It is very probable; but he did not ask her. Her third proposal of marriage came from another partner in the firm, James Taylor, 'my diminutive and red-haired friend,' who, in spite of his smallness and the colour of his beard, had much to recommend him. He was able in his profession, energetic and ambitious, and even Mr. Brontë was inclined to tolerate him. During 1851 he pressed his suit determinedly, both by letter and visit; and it is clear from her letters that Charlotte, who at thirty-five now believed herself assured of a lonely celibacy, would have liked to marry him if she had found it possible. But she could not:

he awoke in her a physical revulsion. 'Now he is away,' she told Ellen after her refusal, 'I feel far more gentle towards him—it is only close by that I grow rigid—stiffening with a strange mixture of apprehension and anger—which nothing softens but his retreat and a perfect subduing of his manner.' Mr. Nicholls must have heard of it with relief when Mr. Taylor withdrew and sailed for India.

Not very long after, Charlotte could not help noticing some particulars of Mr. Nicholls's behaviour which caused her 'dim misgivings.' His spirits were noticeably low, he talked pointedly of going to Australia as a missionary, and hinted that something unspecified was injuring his health—all symptoms which Mr. Brontë (though he did not guess their cause) observed 'with little sympathy and much indirect sarcasm.' The crisis came suddenly.

On Monday evening Mr Nicholls was here to tea. I vaguely felt without clearly seeing, as without seeing, I have felt for some time, the meaning of his constant looks, and strange, feverish restraint. After tea I withdrew to the dining-room as usual. As usual, Mr Nicholls sat with papa till between eight and nine o'clock; I then heard him open the parlour door as if going. I expected the clash of the front door. He stopped in the passage: he tapped: like lightning it flashed on me what was coming. He entered—he stood before me. What his words were you can guess; his manner—you can hardly realise—never can I forget it. Shaking from head to foot, looking deadly pale, speaking low, vehemently yet with difficulty—he made me for the first time feel what it costs a man to declare affection where he doubts response.

The spectacle of one ordinarily so statue-like, thus trembling, stirred, and overcome, gave me a kind of

strange shock. He spoke of sufferings he had borne for
months, of sufferings he could endure no longer, and
craved leave for some hope. I could only entreat him to
leave me then and promise him a reply on the morrow.
I asked him if he had spoken to papa. He said, he dared
not. I think I half led, half put him out of the room.
When he was gone I immediately went to papa, and told
him what had taken place. Agitation and anger dis-
proportionate to the occasion ensued; if I had *loved*
Mr Nicholls and had heard such epithets applied to him
as were used, it would have transported me past my
patience; as it was, my blood boiled with a sense of injustice, but papa worked himself into a state not to be
trifled with, the veins of his temples started up like
whipcord, and his eyes became suddenly bloodshot. I
made haste to promise that Mr Nicholls should on the
morrow have a distinct refusal.

From that moment Charlotte was—partially at
least—on Mr. Nicholls's side. Her father's rage had defeated its own object by sending her to his defence, and
she had been changed, too, by the discovery that the despised curate was as capable as herself of suffering and
passion.

Papa's vehement antipathy to the bare thought of anyone thinking of me as a wife, and Mr Nicholls's distress,
both give me pain. Attachment to Mr Nicholls you are
well aware I never entertained, but the poignant pity
inspired by his state on Monday evening, by the hurried
revelation of his sufferings for many months, is something galling and irksome. That he cared something for
me, and wanted me to care for him, I have long suspected, but I did not know the degree or strength of his
feelings.

The next few days were passed in embarrassing discomfort. Mr. Nicholls took sanctuary in his lodgings, 'en-

tirely rejecting his meals,' and replying by letter to the pitiless attacks of Mr. Brontë, who pursued him with 'a hardness not to be bent, and a contempt not to be propitiated.' Charlotte was so much shocked by her father's cruelty that she felt compelled to write to Mr. Nicholls herself, since although he 'must never expect me to reciprocate the feeling he had expressed, yet at the same time I wished to disclaim participation in sentiments calculated to give him pain.' This letter naturally encouraged Mr. Nicholls to reply, which distressed Charlotte still further, since the last thing she intended was to encourage him. She could not share her father's indignation, but her own objections were almost as unanswerable, resting as they did on 'a sense of incongruity and uncongeniality in feelings, tastes, principles . . .' Even the sexton, with whom he lodged, even the parsonage servants took sides against him. He was, Charlotte told Ellen, 'the one . . . person whom nobody pities but me. Martha is bitter against him. John Brown says *he should like to shoot him.* They don't understand the nature of his feelings—but I see now what they are. Mr N. is one of those who attach themselves to very few, whose sensations are close and deep—like an underground stream, running strong but in a narrow channel. He continues restless and ill . . .'

The situation was becoming unmanageable. Mr. Nicholls resigned his curacy, dropping despondent hints about offering himself as a missionary; then lost his head and wrote again to Mr. Brontë, begging permission to withdraw the resignation. Finding his victim thus delivered into his hands, Mr. Brontë made an ultimatum: Mr. Nicholls might remain at Haworth if he signed an undertaking never again to mention the subject of marriage. Mr. Nicholls refused, so the resignation must stand. Relations between the two clergymen became evilly strained.

In the midst of all this, who should visit Haworth but the Bishop of Ripon, that Dr. Longley who was later to become Archbishop of Canterbury. The parsonage was thrown into a flutter. 'It is all very well to talk of receiving a Bishop without trouble,' Charlotte complained, 'but you *must* prepare for him.' She had got in some extra help for the kitchen, and the local parsons were invited to supper and tea. The Bishop proved, when he came, to be delightful, 'a most charming little Bishop; the most benignant little gentleman that ever put on lawn sleeves'; and everything went off successfully apart from the fact that Mr. Nicholls, whose nerves were at breaking-point, behaved 'not quite pleasantly.' 'I thought,' Charlotte told Ellen, 'he made no effort to struggle with his dejection, but gave way to it in a manner to draw notice; the Bishop was obviously puzzled by it.' (She later learned that the Bishop had *not* been puzzled, but had divined the trouble; and being sorry for Mr. Nicholls had singled him out for a handshake and a kind word at parting. She, however, found her antipathy renewed by his behaviour, which was the sheer folly of misery, but which the servant, who was against him, contrived to dramatize until it appeared quite sinister.) He had even—unheard-of recklessness—

showed temper once or twice in speaking to papa. Martha was beginning to tell me of certain 'flaysome' looks also, but I desired not to hear of them. The fact is [Charlotte confessed] I shall be thankful when he is well away; I pity him, but I don't like that dark gloom of his. He dogged me up the lane after the evening service in no pleasant manner, he stopped also in the passage after the Bishop and the other clergy were gone into the room, and it was because I drew away and went upstairs that he gave me that look that filled Martha's soul with horror. She, it seems, meantime, was making it her business to watch him from the kitchen door. . . .

The weeks went by, and soon it was Mr. Nicholls's last Sunday. It was Whit Sunday, in the middle of May, and Charlotte, who had looked forward to his departure as a relief, found herself shocked once more into emotional sympathy. Mr. Nicholls was taking the Communion Service, and when he reached Charlotte with the wafer 'he struggled, faltered, then lost command over himself, stood before my eyes and in the sight of all the communicants, white, shaking, voiceless. Papa was not there, thank God! Joseph Redman spoke some words to him. He made a great effort, but could only with difficulty whisper and falter through the service.' Mr. Brontë had not been there, but the sexton or some other well-wisher hastened to report. The news 'excited only anger, and such expressions as "unmanly driveller." Compassion or relenting,' wrote Charlotte bitterly, 'is no more to be looked for from Papa than sap from firewood.' As for herself, 'I never saw a battle more sternly fought with the feelings than Mr. Nicholls fights with his, and when he yields momentarily, you are almost sickened by the sense of the strain upon him.'

Nor was this the end, though the presentation of a gold watch and a testimonial from the parishioners would seem to have brought the situation into some final decorum. But no; there was still the last leave-taking, and this was exquisitely painful. After taking his formal farewell of Mr. Brontë,

He went out thinking he was not to see me, and indeed, till the very last moment, I thought it best not. But perceiving that he stayed long before going out at the gate, and remembering his long grief, I took courage and went out trembling and miserable. I found him leaning against the garden door in a paroxysm of anguish, sobbing as women never sob. Of course I went straight to him. Very few words were interchanged, those few barely articulate. Several things I should have liked to ask him were swept entirely from my memory. Poor fellow! But he wanted such hope and such encouragement as I *could* not give him.

Mr. Nicholls went to the south of England for a few weeks, then to the curacy of Kirk Smeaton, near Pontefract. Another of the troublesome race of curates, a Mr. de Renzy, succeeded him at Haworth, and gradually an exhausted peace settled on the place. Mrs. Gaskell paid her first visit to Haworth, and in the course of confidential evenings by the fire learned that Charlotte was still worrying about Mr. Nicholls. Who was looking after him at Kirk Smeaton? Was his health suffering? 'I was aware,' wrote Mrs. Gaskell discreetly in her biography, 'that she had a great anxiety on her mind at this time; and being acquainted with its nature, I could not but deeply admire the patient docility which she displayed in her conduct towards her father.'

But Mr. Nicholls had no intention of remaining at Kirk Smeaton. Months before, at the very moment, in fact, of giving his six months' notice to Mr. Brontë, he had precipitately written to the Society for the Propagation of the Gospel, offering himself as a missionary. He was 'perfectly unencumbered,' he told them, having neither wife nor personal property. Haworth had been his only curacy; he was not in debt. His health he described as 'very good—except that I have been affected with rheumatism this winter, but never so severely as to be incapable of duty.' He would, he said, prefer Australia as his field—not, as one might suppose, because it lay at the greatest imaginable distance from Haworth, but because he had 'a strong inclination to assist in ministering to the thousands of our fellow-countrymen who, by emigration, have been in a large measure deprived of the means of grace.' This was in January, at the time of his bitterest conflict with Mr. Brontë, and it was Mr. Brontë whom he was obliged to ask for a reference. This he may well have done with some misgiving, but if he did, his apprehensions were unfounded. Mr. Brontë could be both prejudiced and violent, but he had too much honesty (or too much sense) to spoil Mr. Nicholls's reference from sheer rancour. Besides, he was himself in the mood for sending Mr. Nicholls to Australia, and his written reference (still, by a happy chance, in the archives of the Society) strikes precisely that note of evasive magnanimity that one finds in the references of servants whose employers have been thankful to see them go.

The Rev. Arthur Bell Nicholls, A.B. . . . has been my curate for seven years, and during that time has behaved himself wisely, soberly and piously. He has greatly promoted the interest of the National Sunday Schools; he is a man of good abilities, and under no pecuniary embarrassment that I am aware of, nor is he, I think, likely to be so, since in all pecuniary and other matters as far as I have been able to discover, he is wary and prudent. In principles he is sound and orthodox, and would, I think, under Providence, make an excellent missionary.

The other testimonials which he was able to offer, all of them from fellow clergymen, were equally valuable. The Rev. George Sowden, vicar of Hebden Bridge, stated that 'his temper is firm, but guided by a wise judgment and much discretion. He has tact . . .' The headmaster of

Skipton Grammar School, considering Mr. Nicholls's
virtues, was all but carried away.

In the whole course of my ministerial career for the last
20 years (and I do indeed speak advisedly) I never met
with a young man whom in every respect as to his general demeanour and professional qualities I so much
admired. . . . Mr Brontë has often detailed to me his
invaluable services and has frequently said, that should
he leave him, he should not know how to supply his
place. . . . A more upright, truthful and amiable man
exists not in the diocese.

In spite of the excellence of his references, the society
took a long time to deliberate, and he wrote again, de-
manding a definite answer. On this, he received a letter
asking him to go to the society's headquarters in London
for an interview, and this suggestion (though it was what
he had been pressing for) seems to have thrown Mr.
Nicholls into something of a panic. He had not yet actually left Haworth; his boats were still unburned. If the
interview were favourable, and he were recruited for Australia, could he ever—in any circumstances—honourably
withdraw? This was just at the time of the Bishop's visit:
was it that sympathetic pressure of the hand, or some
chance word of Charlotte's, that undecided him? At all
events, something did; his next letter to the society suggests that he had perceived—or thought he perceived—
encouragement. 'Owing to the solicitations of friends
some doubts have occurred to me as to the desirableness of
leaving the country at present—when I have fully made
up my mind upon the point I will again communicate
with you.' No hope, however, was in fact held out to him.
The testimonial was subscribed for, the gold watch presented, and he parted from Charlotte with anguish at the
garden gate. Nobody, not even Charlotte (though she had

her moments of compassion and even of doubt), was sorry to see him go.

> He is now grown so gloomy and reserved [she told Ellen] that nobody seems to like him; his fellow curates shun trouble in that shape, the lower orders dislike it. Papa has a perfect antipathy to him, and he, I fear, to papa. Martha hates him. I think he might almost be *dying* and they would not speak a friendly word. . . . In this state of things I must be, and I am, *entirely passive*. I may be losing the purest gem, and to me far the most precious life can give—genuine attachment—or I may be escaping the yoke of a morose temper.

It seemed certain, as Charlotte said, that 'the termination will be—his departure for Australia.'

But Mr. Nicholls's love story was not over, as we know, and as even Mrs. Gaskell was able without indiscretion to reveal. 'By degrees,' she wrote, 'Mr. Brontë became reconciled to the idea of his daughter's marriage'; in her private communications she was more explicit. She had secretly obtained Mr. Nicholls's address from the Haworth postmaster, and had passed it on to her friend Richard Monckton Milnes, the philanthropist, who undertook to write to Mr. Nicholls. 'With skilful diplomacy,' she wrote to him, 'for which I admire myself extremely, I have obtained the address we want. . . . I felt sure you would keep the story secret—if my well-meant treachery becomes known to her I shall lose her friendship, which I prize most highly,' and at the end of her letter added, with some shrewdness, 'Her father's only reason for his violent and virulent opposition is Mr. Nicholls's utter want of money, or friends to help him to any professional advancement.' Six months later, when the ruse had worked, she wrote to Milnes, 'I can't help fancying your kind words may have made him feel that he was not so friendless . . .

as he believed himself to be at first; and might rouse his despondency up to a fresh effort.' The effort had been made. 'He wrote to her very miserably; wrote six times, and then she answered him—a letter exhorting him to heroic submission to his lot, etc. He sent word it had comforted him so much that he must have a little more, and so she came to write to him several times.' This secret correspondence weighed heavily on Charlotte's conscience, and she summoned up her courage to tell her father. It was 'very hard and rough work at the time,' but at length she persuaded him to let the correspondence continue.

Charlotte's argument was not the only thing that influenced Mr. Brontë. There was something else, and that something may, of the two, have been the more persuasive. The new curate, Mr. de Renzy, was *not* satisfactory. Mr. Brontë had grown accustomed to Mr. Nicholls's ministrations, and everything seemed troublesome now that he was gone. He began even to glance at the possibility that Mr. Nicholls might be permitted to return. There was, at least, no harm in allowing a visit. 'This was about Christmas. Miss Brontë had not then made up her mind; but when she saw him again' (transfigured and improved, as we may guess, by this sudden hope) 'she decided that she could make him happy, and that his love was too good to be thrown away by one so lonely as she is.' In the light of this happy change, there is no mystery about the sudden collapse of Mr. Nicholls's missionary ambitions.

As, owing to the severity of the weather [he wrote in his final letter to the Society for the Propagation of the Gospel], the rheumatic affection with which I have been troubled during the winter has not abated as rapidly as I expected, I have been induced by my friends to relinquish for the present my intention of going abroad.

Will you therefore convey to your Committee my sincere thanks for their kindness in entertaining my application; and also my hope that I shall meet with a like consideration, if in a few months I should wish to renew the subject.

There was no need to renew it, for now everything went, by contrast, marvellously well. The wedding was not, it is true, prepared for in the conventional atmosphere of excitement and happiness, but the story, well known though it is, remains as deeply moving as the end of a great novel. No novelist of genius, not Charlotte herself, not Proust, could have more delicately and surely brought about the complete change in their relations which gradually took place, nor the discoveries of truth that Charlotte made, nor the blossoming of all that was good in Mr. Nicholls's character. Not Tolstoy nor Hardy could have imagined a fitter, more poetic, or more tragic end.

If the story of Mr. Nicholls existed only as a work of the imagination, we should find particularly satisfying, particularly illuminating after the manner of Proust's reversals and surprises, the discovery made by Charlotte, the romantic, of the peaceful and comforting aspects of domestic love. Her heroes, from childhood, had been wildly, ludicrously different from Mr. Nicholls. All the writings of her adolescence had been centred round wicked, brilliant, handsome marquesses and dukes in the Byronic pattern, with flashing eyes and sable crests and passionate mistresses. The boldly erotic strain in all her uncensored secret writing reveals, to a modern eye, possibly more than she knew about herself. She was aware of the danger in all this luxurious extravagance, and had purposely kept it out of *Villette* and *The Professor;* but the Byronic hero, in the person of Rochester, had triumphantly reared his sable crest in *Jane Eyre.*

There was nothing in the least Byronic about Mr. Nicholls. He was as unlike those irresistible sardonic heroes as he was unlike the lively, quick-tempered French intellectual whom Charlotte had loved. He was dull, he was unprepossessing, he was undistinguished. He was, in fact, in many ways the male counterpart of those poor, plain, and silently suffering governesses who were variants of Charlotte's only heroine. Like theirs, his calm exterior concealed depths of passion; like them, he was capable of tragic constancy. But he was outwardly, and in everyone's view, a disappointing choice; and it is not surprising that Charlotte, now the marriage was finally settled, should find herself 'very calm, very inexpectant.' 'What I taste of happiness,' she confessed to Ellen, 'is of the soberest order. I trust to love my husband—I am grateful for his tender love to me. I believe him to be an affectionate, a conscientious, a high-principled man; and if, with all this, I should yield to regrets, that fine talents, congenial tastes and thoughts are not added, it seems to me I should be most presumptuous and thankless.' She clung for support to the idea that Mr. Brontë's comfort would be served by the marriage. He would have his best curate back; he would not lose his daughter, since Charlotte and her husband would live with him at the parsonage; and Mr. Nicholls, out of his hundred a year, would contribute to the household. Mr. Brontë's seclusion, moreover, would be in no way disturbed, for a little stonefloored room, scarcely bigger than a cupboard, where they had been accustomed to store turf, was being converted into a study for Mr. Nicholls.

The details of the marriage itself, with Mr. Brontë staying at home, the bride being given away by her old schoolmistress, Miss Wooler, and coming out of the church in white embroidered muslin and white bonnet, looking 'like a snowdrop,' are well enough known from the pages of Mrs. Gaskell, whose delicacy, however, forbade her to follow further. Her instinct was right; but we, at our impersonal distance, need not shrink from learning anything that the letters of the next nine months can tell. All that we learn is good; it is wonderful to see how, in the sudden climate of happiness, Mr. Nicholls improves.

After the wedding they left by train for North Wales, and after a tolerable railway journey, and a superb drive through the mountains from Llanberis to Beddgelert, reached Conway and spent the night at a comfortable inn. Thence, by way of Bangor where they also spent a night, they crossed from Holyhead to Dublin, and after an interlude of sight-seeing went on to Banagher. Here Charlotte was agreeably surprised by everything she saw. Dr. Bell's house, where Mr. Nicholls had been brought up, was 'very large and looks externally like a gentleman's country seat—within most of the rooms are lofty and spacious and some—the drawing-room, dining-room etc.—handsomely and commodiously furnished.' The note of surprise, though polite, is unmistakable. Remembering her father's peasant origins, perhaps, she had clearly prepared herself for something humble; but the house was quite imposing and the other male members of the family seemed 'thoroughly educated gentlemen.' 'I must say,' she told Miss Wooler, 'I like my new relations. My dear husband too appears in a new light here in his own country.' And to Miss Wooler's sister, 'I was very much pleased with all I saw—but I was also greatly surprised to find so much of English order and repose in the family habits and arrangements. I had heard a great deal about Irish negligence . . .'

They went on to Killarney and the south-west coast, Charlotte all the way deriving an exquisite and specially feminine pleasure from 'the kind and ceaseless protection which has ever surrounded me, and made travelling a different matter to me from what it has heretofore been'; and finding to her delight, when at last they confronted the wild and grand Atlantic, that Mr. Nicholls was by no means an insensitive and unimaginative companion.

> My husband is not a poet or a poetical man [she wrote] —and one of my grand doubts before marriage was about 'congenial tastes' and so on. The first morning we went out on the cliffs and saw the Atlantic coming in all white foam. I did not know whether I should get leave or time or take the matter in my own way. I did not want to talk—but I *did* want to look and be silent. Having hinted a petition, license was not refused—covered with a rug to keep off the spray I was allowed to sit where I chose—and he only interrupted me when he thought I crept too near the edge of the cliff. So far he is always good in this way—and this protection which does not interfere or pretend is I believe a thousand times better than any half sort of pseudo sympathy. I will try with God's help to be as indulgent to him whenever indulgence is needed.

Mr. Nicholls had, in fact, in his less articulate way, enjoyed it as much as she had, and took the trouble to report to a clerical friend that it had been 'most refreshing to sit on a rock and look out on the broad Atlantic boiling and foaming at our feet.'

He was changing, under Charlotte's very eyes, into something she had never believed possible. The toad was becoming, if not a prince, at least something very interesting and likable. He now looked 'quite strong and hale,' and had gained twelve pounds during the four weeks in Ireland. Now, in letters to Ellen, he is no longer Mr. Nicholls, but 'Arthur—excuse the name, it has grown natural to use it now'; and by the time they are back at Haworth he is 'my dear Arthur,' 'my dear boy,' and the letters are full of him. He is punctual and practical; every morning he is in the National School by nine o'clock; he calls her away from her writing to go for walks; he likes her, when he is at home, to pursue only 'occupations in which he can share, or which will not at least divert my attention from him.' He is proving, in short, fond, authoritative, possessive. 'My life,' she told Ellen, 'is changed indeed—to be wanted continually—to be constantly called for and occupied seems so strange: yet it is a marvellously good thing.' Even when, with Victorian gravity, he took it upon himself to censor her letters to Ellen, she was too much amused by his strictures to resent them. 'Arthur has just been glancing over this note. He thinks I have written too freely. . . . Arthur says such letters as mine never ought to be kept, they are dangerous as lucifer matches, so be sure to follow a recommendation he has just given, "fire them" or "there will be no more," such is his resolve. I can't help laughing, this seems to me so funny.' His authority was, in fact, one of the things about him that she most enjoyed, and Mrs. Gaskell had been as shrewd as usual when she had written to John Forster, at the time of the engagement, 'with all his bigotry and sternness . . . I am sure that Miss Brontë could never have borne not to be well ruled and ordered.'

Happy she certainly was, and in her gradual discovery of the contentment, even the rare emotional experience which outwardly unpromising people can bestow, she reached a new level of maturity. If it could have lasted, if Mr. Nicholls could have spared her time to write, we might have found her later work enriched with newly discovered harmonies. Alas, having so nearly reached our happy ending, we are all too abruptly hurried to the deathbed. The new novel, of which she was reading the first chapters to her husband when she sickened, was in its very beginning laid aside. A cold, as Mrs. Gaskell relates, caught on a winter walk, lingered and would not improve; and weakened as she was by this and by the nauseas of early pregnancy, she fell all too easily a victim of the disease which had preyed on the family from the beginning—the consumption which had killed her mother, Maria, Elizabeth, Branwell, Emily, and Anne.

No great novelist has ever devised a more tragically fitting, or more poignant ending than the famous, the almost unbearable last pages of Mrs. Gaskell's biography. Slowly dying, Charlotte had written a last pencilled note to Ellen, crowning with one unforgettable chord the long-sustained crescendo of Mr. Nicholls's love.

'I must write one line out of my dreary bed. . . . I want to give you an assurance, which I know will comfort you —and that is, that I find in my husband the tenderest nurse, the kindest support, the best earthly comfort that ever woman had. His patience never fails, and it is tried by sad days and broken nights. . . .'

Long days and longer nights went by; still the same relentless nausea and faintness and still borne on in patient trust. About the third week in March there was a change; a low wandering delirium came on; and in it she begged constantly for food and even for stimulants. She swallowed eagerly now; but it was too late. Wakening for an instant from this stupor of intelligence, she saw her husband's woe-worn face, and caught the sound of some murmured words of prayer that God would spare her. 'Oh!' she whispered forth, 'I am not going to die, am I? He will not separate us, we have been so happy.'

Early on Saturday morning, March 31st, the solemn tolling of Haworth church-bell spoke forth the fact of her death to the villagers who had known her from a child, and whose hearts shivered within them as they thought of the two sitting desolate and alone in the old grey house.

It was to this house, inhabited only by the two mourning clergymen, who must now make shift somehow to live together, that Mrs. Gaskell came the following July, summoned by Mr. Brontë's unexpected request that she should write some sort of memorial of his daughter. The situation, for a biographer, was extremely delicate. Charlotte had been only four months dead; her husband and father were in deep mourning, and both, separately, wept. Mrs. Gaskell was aware of their quivering susceptibilities. She was made instantly aware, too, of Mr. Nicholls's covert hostility to the idea of a biography. Unlike Mr. Brontë, he had no ambitious pride to be comforted by a 'life'; he had loved Charlotte long before he knew that she was anything more than a plain parson's daughter, and in the nine months of marriage had certainly never recognized his own position as the husband of genius. He had been not hostile to her fame but a little jealous of it; he saw it, rightly, as a threat to his possessiveness, and as far from being the most important attribute of the woman he had married. He had not discouraged her from writing; he had even, in the month before her final illness, listened attentively to the first chapters of her new novel, *Emma*, and had warned her that the public might find the theme repetitive; but he was firmly settled that her married life should be that of a curate's wife; her leisure would be sufficient for the writer.

Now, confronted by Mrs. Gaskell, he showed himself more worldly than Mr. Brontë. He knew that it was no formal memorial to the writer, but a minute account of Charlotte's private life that would be wanted. His imagi-

nation failed to grasp that there was anything worth telling, and his reserve shrank from the thought of such
exposure. 'I confess,' he told Ellen Nussey, 'that the
course most consonant with my own feelings would be to
take no steps in the matter, but I do not think it right to
offer any opposition to Mr Brontë's wishes.' So he made no
explicit objection, but directed Mrs. Gaskell to Ellen Nussey for early letters, and sat silently by while Mr. Brontë
occupied himself with long, valuable (though not always
perfectly accurate) letters to his daughter's biographer.
The work was begun. Mrs. Gaskell pursued her inquiries
with conscientious thoroughness, going even as far as
Brussels and interviewing M. Héger; and the further she
progressed the more she became aware of Mr. Nicholls as
an inhibiting influence, always watching her, so to speak,
from the parsonage, and increasingly costive in the provision of material. He had not shown her Charlotte's letters
to himself, nor his to her, and was not likely to do so.
(These, indeed, have never come to light.) She had the
frustrating impression that he was in possession of more
than he ever intended to divulge. 'I still want one or two
things to complete my materials,' she told Ellen Nussey,
'and I am very doubtful if I can get them—at any rate, I
think they will necessitate my going to Haworth again,
and I am literally *afraid* of that.' She wished to see M.
Héger's letters to Charlotte, which the professor himself
had told her, 'contained advice about her character, studies, mode of life'; but 'doubt much if Mr Nicholls has not
destroyed them.' She also wished to see the fragment of
the new novel which Charlotte had laid aside in her last
illness, since 'her happy state of mind during her married
life would probably give a different character of greater
hope and serenity to the fragment'; 'but I doubt much if
Mr Nicholls won't object to granting me the sight of these

things.' Mr. Brontë's permission in these matters was not, she found, enough ('It seems as if Mr Brontë's own consent or opinion had very little weight with Mr Nicholls') and she found herself close to unadmitted tensions between the two clergymen.

These tensions were to increase after the biography was published, and all the quarrels and troubles it precipitated had shown that Mr. Nicholls had perhaps been right in his preference for silence. Trouble on account of Mr. Brontë, whose eccentricities had been too simply accepted, too dramatically underlined: trouble in the shape of a threatened libel action from the lady with whom Branwell had been in love: trouble with Cowan Bridge School, fought out as a long and bitter quarrel in the newspapers. Mrs. Gaskell's hard-won pleasure in her success was ruined, and she herself made miserable.

The Cowan Bridge controversy, though it was not the most dangerous (since no libel action was threatened) proved the most long-drawn and acrimonious, and to everyone's surprise it was Mr. Nicholls who undertook to defend Mrs. Gaskell and his wife against the Clergy Daughters' School and its supporters. The descriptions of Lowood School in *Jane Eyre* had long ago given offence to the Rev. W. Carus Wilson, the school's founder and director, but no protest had been made until after Charlotte's death, when obituary notices identified the school with Cowan Bridge and accepted the description as true: and the real storm did not break until after the publication of Mrs. Gaskell's biography, in which, after careful inquiry and with anxious concern for her own fair-mindedness, Mrs. Gaskell had firmly come down on Charlotte's side. The *Leeds Mercury* and the *Halifax Guardian* were now enlivened, almost daily, by rude and bitter letters—the Carus Wilson faction angrily impugning Charlotte Brontë's truthfulness and Mr. Nicholls as angrily upholding it. The correspondence makes fascinating reading; the evidence is so copious, so contradictory; and Mr. Nicholls emerges, rather surprisingly, as a spirited and venomous fighter. The argument is long, and not altogether conclusive; we have better evidence today, fully supporting Mr. Nicholls's statement that 'To the day of her death "Currer Bell" maintained that the picture drawn in *Jane Eyre* was on the whole a true picture of Cowan Bridge School, as she knew it by experience'; but at the time the testimony was so contradictory that Mr. Nicholls eventually withdrew from the controversy in disgust. He believed that Charlotte had told the truth, and that in publicly supporting her he had done his duty. 'Henceforth Charlotte Brontë's assailants may growl and snarl over her grave undisturbed by me.'

A sterile peace descended on the parsonage. The two clergymen, so dissimilar, fundamentally so uncongenial, 'still *ever near* but *ever separate*' as the sexton said, must now for the next six years live tolerantly together, smothering their hostilities. On the surface the relationship was smooth enough, Mr. Nicholls perpetually busy in church and parish, doing at first nine tenths of the work and then the whole of it, Mr. Brontë preaching an occasional sermon for a year or two and then retiring to bedridden seclusion in his room upstairs, where, as Mrs. Gaskell's daughter saw it, 'everything was delicately clean and white, and there he was sitting propped up in bed in a clean night-gown, with a clean towel laid just for his hands to play upon'; Mr. Nicholls meanwhile promoting himself from the stone-floored closet to the use of the front parlour. If ever their old hostility looked out for a moment under the convention and duty clamped down like a lid upon the past, it was more likely than not to be over some irritable question of Charlotte's fame. Mr. Nicholls detested sight-seers; Mr. Brontë thought they showed a proper respect. When a new memorial was carved for the Brontë graves, Mr. Nicholls had the old tablet-stone broken into small pieces, and himself watched while the sexton carried out his instructions of burying it four feet deep in the parsonage garden, 'for fear,' as Meta Gaskell said, 'anyone should get hold of a piece for a relic.' Passionately possessive in marriage, it now seemed as though he were jealous of even the most reverent touch on Charlotte's memory. When a child in the village was to be christened 'Brontë' he announced that he would not christen it, so that the intimidated parents, not wishing to give up the project and not knowing what else to do, kept the infant unbaptized for the space of six months; by which time it was so sickly that Mr. Brontë became alarmed, and sent for and privately christened it in his bedroom. 'Eh, Mr Nicholls was angry a' that,' the sexton told Meta Gaskell, for the next time he christened a baby he found the offending entry in the register, and 'there and then he strode straight back to the parsonage, and up into Mr B.'s bedroom; and "So I see you have christened your namesake." ' Mr. Brontë resourcefully 'got out of it by saying that he had done it to save Mr N. from the terrible scrape in which he would have found himself, had the child died unchristened, etc.' All relics of Charlotte, all her books and papers, Mr. Nicholls kept very strictly to himself.

When Mr. Brontë died in 1861 at the age of eighty-four, Mr. Nicholls was not appointed to succeed him. It is said that the casting vote against him was given by a trustee of the living who was also a dissenter, and who smelt the rack and screw in his horror of heretics. Disappointed and at a loss, since for years he had been waiting for the incumbency, Mr. Nicholls packed his belongings.

There was a sale at the parsonage, scattering the modest possessions and furniture which are still, after nearly a century, finding their way back to Haworth as museum exhibits. All Charlotte's personal relics, her childish writings and Branwell's, and also Branwell's paintings of his sisters, Mr. Nicholls took back with him to Ireland.

He was now forty-two, thickly bearded, a widower, and still a curate. Was it disappointment, distaste, or the temptation of a quiet life in Banagher which made him give up the church? It is said that some kind of throat trouble disinclined him from further curacies. We cannot tell. The only certainty is that once settled in his boyhood home he made no move to leave it, and drifted presently into farming, in a respectable, amateurish, small gentleman Irish way; and eventually, in 1864, after nine years of celibacy, married a cousin, Miss Bell, who is said to have loved him from the days before he left Ireland.

This second marriage was childless, and evidently happy. When in 1895 Mr. Clement Shorter went to Banagher to see him he was apparently much mellowed by age (he was seventy-six) and astonished even that literary filibuster by allowing him to buy, on behalf of T. J. Wise, the collector, most of his Brontë letters and material. What extraordinary change of feeling can have taken place in Mr. Nicholls, the reticent, the jealously reserved, which allowed him to put his privacy into the hands of men like Shorter and Wise, with their smell of the literary gossip column and the sale-room? None, perhaps, that forty years cannot after all gently and unnoticeably make. For years before Mr. Shorter's visit the Brontës had been discussed and written about in books, newspapers, and magazines, and in some of these both Mr. Nicholls and Mr. Brontë had cut sorry figures. Even the intimate letters which Charlotte had written to Ellen Nussey about her marriage had been privately printed by that lady, and a dozen copies were known to be in different hands; so that Mr. Nicholls was abandoning a reserve which had already become meaningless. Still, in handing over the letters, fragments and microscopic *juvenilia* to Shorter and Wise he showed more than a touch of innocence. Most of the papers, he wrote to Mr. Shorter, he had 'found in the bottom of a cupboard tied up in a newspaper, where they had lain for nearly thirty years, and where, had not it been for your visit, they must have remained during my lifetime, and most likely afterwards have been destroyed.' Their fate was now to be broken up by T. J. Wise for the sale-room, and to be bought at high prices for private collections in England and America.

Mr. Nicholls died at Banagher in 1906, a month be-fore his eighty-eighth birthday. Some eight years later his wife, still living in the same house, was superintending the turning out of an old wardrobe when two brown-paper parcels came to light. Unwrapping these, she found them to contain two cracked and faded canvases—one, Bran-well's moving portrait of Emily cut out by Mr. Nicholls from a group of the three sisters in which he considered the faces of Charlotte and Anne to be poor likenesses, and the other, cracked and folded in four, an amateurish but unmutilated group, the very painting which Charlotte had held up for Mrs. Gaskell to see, the 'rough common-looking oil-painting, done by her brother, of herself—a rather prim-looking girl of eighteen—and the two other sisters, girls of sixteen and fourteen, with cropped hair, and sad, dreamy-looking eyes.' Mrs. Nicholls presented these two paintings to the nation, and they are both now in the National Portrait Gallery.

The second Mrs. Nicholls survived her husband by just over eight years, dying at Banagher during the First World War, in February 1915.

The Mysterious Genius
of Emily Brontë

ANY PEOPLE BELIEVE THAT EMILY
Brontë left a second novel, the successor
to *Wuthering Heights*, unfinished when
she died. This lost novel has never been
found, and if she wrote it, it is almost certain that Charlotte Brontë must have destroyed it after Emily's death, as
she probably did her juvenile writings and her letters.
The only evidence for its existence is a single letter which
was found in the little folding desk Emily always wrote
on, and in which she kept her papers. This letter is from
J. C. Newby, the rather unsatisfactory publisher who had
already published *Wuthering Heights* and *Agnes Grey*
(Anne Brontë's first novel), and it refers to the progress
of a second work. 'Dear Sir'—the Brontë sisters, having
written under the pseudonyms Currer, Ellis, and Acton
Bell, were at first thought to be men—'Dear Sir, I am
much obliged by your kind note and shall have great
pleasure in making arrangements for your next novel. I
would not hurry its completion, for I think you are quite
right not to let it go before the world until well satisfied
with it, for much depends on your next work. If it be an
improvement on your first you will have established yourself as a first-rate novelist, but if it falls short the critics
will be too apt to say that you have expended your talent

in your first novel.' This was in February 1848, and nine months later Emily Brontë was dead.

It is conceivable that one day this lost novel will be discovered in some forgotten box or cupboard, as Charlotte's early writings were, and the portrait group of the three sisters, painted by their brother Branwell, which now hangs in the National Portrait Gallery; but more than a hundred years have passed and such an interesting discovery grows less likely. The thought of it is particularly tantalizing—more so even than those intimate letters of Jane Austen's which her sister Cassandra burned—because Emily Brontë is such a mysterious genius. How it came about that this Yorkshire parson's daughter, a recluse even in her secluded situation, *farouche* and shy, without experience of life, could sit down at twenty-seven and write one of the most powerful and haunting novels in all literature, has never been explained. Even Charlotte, who loved and understood her as only a sister and a woman of genius could, was baffled by it. 'I am bound to avow,' she wrote after Emily's death, 'that she had scarcely more practical knowledge of the peasantry among whom she lived, than a nun has of the country people who sometimes pass her convent gates. Though her feeling for the people round was benevolent, intercourse with them she never sought; nor, with very few exceptions, ever experienced.'

However we puzzle, we are always driven back at last to the conclusion that Emily Brontë's genius was nourished solely from her own imagination. Whatever contacts she had with the actual world had less to do with it than her secret preoccupations with good and evil, man and nature, God and the soul. Her poems, that other manifestation of her peculiar genius, throw some light on the extraordinary nature of her mind, but they set as many problems as they solve. She left a considerable mass of poetical fragments and a few lyrics that are as pure, wild, and strong as anything in the language; but they give us no straightforward answer to the questions it is impossible not to ask—What was Emily Brontë *like?* What did she believe? What were the foundations of that self-contained strength, that mystic stoicism, which are so hard to relate to the sheltered life of a country parson's daughter?

If Emily Brontë, like Charlotte, had left behind her a vast mass of personal letters, we might not be so much at sea; we might know as much about her thoughts and character as we do about Charlotte's, which is a great deal. But the only letters of Emily's that escaped destruction are three little nondescript notes addressed to Charlotte's intimate friend, Ellen Nussey, and they tell us nothing. Here, then, is this mysterious genius, whose one novel and handful of poems have made a tremendous impact, and of whom we know so little. How eagerly we should seize on that lost novel if it were ever found, or a few more undiscovered letters or poems, or on any scraps of hers that would tell us anything! It so happens that a few scraps have survived which came to light some years ago in America. These are three essays on diverse subjects which Emily Brontë wrote when she was twenty-four, and which were translated and published, first by Miss Fannie Ratchford, and later in the Transactions of the Brontë Society.

That surprising word 'translated' needs explaining. We remember that when Charlotte Brontë was twenty-six and Emily two years younger they went to school in Brussels, to improve their French and better to equip them for starting a school of their own, which at that time seemed the only possible plan for earning a living. They became pupils at the Pensionnat Héger in the Rue Isabelle, where

Emily stayed for one year and Charlotte for two, under the direction of M. Constantin Héger, who quickly perceived the extrardinary powers of mind hidden under the frumpish exterior of these two grown-up schoolgirls. It was part of his teaching plan that his pupils should be allowed to write freely on subjects chosen by themselves, the finished essays being then submitted to minute criticism. After a few months in Brussels the two Brontës both spoke and wrote French with some facility, and wrote numerous essays for the sharp critical eye of M. Héger.

We know from Mrs. Gaskell that he thought Emily the more brilliant of the two, and this in spite of the fact that she proved an intractable pupil, disposed to argue and disagree, and by difficult silences to express a certain resentment of his authority. He for his part was of that dynamic temperament which insists on an emotional *rapport* between master and pupil; he felt obliged to dominate and control, or he could not teach. Emily refused to be dominated, and she was emotionally inaccessible. 'Emily and he don't draw well together at all,' Charlotte wrote regretfully to Miss Nussey. Nevertheless, Emily made remarkable progress, and her work impressed M. Héger to the extent of his telling Mrs. Gaskell ten years later that Emily had the makings of a fine historian; also—and one feels he considered this the greater tribute—that she should have been a man.

In her *Life of Charlotte Brontë* Mrs. Gaskell reproduced the whole of one of Charlotte's French *devoirs*, an imaginative essay on the death of Napoleon; but she did not see—or if she saw she was not interested in—the essays of Emily. Nevertheless, five of these have survived to the present day, though I imagine very few people have had access to them. Two of the five at least are extremely interesting, and perceptibly enlarge our knowledge of

Emily. Where have they lain all this time? Two essays (the least interesting) are in the Bonnell Collection in the Brontë Museum at Haworth; they were published in the Brontë Society Transactions of 1947. The other three are in America—two in the Berg Collection in the New York Public Library, and one in the Stark Collection belonging to the University of Texas. These three might have remained unknown if it had not been for the sharp eye of Miss Fannie Ratchford, librarian of Texas University, whose monumental researches into the strange mass of Brontë *juvenilia* have produced the most important modern contribution to the study of the Brontës.

In two of these short essays, which are about five hundred words apiece, we find new and valuable clues to Emily Brontë's mind. One is called 'The Cat' and the other 'The Butterfly.' 'I can say with sincerity,' Emily begins, 'that I like cats; I can also give very good reasons why those that hate them are wrong.' At first sight this appears to be simply an essay on the character of animals, and so on comparatively familiar ground, since one of the few things we know about Emily is that she was passionately attached to animals and bestowed on them the intense love which she always seemed to withhold from human beings. But we soon discover it is more than this: in comparing the human with the feline character she reveals her general opinion of mankind, and it is a pessimistic and disillusioned one. 'We cannot,' she writes, 'stand up under comparison with the dog, he is infinitely too good.' (We are reminded here of her own fierce mastiff, Keeper, who walked behind the coffin at her funeral, and never, as Mrs. Gaskell tells us, 'rejoiced, dog fashion, after her death.') 'But the cat, although he differs in some physical traits, is extremely like us in disposition. In truth, there may be people who would say that the resemblance is close only to the meanest human beings, that it is limited to their excessive hypocrisy, cruelty and ingratitude—detestable vices in our race and equally odious in the cat's . . . I answer, that if hypocrisy, cruelty and ingratitude are the characteristics exclusively of mean people, this class includes everyone; our education develops one of these qualities to great perfection, the others thrive without cultivation, and we, far from condemning them, look upon all three with great complaisance.' She goes on to describe the soft and gentle manners which the domestic cat displays to his owner, concealing his real nature, which is primitive and cruel: and observes, 'Such finesse in him we call hypocrisy, but in ourselves we give it another name, politeness, and any person not using it to disguise his true feelings would soon be driven from society.'

Here, then, is a clue to that reserved and *farouche* side of Emily's nature which so disconcerted everyone who came near her. Soft manners and politeness are hypocrisy; her uncompromising honesty will have none of it. Cruelty and ingratitude she sees as universal human traits, and this seemingly misanthropic opinion of mankind gives us a valuable clue to the strangely cruel, passionate and ungrateful characters of *Wuthering Heights*. 'If,' said Charlotte, who had heard the novel read aloud in manuscript, 'one shuddered under the grinding influence of natures so relentless and implacable, of spirits so lost and fallen; if it was complained that the mere hearing of certain vivid and fearful scenes banished sleep by night and disturbed mental peace by day,' Emily 'would wonder what was meant, and suspect the complainant of affectation.' Emily was not aware that in the characters of *Wuthering Heights* she was portraying people unusually remorseless and intractable. That was how she saw mankind, without any softening drapery of sentiment. Cruelty and ingratitude were in us all, and in refusing to subscribe to polite fictions she believed she was only setting down the truth without hypocrisy.

If Emily Brontë's view of humanity was essentially a dark one, so, too, if we are to take her essay called 'The Butterfly' as evidence, was her view of life and indeed of the whole universe. In this short and singularly moving piece of writing she describes herself walking in summer on the edge of a wood, in a dark mood, 'one of those moods,' she says, 'which sometimes lay hold on us, when the world of imagination suffers the blight of winter.' She sees nature, not in its beauty, but in its cruelty, and wonders why the nightingale should sing so gloriously when its clearest notes will only guide some enemy to its nest. But 'All creation,' she says, 'is equally insane. There are those flies playing above the stream, swallows and fish diminishing their number each minute: these will become, in their turn, the prey of some tyrant of earth or water and man for his amusement or for his needs will kill their murderers. Nature is an inexplicable puzzle; life exists on a principle of destruction; every creature must be the relentless instrument of death to the others, or himself cease to live. Nevertheless we celebrate the day of our birth, and we praise God that we entered such a world.'

She goes on to consider the part that man must play in this monstrous scheme. 'Why was man created? He torments, he kills, he devours; he suffers, dies, is devoured—that's his whole story. It is true that there is a heaven for the saint, but the saint leaves enough misery here below to sadden him even before the throne of God.' She sees no gleam of light or hope, and almost reaches the point of reviling her Creator. 'At the moment the universe appeared to me a vast machine constructed only to bring

forth evil: I almost doubted the goodness of God for not
annihilating man on the day of his first sin.' At that very
moment, however, a butterfly appears, hovers and flutters
for a moment of pure beauty, and vanishes in the sunshine. Emily Brontë feels herself rebuked for her savage
judgement, and accepts the butterfly as the symbol of
what she believes to be a philosophical truth—that nature
is a balanced creation, that every horror, every suffering,
has its compensation, and that the seemingly cruel
schemes of God are designed to lead in the end to mercy
and peace. 'Here,' she says, 'is a symbol of the world to
come. Just as the ugly caterpillar is the beginning of the
splendid butterfly, this globe is the embryo of a new
heaven and of a new earth whose meagrest beauty infinitely surpasses mortal imagination. When you see the
glorious outcome of what now seems to you so mean, how
you will despise your blind presumption in blaming Om-
niscience for not having destroyed nature in its infancy.'

It has been the fashion among Emily Brontë's biographers to regard her as what is called a pagan. Some of her
poems, her extreme reticence in religious matters in an
outspokenly religious age, and the completely amoral tone
of *Wuthering Heights* have sustained this view. In this
short essay, however, she is outspoken enough, and makes
it clear that her religion, remote though it may be from
the conventional Methodist-tinged Church of England in
which she was brought up, nevertheless fits firmly within
the Christian framework. She is peculiarly sensitive to the
suffering and cruelty of life, and her imagination is per-
manently darkened by it; but she clings as to a rock to the
conception of divine justice and mercy, to a belief in ulti-
mate peace, and to a glorious and certain immortality.
This belief, however she arrived at it, was necessary to a
mind like hers, which perceived the shadows more readily

than the light. Without it she would have been committed to a despair to which even her spiritual stoicism would have been unequal.

This is a subject on which she had brooded much: her preoccupations are less with ordinary life than with the abstract and the philosophical: she is less concerned with man than with the soul: and it is on this abstract plane that her imagination moves most freely, in an atmosphere at once spiritual and profoundly emotional. 'God,' she concludes, 'is the God of justice and mercy; then, assuredly, each pain that he inflicts on his creatures, be they human or animal, rational or irrational, each suffering of our unhappy nature is only a seed for that divine harvest which will be gathered when sin having spent its last drop of poison, death having thrown its last dart, both will expire on the funeral pyre of a universe in flame, and will leave their former victims to an eternal realm of happiness and glory.'

No joy, she seems to say, is fully tasted without preliminary effort or preliminary pain. How logical then, how just, how certain that the suffering implicit in every form of life should lead at last to a proportionate happiness and peace. This is not conventional theology, and one has the feeling that she reached her faith through independent thought, without the help of teaching or the Church. Once reached, that stern but consoling idea laid the foundation of her life and work, and surely shines through that wonderful (if too often quoted) last paragraph of *Wuthering Heights*, where the narrator, after all the suffering and violence of the tale, is touched by the peace of Heathcliff's and Catherine's graves: 'I lingered round them, under that benign sky: watched the moths fluttering among the heath and harebells; listened to the soft wind breathing through the grass, and wondered how anyone could ever imagine unquiet slumbers for the sleepers in that quiet earth.'

Emily Brontë's vision of life, sombre, uncomforting, owing less to any concept of cosmic justice than to a conviction of the necessity of stoicism, has sometimes a curiously prophetic and disillusioned quality. Without wishing to read too much into what is, when all is said and done, only another school exercise of the Brussels period, it is worth while looking at another of her French *devoirs* which came to light little more than a decade ago, among the papers of the Héger family.

This essay—if it can properly be so described—is called 'The Palace of Death,' and in theme and outline it bears a strong resemblance to one of John Gay's *Fables*. Both Charlotte and Emily wrote essays in French on this theme towards the end of their Brussels period, and since both exercises have survived, and are as different as possible from one another, they are clearly not translations of Gay's poem, but imaginative treatments of the same subject, an allegory of the type that recurs in popular literature from the Middle Ages to the end of the eighteenth century. Gay's poem describes the Court of Death, and the 'diseases dire, a ghastly train,' which aspire to the honour of being his chief minister. Fever, Gout, Pox, Stone, Consumption, and Plague present their claims, but the wand of office is awarded to Intemperance, who not only reaps Death's richest harvest but also lines the busy doctors' pockets.

Charlotte's and Emily's essays are not concerned with diseases but with abstract sins and dangers. Charlotte considers Ambition and War before giving the prize to Intemperance; her essay is elaborately descriptive, somewhat in the Angrian manner—Death is pale and veiled and sits in a palace of ice, and so on. It is all rather laboured and the result, one has to admit, is not particularly interesting. In Emily's essay, on the other hand, we hear at once a different and distinctive voice. At *her* Court of Death, Ambition and Fanaticism are the chief contenders, until their claims are swept aside by Intemperance, who works through her friend and ally, Civilization.

'You know me,' said the stranger: 'I come later than the rest, but I know my cause is just. Some of my rivals are terrible, I own, and it is possible I shall be outdone in noisy deeds which impress the vulgar: but I have a friend before whom this whole assembly will be forced to yield: her name is Civilization: in a few more years she will inhabit this globe with us, and every century will increase her power. In the end she will seduce Ambition from your service; Rage she will curb with the restraints of law, she will disarm Fanaticism, drive out Famine among the savages. I alone will flourish under her rule. The power of the others will die with their supporters; mine will exist even when I am dead. When once I am known to the father, my influence will lay its hand upon the son: and before ever men unite to banish me from their midst I shall have changed their very nature, making the entire species your easy prey. So effectively shall I do this, indeed, that Old Age will find his task a sinecure, and your palace will be glutted with your victims.'

'Say no more,' cried Death, descending from her throne to embrace Intemperance—for this was the stranger's name. 'Enough that I know you. For the rest, I have important and profitable work; they shall all be my ministers: but for you alone is reserved the title of Viceroy.'

This curious and macabre production is dated October 18, 1842, that is to say, at the end of Emily's nine months in Brussels, less than a fortnight before Miss Branwell's death recalled the sisters to Haworth. Emily was then twenty-four years old, and it would be nearly another five years before she would begin *Wuthering Heights*. We have nothing else of hers from this Brussels period except two poems, both concerned with the Gondal saga and of little interest or merit.

'The Palace of Death' has the same dark visionary tone as many of the Gondal poems, which are often concerned with dungeons drear, with revenge and violence, and with lonely death. There is in this essay, however, a medieval flavour which is not found in any of the poems. The bone-strewn pavements, Death on her throne, surrounded by allegorical figures, seem to belong more to the fifteenth century than to the nineteenth, like those frescoes that come to light under the flaking eighteenth-century plaster of an old church. But this allegory, like other allegories, is simply the form chosen to express an abstract idea, and the idea so briefly and forcefully set out is that the most obvious evils are not necessarily those most destructive to man. Appearances, in fact, are intrinsically deceptive. Rage and Violence, Envy and Treason, Famine and Pestilence are scarcely glanced at; Ambition and Fanaticism are more dangerous. What did Emily Brontë know of fanaticism? Religious fanaticism, certainly, she knew something of; the Evangelistic movement of the eighteenth century had left some ugly scars in the West Riding; fanatical lay preaching, bigotry, and sectarian hatred were things that all the Brontës had seen and heard. But when Emily herself came to deal with fanaticism, as she did in *Wuthering Heights*, it is of a different order. Nearly all the characters are fanatics. One is tempted to believe that Emily Brontë knew the dangers of fanaticism because there were elements of it in her own nature, and that in *Wuthering Heights* she purged her imagination of a secret burden.

Yet this was not, as she saw it, the worst of the evils threatening mankind. How triumphantly she might have said 'I told you so' if she had lived today! Does it surprise us that she saw civilization itself as a destroyer of life— civilization and the intemperance which it makes possible? 'When once I am known'—it is Intemperance addressing Death—'when once I am known to the father, my influence will lay its hand upon the son; and before ever men can unite to banish me from their midst, I shall have changed their very nature, making the entire species your easy prey.'

At this point our minds fly rather too easily to poor Branwell, the Brontë brother, who died at thirty, as Emily did, of consumption, death in his case being accelerated by opium and drink. But Branwell's death is still six years ahead, and it was not until two months after the writing of this essay that he went as tutor in the family of the Rev. Edmund Robinson, where he was to fall disastrously in love with his employer's wife and set off on his downward course of drink and despair. So that Emily cannot have written as she did about intemperance through having seen her brother morally and physically destroyed by it. Anne Brontë later wrote *Wildfell Hall* as a moral and a warning against drunkenness: she wrote it while Branwell was in his last stages, and it was published less than three months before his death. But the sisters had seen enough, even before Charlotte and Emily went to Brussels, to give them a horror of drunkenness. There is some slight evidence that Mr. Brontë himself was too fond of his whisky, but it would be a mistake to make much of this. But Branwell had already been in disgrace. He already haunted the Black Bull when he had the money, and his companions were drinkers, in spite of the fact that for a time he was secretary of the Haworth Temperance Society—an ironical appointment, as it turned out. And it was in the month before Charlotte and Emily went to Brussels that he was dismissed from his job as railway clerk at Luddenden Foot, partly for drunkenness, partly for some neglect of duty which has never been made clear. So it seems, after all, only too probable that it was Branwell's intemperance, even in its beginnings, that impressed Emily as being so dangerous a vice that in her grim little allegory she advances special arguments for setting Intemperance on Death's right hand, and giving her precedence above the other deadly sins.

There is something particularly interesting in this, for there is a legend, supported (perhaps even invented) by Mme Duclos (Mary Robinson) in her 1883 biography of Emily, that Emily was the one member of the family who did not condemn Branwell in his downfall, who comforted and watched by the drunkard in his delirium, while Charlotte turned disgustedly away. The only person whom we know, from existing letters, to have lain awake and struggled with Branwell in his worst stages, sharing the same room with him, was his father; but in Mme Duclos's picture it is Emily. 'There was one woman's heart,' she wrote, 'strong enough in its compassion to bear the daily disgusts, weaknesses, sins of Branwell's life, and yet persist in aid and affection. Night after night, when Mr Brontë was in bed, when Anne and Charlotte had gone upstairs to their room, Emily still sat up, waiting. She often had very long to wait in the silent house before the staggering tread, the muttered oath, the fumbling hand at the door, bade her rouse herself from her sad thoughts and rise to let in the prodigal, and lead him in safety to his rest.'

This may be true: writing in the eighties, when people were less scrupulous about biographical exactness, Mme Duclos did not give her source of information. She knew Ellen Nussey, Charlotte's lifelong friend, and certainly consulted her, but admitted in her introduction that Miss Nussey 'knew little of Branwell's shames and sorrow.' She may have formed her picture of Emily and Branwell from some piece of genuine information, or she may have imagined it as something touching and probable, in key with Emily's character and therefore safe to assume because there was no evidence to the contrary. But whatever Emily may have done, we now know what she thought: and she evidently agreed that Intemperance was the Viceroy of Death—an idea that would have delighted the Haworth Temperance Society much more than anything Branwell ever said or did during his term of office.

This attitude is perfectly consistent with what little we know of Emily Brontë's nature, and her mysterious genius. Her kind of strength is of the Spartan and Puritan persuasion, however steadily she may regard the powers of evil. Her preoccupation with the wild and solitary is known to us; we would as soon expect an eagle to approve of civilization as she. And the horror of Hindley Earnshaw's self-destruction by drink speaks clearly enough in the pages of *Wuthering Heights*. This essay, written so carefully in French for M. Héger, does nothing more, perhaps, than confirm and underline what we might have supposed. Though I doubt whether many of us would have gone so far as to deduce, without it, that Emily Brontë believed civilization and its indulgences to be even more terrible in their destructive power than famine, fanaticism, or pestilence.

Charlotte Brontë: Emma, A Fragment

I F DEATH HAD NOT SILENCED CHARLOTTE BRONTË when it did, in the thirty-ninth year of her age and at the height of her powers, would she have left us another novel to stand in the canon with *Villette* and *Jane Eyre?* Or would she in any case have remained silent? Speculation is not as idle as it seems, for on the one hand there are those who believe that the Rev. Arthur Nicholls and comparative happiness would have dried up the source of Charlotte Brontë's protest (protest and poetry being the springs of her art), killing her fertility as a writer: and on the other hand we have, we actually have, a fragment.

It is the first two chapters of *Emma*, a novel. (She had at first thought of calling it *Willie Ellin*, and no doubt would have changed the title yet again on account of that other *Emma* whose perfections she found it difficult to assess.) It was published five years after her death in *The Cornhill*, with an unctuous introduction by Thackeray which yet contains some splendidly illuminated phrases, and then, as far as the general reader was concerned, was soon forgotten. It opens the door a fraction of an inch into a nonexistent future; it gives a disturbing glimpse.

'One evening, at the close of 1854,' wrote Thackeray, 'as Charlotte Nicholls sat with her husband by the fire'—they had been married that summer—'she suddenly said to her husband, "If you had not been with me, I must have been writing now." She then ran upstairs, and brought down, and read aloud, the beginning of a new tale. When she had finished, her husband remarked, "The critics will accuse you of repetition." ' Mr. Nicholls was right: certain things in this new beginning are so repetitious as to be startling—they disturb one, like sudden evidences of obsession, and even Charlotte's confident reply 'O! I shall alter that. I always begin two or three times before I can please myself'—hardly drives off the suspicion that she is still not free from the childhood miseries, the dungeon taste she had known at Cowan Bridge.

It is absurd to judge an unfinished work from two short chapters, but there are already in those chapters some of the compulsive strains of Charlotte Brontë's music, as recognizable and as significant as the dark themes running in *basso continuo* through the work of Dickens. Her imagination was more deeply and tenaciously subjective than most; it is her own wounds that cry with the mouth of poetry, the blood of her prose is rich with indignation.

So we see, as we might have guessed, that we are to be shown, as it were through a keyhole, some painful early scenes in the life of an outcast. It is a hackneyed theme, or at least it seems so now, when two generations of children have been brought up on Frances Hodgson Burnett's sentimental and charming working of it in *A Little Princess*—the theme of the petted rich girl in a snobbish school, who suddenly, through the death or ruin of her parents or some other misadventure, is reduced to nothing, and becomes the helpless victim of scorn and hatred. Whether Charlotte Brontë had ever read such a tale, one

cannot tell: she could have, for in 1818 an anonymous novel, *Fatherless Fanny*, had appeared with an iden-
tical beginning, and had enjoyed some success. But in the
Brontë fragment there are already undertones, echoes
from greater depths than can be sounded in the Regency
novel of reputations, orphans, and rakes.

It is almost touching to recognize the dominant Brontë
characters in these first two chapters of *Emma:* Matilda
Fitzgibbon, silent and unattractive little heroine, whom no
one at school can like, hiding a sick heart and a dark
history under a frigid demeanour and (we are sure of it)
an assumed name; Miss Wilcox, coarse-grained insensitive teacher; Miss Scatcherd in new guise, briskly inflict-
ing her pains; Mr. William Ellin, mysterious middle-aged
bachelor, less calm than at first appears—can it be that he
is *Emma*'s hero? And who is Emma? We shall never
know. Charlotte Brontë did not tell her husband how the
story was to develop, and so he could not tell Thackeray,
and Thackeray cannot tell us.

There is an air of serenity about the opening chapters
which suggests—though one must be wary of such guesswork—that she had begun to write in a mood of confidence and optimism. The 'I' of the story is Mrs. Chalfont,
a widow no longer young but apparently comfortably off,
still capable of taking an alert interest in life. Looking
back over her own past she expresses a distinctly unpes-
simistic philosophy:

'A pleasant fancy began to visit me in a certain year,
that perhaps the number of human beings is few who do
not find their quest at some era of life for some space more
or less brief. I had certainly not found mine in youth,
though the strong belief I held of its existence sufficed
through all my brightest and freshest time to keep me
hopeful. I had not found it in maturity. I was become

resigned never to find it. I had lived certain dim years
entirely tranquil and unexpectant. And now I was not sure
but something was hovering round my hearth which
pleased me wonderfully. Look at it, reader. Come into my
parlour and judge for yourself whether I do right to care
for this thing. . . .'

From this moment we learn no more of Mrs. Chalfont
herself: she is recounting a story to prepare us for the
mysterious tale she will now tell, of how 'Fortune, by a
somewhat curious turn of her wheel, placed in my way an
interest and a companion.' We are in a little school for
young ladies run by the Misses Wilcox, a school not
unlike that which the Brontë sisters might have had if
they had been more fortunate. (It is no surprise to learn
that the Wilcoxes have spent some time in France.) The
narrator, while not wholly admiring them, allows them
'some portion of that respect which seems the fair due of
all women who face life bravely, and try to make their
own way by their own efforts.' It is the champion of
governesses speaking; we remember Miss Wooler. 'I
speculate much,' Charlotte had written to Miss Wooler in
1846,

on the existence of unmarried and never-to-be married
women nowadays, and I have already got to the point of
considering that there is no more respectable character
on this earth than an unmarried woman who makes her
own way through life quietly, perseveringly—without
support of husband or brother, and who, having attained
the age of 45 or upwards, retains in her possession a
well-regulated mind, a disposition to enjoy simple pleasures, fortitude to support inevitable pains, sympathy
with the sufferings of others, and willingness to relieve
want as far as her means extend.

Into this modest school, which so far has achieved
only three boarders, fate drops a windfall, a richly dressed
little girl called Matilda Fitzgibbon, unexpectedly deposited and left for the Misses Wilcox to educate and care
for. No expense is to be spared. She is treated with fawn-
ing favouritism by her teachers, but remains unattractive,
solitary, withdrawn. The other girls dislike her, and one of
them (here Emily's shadow seems to fall across the page)
after a particularly flagrant incident is moved to protest.
'There was a girl called Diana . . . a daring, brave girl,
much loved and a little feared by her comrades. She had
good faculties, both physical and mental—was clever,
honest and dauntless. In the schoolroom she set her young
brow like a rock against Miss Fitzgibbon's pretensions;
she found also heart and spirit to withstand them in the
drawing-room. One evening . . . Diana had been called in
to play a long, difficult piece of music which she could
execute like a master. . . .'

So there is a mystery here, as we are soon to be told.
Matilda Fitzgibbon is secretly unhappy; she terrifies the
others by walking in her sleep, and is found one night
unconscious, in a fit. (At once we are back in the red
room with Jane Eyre, wondering for the hundredth time
who it was who had a fit in Haworth Parsonage. It would
be strange indeed to introduce such a thing into the opening chapters of two novels if the writer had neither witnessed nor experienced one.) But there is worse to come.
A letter to the 'tall, fine-looking personage' who had
brought Matilda to the school is returned unopened: both
his name and his address are unknown to the Post Office.
Mr. Ellin undertakes to investigate the puzzle, and returns with grave news—'Conway Fitzgibbon was a man
of straw; May Park a house of cards. There was no ves-

tige of such a man or mansion in Midland County, or in any other shire in England.' The mistress's tenderness for her favourite instantly vanishes, and she is hastily sent for.

' "Keep yourself still, and reply, if you please," said Miss Wilcox, whom nobody should blame for lacking pity, because nature had not made her compassionate. "What is your name? We know you have no right to that of Matilda Fitzgibbon."

'She gave no answer.'

From this point we are left in the dark, for we have almost reached the end of those two chapters which Charlotte Brontë read to Mr. Nicholls. We know only that William Ellin is moved by the child's plight, and is likely to become her champion. 'Say no more to her,' he tells Miss Wilcox. 'Beware, or you will do more mischief than you think or wish. That kind of nature is very different from yours.' We are left with the elements of a Charlotte Brontë novel—the oppressed and friendless child in a hostile world, the hated school, the harsh intolerant schoolmistress, the sensible independent man who will resolve the mystery (from Keighley, surely, related to the Yorkes?)—Gothic elements if you like, tempered by that truthful astringency which so often led her to cut the ground from under her own romanticism. No notes, no indications of plot survive. Mrs. Chalfont, one supposes, is to reappear, and tell Matilda's (or Emma's) story at first hand. Or she may be discarded: a narrator who details scenes and conversations at which she could never have been present is always an awkward and unconvincing device.

It is all guesswork. The opening chapters might have been changed if Charlotte Brontë had lived, but I do not believe the novel would have been abandoned. Mr. Nicholls was a possessive husband, a little jealous of his wife's literary fame and determined that she should concentrate on him; but time would have slackened his intensity; children are not always babies, and even parsonages in that halcyon age were cleaned and cared for by rough, devoted, articulate Yorkshire servants. I do not believe that married life and happiness could stop up the welling spring, the almost alarming force of Charlotte Brontë's creative imagination. They would change it, of course; she would have mellowed and matured, have explored further into the mazy thicket of passionate feeling between men and women. One pictures her writing away in the dining-room of her Parsonage, like Mrs. Gaskell in hers, while Mr. Nicholls comes and goes from the parlour which for a lifetime (but now no longer) was Mr. Brontë's.

But here, of course, we remember, and turn back to the two chapters with a sigh. 'The trembling little hand,' wrote Thackeray, 'was to write no more. The heart, newly awakened to love and happiness, and throbbing with maternal hope, was soon to cease to beat. . . .' We recoil from something in his voice, but that is not his fault; the sexual attitude of his time was mawkish, imposing a false tone, whenever the word 'woman' had to be uttered, on even the greatest man. But there is strong feeling there, and we partly share it. 'Will not the leaf be turned some day, and the story be told? Shall the deviser of the tale somewhere perfect the history of little Emma's griefs and troubles?' Alas, no. It is a great pity. But even a fragment is precious, and is worth study.

Mrs. Gaskell's Task

ORE THAN A HUNDRED YEARS HAVE
passed since Charlotte Brontë died, and
Mrs. Gaskell, acutely sensitive to the
seriousness and to the difficulties of her
task, went by train and gig to Haworth for her first biographer's interview with Mr. Brontë. Since that afternoon, so
pregnant with literary history, much more has been written about the Brontës than Mrs. Gaskell dreamed of; so
that the two volumes of her first edition are at times lost
sight of behind the crowd of books which have taken her
work as a basis to proceed or quarrel on.

So dense is the press, indeed, that the ordinary reader,
stretching up a hand to the appropriate shelf in any well-
stocked library, may well hesitate, and bring it slowly
down again. For if so much has been written since Mrs.
Gaskell's *Life*, it is reasonable to suppose that there is new
material of which Mrs. Gaskell knew nothing; and if that
is so, which of these newer volumes contains the whole?
And then, Mrs. Gaskell has been accused of timid
suppressions on the one hand and libellous blackening of
character on the other: so what is one to believe? Besides,
our attitude to human nature itself, to the luxurious
strangeness of personality, to the mind's hidden motives,
has altered out of recognition since Mrs. Gaskell's day.

We demand a reading of character based on something more complicated and suggestive than the Christian ideal of duty. We ask questions to which Mrs. Gaskell would have been deaf and blind.

At this point the would-be reader perceives his dilemma. Either he must start at one end of the Brontë shelf and read his way steadily through to the other, taking in Clement Shorter, the Wise and Symington collations, the minutely composite results of American research, all the biographers, both mad and sane, who have been drawn into the web of Emily Brontë, even the innumerable Transactions of the Brontë Society—a lengthy but absorbing course: or, feeling that the whole subject has become unmanageable, he is bound to put his hands in his pockets and wander off to another part of the library.

And that would be a pity; for though it is true that Mrs. Gaskell suppressed some things and exaggerated others, that important material has come to light of which she knew next to nothing, and that we, her readers, are in some ways fundamentally changed, still, her great biography remains a stirring and noble work, one of the first in our language. More, it is still in essence 'truer' than anything about the Brontës which has been written since, and it needs only to be read with a full knowledge of the new, suppressed, or now differently apprehended material, and of her special difficulties and advantages as a biographer, to emerge more than ever clearly and splendidly as a work of art. It is, indeed, a surprisingly stimulating and rewarding experience to read it, so to speak, over her shoulder, with a never relaxed consciousness of her problem, approach, and performance as Charlotte Brontë's biographer.

For Mrs. Gaskell, arriving in Haworth from Manchester that summer afternoon in 1855 and making her way from Keighley Station to the parsonage with, one imagines, mixed feelings of excitement and apprehension, possessed advantages and confronted difficulties greater than have fallen to the lot of any subsequent biographer of the Brontës. She had the supreme advantage of being first in a field which was destined to be very highly cultivated. For the past five years she had been Charlotte's friend, on an extremely interested and sympathetic, if not intimate level; and she had been profoundly moved, both as a woman and a writer, by her contacts with Miss Brontë, whose work she recognized as being of the first order and to whose rare personality and sombre setting she responded with the sensitive imagination of the novelist. While Charlotte, after that first meeting (an event of perfectly mutual interest, since they were both at the height of their living fame) described Mrs. Gaskell in a letter as 'a woman of the most genuine talent—of cheerful, pleasing and cordial manners and—I believe—of a kind and good heart,' Mrs. Gaskell was writing to her friend Catherine Winkworth, 'Such a life as Miss B.'s I never heard of before,' and dashing off page after eager page, hastily recording the details that she had gleaned from Charlotte herself and everything she had been able to learn from their hostess, Lady Kay-Shuttleworth.

Everything about Miss Brontë had startled her imagination with such a vibrant touch that she must have been pleased, however soberly, when Mr. Brontë, less than four months after Charlotte's death, wrote and asked her to undertake a biography. Like most bereaved relations who sanction such things, he had no clear conception of the form it was likely to take. He had in mind 'a brief account of her life,' with perhaps 'some remarks on her works'—what Mr. Nicholls, Charlotte's husband, called 'some authentic statement.' Something, in a word, which would put a stop to those fanciful speculations which kept cropping up, to their pain, in the magazines.

Mrs. Gaskell must have seen at once the attraction of the task, for she came to Haworth within a few days of getting Mr. Brontë's letter; she was also very much alive to the peculiar difficulties. Chief among these were the two clergymen whom she had come to interview, and who were now living together in the parsonage in a sort of silent neutrality induced by sorrow but with nothing else in common. Mr. Brontë, whom she had had opportunities of observing when she had stayed at Haworth the year before Charlotte's marriage, she already knew as an odd and difficult character; and she had since heard enough, from Lady Kay-Shuttleworth and from Charlotte herself, to deepen this impression. Mr. Nicholls, the widower, was still more or less an unknown quantity, though Mrs. Gaskell before the marriage had fancied him 'very good, but *very* stern and bigoted,' and had been somewhat repelled (she was an intellectual Unitarian and the wife of a dissenting minister) when Charlotte had said, 'He is *not* intellectual. . . . He is a Puseyite and very stiff; I fear it will stand in the way of my intercourse with some of my friends.' So she was prepared with a faint wary dislike, though in all fairness she had admitted, discussing the marriage with her friends, that 'it must be charming to be loved with all the strength of his heart,' which she knew Charlotte was; and that Charlotte, moreover, 'would never have been happy but with an exacting, rigid, law-giving, passionate man.' Astute Mrs. Gaskell!—to perceive not only the special quality of her friend's emotional nature, but to see also that the erotic blend of authority and passion which alone could satisfy it lay concealed under the black habit and strict demeanour of this Victorian clergyman.

The surviving relations of genius can be a mixed blessing to biographers. The information which it is in their power to bestow is invaluable, but they rarely approach their subject with detachment, and their prejudices, preferences, and personal scruples can be highly inhibitive. Mr. Nicholls was reticent, if not indirectly obstructive; he had been against any idea of a biography, and had yielded at length only to Mr. Brontë's 'impetuous wish.' However, he produced a few of his wife's letters to her sisters, and directed Mrs. Gaskell, as he could hardly have avoided doing, to the rich mine from which all her best ore was to be extracted—to Charlotte Brontë's lifelong friend Ellen Nussey.

This was encouraging; but still, Mrs. Gaskell knew, she would sooner or later have to face the subject of Charlotte Brontë's marriage, and with Mr. Nicholls alive and watchful at the parsonage it was going to be difficult. Worse than this, Mr. Brontë himself would have to be explained; and as she had once described him privately as 'half-mad,' and believed that the tragic frustrations of Charlotte's life were due chiefly to his selfishness and eccentricity, this, too, was going to be critical. 'I can never think without gloomy anger,' wrote Mary Taylor, Charlotte's other lifelong friend, to Ellen Nussey, 'of Charlotte's sacrifices to the selfish old man. . . . But how on earth is all this to be set straight! Mrs Gaskell seems far too able a woman to put her head into such a wasp nest, as she would raise about her by speaking the truth of living people.' Mrs. Gaskell saw the wasp nest well enough, but underestimated its danger. And now here was Mr. Brontë himself, seeing her off at the front door and crying in innocent encouragement, 'No quailing, Mrs. Gaskell. No drawing back!'

Mrs. Gaskell quailed, fortunately for posterity, very

little. Indeed, the marvel is that she was so wonderfully reckless, so obsessed by the belief that biography is worthless unless *in essence* true, whatever the consequences, that she took risks which no modern biographer would dream of taking. The libel laws in the eighteen-fifties were not the series of concealed man-traps that they have since become, but they existed; and one's blood runs cold to see the earnest single-mindedness with which Mrs. Gaskell ignored them.

It is wonderful that she showed so little timidity in writing about Mr. Brontë. Her impression of him was that he was a selfish man of passionate temper, possessed of undoubted mental vigour and originality. Stories she was told confirmed this view, and she so described him. It is odd that Mr. Brontë never stipulated (that stipulation so fatal to sincere biography and so often made) that he should see Mrs. Gaskell's book before publication; but apparently he did not, and had his first glimpse of the work when it was published. Even so, with a moral robustness extremely characteristic of him, he read her descriptions at first without disapproval, making only one small correction; but it was not long before his acquaintance on all sides were assuring him that he had been held up to censure, and a chill fell across his relations with Mrs. Gaskell. He began to put it about that she had been taken in by spiteful and silly stories, and so to some extent discredited her; so that even three and a half years later, when she visited Haworth with her daughter, she 'fancied he would not like to see her, because so many reviews, letters in newspapers, etc., which she knew had reached him, dwelt on the way in which, while pretending to have been his daughter's friend, she had held up his character to ridicule.'

The Cowan Bridge controversy, as we have already

seen, was a more serious matter, and one in which Mrs. Gaskell was singularly unfortunate. In the 'Lowood' of *Jane Eyre* Charlotte Brontë had described the school of her early childhood, the Clergy Daughters' School, from which her two elder sisters had been removed in a dying condition, and where she herself had suffered enough for the marks on her mind to be indelible. In thirty years, however, the school had been improved and removed to a much healthier situation, so that the friends of the Rev. Carus Wilson had some appearance of justice on their side when they indignantly denied the truth of her descriptions. Mrs. Gaskell knew that she must be careful when she came to deal with Charlotte's nine months at Cowan Bridge; she believed the descriptions in *Jane Eyre* to be in essence true, because Miss Brontë had assured her that they were; but she was anxious to sift every shred of evidence and to do everybody justice. Anyone who has ever looked into Mrs. Carus Wilson's religious works for children, admonitory tales full of whippings, sudden deaths, and naughty children being tortured in hell, is bound to believe that Charlotte Brontë did no injustice to the 'black marble clergyman,' and that Mrs. Gaskell's treatment of him is even tender, so anxious is she to omit no favourable word that can be said. But the favourable words were still too few for Mr. Carus Wilson's supporters, and because Mrs. Gaskell did not openly condemn the description of Lowood as a libel on Cowan Bridge, but seemed, however, hesitantly and judiciously, to support it, they attacked her with a ferocity and persistence far greater than they had shown to Charlotte Brontë.

The Cowan Bridge controversy, however, prolonged and dangerous though it was, was nothing to the unpleasantness over Branwell Brontë's love affair with Mrs. Robinson. This episode in the Brontë legend, and indeed the

whole fascinating story of Branwell, is one which irresisti-
bly tempts the modern biographer. We feel that we understand him better than Mrs. Gaskell did; our moral scales
are not so implacably weighted; we feel less distaste for
the specimen before us, and have developed different instruments of dissection. The whole question of Branwell's
putative genius and the facts of his disgrace are more
suggestive to us today than they were to his contemporaries, and we are drawn on to speculate and theorize where
Mrs. Gaskell could only shudder and condemn.

Where she condemned, however, she did it thoroughly; and the modern reader, brought up under libel
laws as tricky in interpretation as the pronouncements of
an oracle, must regard her shocked sincerity as reckless.
Mrs. Gaskell, a minister's wife herself, could not conceive
of anything more wicked than the temptation which she
believed Mrs. Robinson, a clergyman's wife and a mother,
had trailed in the path of Branwell; and the frightened
withdrawal from the third edition of the *Life* of everything relating to Mrs. Robinson, and the apology, made
under threat of legal action, published in *The Times*, are
familiar literary history. Fortunately, it all happened long
enough ago to have become safe again, and the version of
the Branwell-Robinson affair which we read today is as
Mrs. Gaskell wrote it. The truth can never be known with
any certainty, and our assessment of Branwell is unlikely
to be the same as Mrs. Gaskell's. The story is significant
today only because Branwell was a Brontë.

Mrs. Gaskell's reckless regard for truth, for which we
are so grateful, was of necessity suppressed when she
came to deal with Charlotte Brontë's own emotional history; and for this suppression we must blame (if blame is
the word, for widowers and other surviving relations commonly cannot *help* being the blight of biography) the

Rev. Arthur Bell Nicholls, that silent but utterly inhibiting presence sitting alone with his sermons in Haworth Parsonage. There seems to be no doubt about Mrs. Gaskell's knowledge of Charlotte's unhappy love for M. Héger, from which she recovered slowly, as from a long secret illness. Ellen Nussey, too, knew something of it, for in their letters she and Mrs. Gaskell exchanged veiled glances. Mrs. Gaskell, when she visited M. Héger in Brussels, must have been shown those four letters of Charlotte's to her schoolmaster which, with their authentic and unmistakable cry, are still such painful reading; for she quoted from them, slightly and very discreetly, in her biography. Whether M. Héger showed her the whole, or only extracts, we do not know.

He may possibly, to prove how correctly discouraging he himself had been, have shown passages from Charlotte's final letter: 'To write to an old pupil cannot be a very interesting occupation for you, I know; but for me it is life. Your last letter was stay and prop to me—nourishment to me for half a year. Now I need another and you will give it to me; not because you bear me friendship—you cannot have much—but because you are compassionate of soul and you would condemn no one to prolonged suffering to save yourself a few moments' trouble. To forbid me to write to you, to refuse to answer me, would be to tear from me my only joy on earth, to deprive me of my last privilege. . . . So long as I believe you are pleased with me, so long as I have hope of receiving news from you, I can be at rest and not too sad. But when a prolonged and gloomy silence seems to threaten me with the estrangement of my master—when day by day I await a letter, and when day by day disappointment comes to fling me back into overwhelming sorrow, and the sweet delight of seeing your handwriting and reading your counsel escapes me as a vision that is vain, then fever claims me—I lose appetite and sleep—I pine away.' At all events she saw enough (and her suspicions must have been deepened by Mme Héger's pointed refusal to see her) to make her write to Ellen Nussey, 'I believed him to be too good to publish those letters.'

Yet what, if she fully realized Charlotte's case, was Mrs. Gaskell to do? To be in love with a married man, however hopelessly and virtuously, was a shameful disaster from which the Victorian woman (or at least that ideal conception of woman which Charlotte Brontë and Mrs. Gaskell shared) shrank back in horror. To have hinted, even, at Charlotte's plight would have been a betrayal: a woman of Mrs. Gaskell's delicacy simply could not have done it. And even if she had been willing to do Charlotte's memory this injury, there was always Mr. Nicholls, disconcertingly watchful and always a little uneasy at the thought of what might come to light in his wife's letters. No, the only possible course was to keep silence; as she must keep silence, too, about Charlotte's real view of her husband before their marriage. Mrs. Gaskell hid from the whole problem behind a draped screen of womanly reverence.

What, of course, she could not foresee was the future history of those very letters which M. Héger seems to have shown her in Brussels, and which he afterwards tore up and threw away. She could not guess that Mme Héger (more like Mme Beck than ever, and appearing to glide straight out of the pages of *Villette*) would search the wastepaper basket, find the pieces, fit them together, mount them with glue and lock them away in her jewelcase with unexplained motives—with a sense, one suspects, of power in a concealed weapon. There they remained untouched until after her death, and came into M.

Héger's hands again when he was going through her papers. Astonished—so his daughter maintained—at finding these worthless fragments so jealously preserved, he threw them away once more; and now it was his daughter who retrieved the pieces and hid them away until she was an old woman. And in 1913, near the end of her life, Mlle Louise Héger and her brother, feeling that the letters had a more than personal importance, gave them to the British Museum, whence they found their way to the public through the columns of *The Times*. Mrs. Gaskell's reticence no longer availed, and there is a poetic fitness in this defeat of her discretion, for there is a boundary in time which genius inevitably reaches, stepping out of the claims of family and friends and into a region of freedom, and Charlotte Brontë has crossed it long ago.

One other important area of Charlotte Brontë's life Mrs. Gaskell left untouched, and this not deliberately, but because she did not know that it was there. It has remained for the patience, the almost inconceivable patience of American scholarship, to turn over the dark, close-packed and seemingly sterile mould of the *juvenilia* and to unearth whole buried cities of the imagination, alive still in their own peculiar atmosphere, at once tense and languorous, like the climate of erotic dreams. If Mrs. Gaskell had possessed the key to this uninviting and uncharted mass she would not have cared for everything to be found there. The conclusions to be drawn would not have fitted her conception of Charlotte Brontë; so perhaps it was the artist's instinct of selection which led her to pass so lightly over the microscopic volumes, and to describe the rich collection which Mr. Nicholls had preserved as simply a 'curious packet.'

If it had not been for Sir James Kay-Shuttleworth, who accompanied her on her final visit to Haworth, she would never even have known that the packet existed. A dictatorial man, founder of the modern system of education and a determined philanthropist, he had insisted on going with her, though she shrank from the suggestion, knowing how likely he was to prove an embarrassment. But as things turned out, his blunt methods made unexpected headway with Mr. Nicholls. 'He had not the slightest delicacy or scruple,' Mrs. Gaskell wrote afterwards, 'and asked for an immense number of things, literally taking no refusal. Hence we carried away with us an immense heap of those minute writings . . . the beginning (only about 20 pages) of a new novel which she had written at the end of 1854, before marriage, and I dare say when she was anxious enough. This fragment was excessively interesting.' More to her purpose, when later she re-examined the 'immense heap' at leisure, were 'quantities of fragments very short but very graphic written when she was about 12, giving glimpses of her life at that time, all of which I had to decipher, and interweave with what I had already written—in fact I had to rewrite about 40 pages. They give a much pleasanter though hardly less *queer* notion of the old father.'

Yet, even with its untouched and fallow areas, what a wonderful field to be the first in! For the Brontës, like Dr. Johnson and Byron, are possessed of that strange potency of personality which is unaffected by time, and which makes the least detail which concerns them interesting. The drama of their setting, the poignancy of their lives, the marvel of their achievement (to speak only of Charlotte and Emily) the strong, the bitter undercurrent which is never absent and which comes again and again disastrously to the surface—what biographer, unless perhaps Boswell, has ever closed his hand on a more fertile subject? Mrs. Gaskell's very quietness of demeanour is an added strength, supporting, with a well-bred and unhurried air, her antique theme of moral struggle, human greatness, and implacable fate; just as the harsh but satisfying tragedy of the story thrusts her at times into positions which, as a novelist, she would never have considered. Charlotte's death, after the one brief gleam of quiet hapiness, is a final blow which few Victorian novelists would have had courage to deal—and certainly not Mrs. Gaskell. Yet it is the perfect ending; unbearable, lacerating, and at the same time marvellously quiet, so that we close the book with a sense of exhaustion and relief, and a feeling that we have learned something of importance to us for ever—though we cannot, perhaps, say what. Charlotte Brontë's death, forcing itself on Mrs. Gaskell's recording hand, is a curious example of nature imitating art.

It is saddening to reflect that this beautiful achievement, in the two years' writing of which, as she said, she had 'weighed every line with my whole power and heart,' brought Mrs. Gaskell so much unhappiness that she was 'frightened off her nest,' in the literary sense, for the next six years, and even came to the conclusion that all forms of biography were undesirable. So harassed was she by the assaults made on her, not only by Carus Wilson and the Robinsons, but by innumerable busybodies who took exception to one detail after another, that her health suffered; and she is said to have made a solemn request to her daughters that no biography of herself should ever be written. Certainly there is no comparable *Life of Elizabeth Gaskell,* and the last person to remember her is long dead. It is a pity. Yet in a sense it is true, as her American friend Charles Norton wrote to James Russell Lowell, that this biography 'is almost as much an exhibition of Mrs. Gaskell's character as of Miss Brontë's'; and if our fullest intimacy with her is in watching over her steady shoulder as she pursues her literary life's most splendid task, we shall find our vigilance rewarded by a strange impression, as of a double exposure, in which a second figure, more delicate and shadowy than the first, stands close beside it, and with this unemphatic wraith we must rest content.

Mrs. Gaskell: Wives and Daughters

IN JANUARY 1866 MRS. GASKELL'S FINAL NOVEL broke off in *The Cornhill* in the middle of a chapter, never to be finished. Two months before, sitting by the fire in the house she had secretly bought for her husband's retirement at Holybourne in Hampshire, her voice had stopped—'*quite* suddenly, without a moment's warning, in the midst of a sentence,' as her daughter Meta wrote to Ellen Nussey—and she had fallen slowly forward from her chair, dead. She was only fifty-five and at the height of her powers, as the unfinished novel already triumphantly demonstrated.

And perhaps, after all, it is pedantic to call it unfinished, since there was only a short chapter still to be written and it is clear that a few more pages would have brought her in sight of a happy and satisfying ending. The novel is a long one, unhurried, warm, expansive, and in every important respect artistically complete. The pious 'Concluding Remarks' by the editor of *The Cornhill* (in which magazine the novel had been running as a serial for the past eighteen months) though proper enough at the time are really superfluous. We know what will happen, as inevitably as though we were in Mrs. Gibson's drawing-room and heard her final inconsequential remarks. It is as satisfying as though we had come to the last page.

Is it as satisfying now, after all these years? Why, as a critic recently asked himself in print, should anyone read Mrs. Gaskell today? Novels are rare which trium-phantly survive so long, but the mid-nineteenth century produced a fine harvest of survivors, and *Wives and Daughters* can fairly be called one of them. It takes us at once into a vanished world, a rural England before the days of railways and the Industrial Revolution, and so into a climate of life and modes of behaviour that in some aspects are as strange to us as though they belonged to beings of another planet. Yet Mrs. Gaskell's tone of voice is curiously modern; she is a sophisticated writer, humor-ous and ironic as well as tender; less sentimental by far than some of her contemporaries and with a knowledge of the social scene and of the human heart which time has done nothing to diminish. Her style is plain and unforced, like good conversation, and if there is one thing that makes her seem unfashionable today it is her conviction that there is great good to be found in ordinary people, and that open dealing and upright behaviour are both desirable and possible.

Of course, there are things to strike amazement into the reader who comes upon them now for the first time, and this is one of the pleasures of reading Mrs. Gaskell: there are so many contrasts between then and now. The sacredness of the 'engagement,' for example—even a promise of marriage extracted in secrecy and under duress from a girl of sixteen. Such a conception of honour seems unreasonable and absurd, yet in Molly Gibson's and Cyn-thia Kirkpatrick's day such clandestine promises were seri-ous affairs which could give rise to scandal and suffering. An engagement, however improperly contracted, could properly be dissolved only by mutual consent, and many marriages took place for the simple reason that to jilt, or to be jilted, was more disgraceful than to enter stoically into a loveless partnership.

Her characters indeed are all caught in the net of what was then considered decent behaviour, and the meshes of that net are fine enough to make the reader tremble. Cynthia Kirkpatrick, one of the freshest and most entrancing creations of any period of fiction, transgresses the code, it is true, knowingly and without serious regret, and gets off scot-free, as she would in life, leaving a satisfying trail of damaged hearts behind her. But the terrors and risks of the net encompass them all.

Molly Gibson, the doctor's daughter, is conceived in the best tradition of Victorian heroines—spirited but dutiful, more prone to tears and silent endurance than would be thought reasonable nowadays, but too warm and direct to be exasperating. She is perfectly adequate; one grows gradually and genuinely fond of her. But it is Cynthia, enchanting in face and manner, wanting in principle, and still more her shallow, selfish, worldly-minded mother, who are Mrs. Gaskell's triumphs in the novel. She is tender to Cynthia despite her faults, for the sake of her ravishing charm and her instinct to please. To charm, to set out to attract any man who comes within range, of whatever age or condition, is an instinct that Cynthia obeys as naturally as she breathes. Her sexual responses are facile and uncalculating, and being the charming creature that she is, and quite free from illusions about herself, she is naturally, as Mrs. Gaskell observes, 'not remarkable for unflinching morality.' Charlotte Brontë would have made heavy weather of Cynthia Kirkpatrick, whose behaviour, if she had described it, she would condemn; but Mrs. Gaskell is more worldly and tolerant, and knows there is something to be said for a temperament that can forget her tears and troubles and 'throw her soul into millinery.' It is her mother, Mrs. Kirkpatrick, the attractive widow who was once governess to the great family of the neighbourhood and who marries the country doctor for the sake of her bread and butter, who is dissected slowly and delicately, without mercy. We are left at the end knowing her as selfish, trivial, and insensitive, a dry husk of a human being who at first had shown all the charms of a desirable woman.

Her surface attraction and basic selfishness are suggested by oblique but telling detail. To look like a lady on the salary of a governess is an exhausting business, and Mrs. Kirkpatrick's hollowness is slyly conveyed in terms of preoccupation with appearance and money.

She was very pretty and graceful; and that goes a great way towards carrying off shabby clothes; and it was her taste more than any depth of feeling that had made her persevere in wearing all the delicate tints—the violets and greys—which, with a certain admixture of black, constitute half-mourning. . . . Her beautiful hair was of that rich auburn that hardly ever turns grey; and partly out of consciousness of its beauty, and partly because the washing of caps is expensive, she did not wear anything on her head; her complexion had the vivid tints that often accompany the kind of hair which has once been red; and the only injury her skin had received from advancing years was that the colour was rather more brilliant than delicate, and varied less with every passing emotion. . . . Her figure was a little fuller than it used to be, but her movements were as soft and sinuous as ever. Altogether, she looked much younger than her age, which was not far short of forty.

It is a little startling to find that her hair and complexion showed the effects of 'advancing years' in her late thirties, but Mrs. Gaskell was not writing in a cosmetic age, nor one in which youth was supposed to last for ever. We sympathize with Mrs. Kirkpatrick's 'elegant economies,' but no sooner do they touch us than we perceive the shrewd self-seeking that they serve. 'One would think it was an easy enough thing to deck a looking-glass like that with muslin and pink ribbons,' she grumbles to herself when she visits her old employer, Lady Cumnor, at The Towers,

and yet how hard it is to keep it up! People don't know how hard it is till they've tried as I have. I made my own glass just as pretty when I first went to Ashcombe; but the muslin got dirty, and the pink ribbons faded, and it is so difficult to earn money to renew them; and when one has got the money one hasn't the heart to spend it all at once. . . . Now here, money is like the air they breathe. No one ever asks or knows how much the washing costs, or what pink ribbon is a yard. Ah! it would be different if they had to earn every penny as I have! They would have to calculate, like me, how to get the most pleasure out of it. I wonder if I am to go on all my life toiling and moiling for money? It's not natural. Marriage is the natural thing; then the husband has all that kind of dirty work to do, and his wife sits in the drawing-room like a lady.

Her charming appearance and good manners persuade Dr. Gibson, too deeply engrossed in a large country practice to think these things out as carefully as he should, to believe she will make an affectionate stepmother for Molly and even, perhaps, a desirable wife for himself. (He only once, so far as we are told, pauses to consider her physical attractions.) But no sooner is the honeymoon over than Molly (and the reader) are given a glimpse of her real preoccupations. The doctor's hand-to-mouth household is now transformed. 'New paint, new paper, new colours; grim servants dressed in their best, and objecting to every change—from their master's marriage to the new oilcloth in the hall, "which tripped 'em up, and threw 'em down, and was cold to the feet, and smelt just adominable." ' The new Mrs. Gibson is tired, and inclined to be fretful.

'I feel so lonely, darling, in this strange house; do come and be with me, and help me to unpack. I think your dear papa might have put off his visit to Mr Craven Smith for just this one evening.'
　　'Mr Craven Smith couldn't put off his dying,' said Molly bluntly.
　　'You droll girl!' said Mrs Gibson, with a faint laugh. 'But if this Mr Smith is dying, as you say, what's the use of your father's going off to him in such a hurry? Does he expect any legacy, or anything of that kind?'

And here, indeed, contemplating the marriage of Mrs. Kirkpatrick to the sardonic and handsome doctor, the present-day reader is brought to a curious pause. Mr. Gibson's sexual attractiveness is never in doubt, in spite of Mrs. Gaskell's half-hearted assumption that a good-looking widower of forty-five is past the age of being susceptible to a pretty woman. He marries her because his household needs a mistress and his daughter a mother, and there is no hint anywhere that Mrs. Kirkpatrick's personal attractions, her elegant dress and winning manners, have made more than a momentary appeal to his masculine senses. True, he repents at leisure, and is forced to make the best of a bad bargain, but to the intimate stages of his disillusion we are given no clue.

Such reticence in a novelist would be unthinkable today. We would be left in no doubt as to whether or not he had embarked on a *mariage blanc*, but in Mrs. Gaskell's time the conspiracy of silence was inevitable. Novels were written for family reading, instalment by monthly instalment in the family circle, and such matters were no more to be touched on in print than in conversation. How could it be otherwise? Is it such a bad thing, after all, that the reader should provide the answer according to his own judgement and experience? Mr. Gibson had had love affairs before, but was settled in habits of overwork and celibacy. Dynamic though he is, he does not make a sensual impression, and it is well to remember, in spite of what some notable present-day novelists would have us believe, that there do exist normal, intelligent, and attractive persons to whom sexual gratification is not the only consideration in life. So we are free to interpret his marriage as being entirely for practical motives or not, as we choose. For Mrs. Kirkpatrick, self-seeking and self-absorbed, essentially frigid, to be a *maitresse-femme* would be out of character as well as out of period.

It is not a point of great importance. The Gibsons are as alive to us today as if we knew them and frequented the doctor's modest house in Hollingford. So, indeed, are most of the people of the neighbourhood, for within the limits of her time Mrs. Gaskell is a realist. The aristocratic family at 'The Towers,' arbiters of local society, are drawn with an outrageous yet tender eye for their absurdity; even Lady Cumnor, the 'dear Countess' of Mrs. Kirkpatrick's adulation, in spite of her thick-skinned arrogance has some respectable qualities. For Mrs. Gaskell, married to a hard-working Unitarian minister in Manchester, knew at first hand more about social and economic conditions than most of her contemporaries, and to her eye the Countess and her like were already anachronisms, survivals to be laughed gently off the scene, not tumbril-fodder.

To Squire Hamley, head of an older but impoverished county family, she is kinder because she values him, but she is still severe. He is (and they still existed in those days) a relic of the eighteenth century; in his ignorance, bluster, and bad temper he might almost be one of Fielding's domineering squires. Yet she knows the inner helplessness of the man and the impossibility of his playing a rational part in the rapidly changing world of the nineteenth century.

For the future she looks to his younger son, Roger Hamley, who serves somewhat stodgily as the hero of the story and is distinguished by being its only comparative failure. Roger is plain and clever and worthy, and comes out, it must be admitted, as a bit of a prig. (Trollope would have allowed him a few faults.) Mercifully he is shipped off to Africa on a scientific expedition and becomes, improbably enough, a minor Darwin. It is difficult to make solid worth attractive; even a hundred years ago it could be a pitfall for the novelist, and Roger Hamley by any standard is dull. But then so are many young men in everyday life, and they may fall in love with a Cynthia or be loved by a Molly without anyone being astonished. With such a broad, homely scene before us, so lovingly evoked and skilfully explored, to carp because Roger is neither a hero nor an anti-hero is to miss Mrs. Gaskell's point. She does not deal in conventional heroics.

Of all her novels *Cranford* is perhaps the only one that is widely read today. This is a pity. *Wives and Daughters* is a work of far greater stature, wider sympathies, maturer grasp of character, and no less humour. It creates the illusion of a return to a rigidly exacting but more stable and innocent world than ours, from which we emerge consoled and refreshed in spirit. We feel, indeed, 'caught out of an abominable wicked world, crawling with selfishness and reeking with base passions, into one where there is much weakness, many mistakes, sufferings long and bitter, but where it is possible for people to lead calm and wholesome lives.'

These words, oddly enough, were not written recently. They are from *The Cornhill* editor's 'Concluding Remarks,' published with the unfinished chapter in 1866.

Mrs. Gaskell and the Fallen Woman

ONE OF THE SIDE EFFECTS OF THE SEXUAL revolution is that the generation that has grown up with it tends to look with impatience on novels written before the liberation. Can the young reader today care for the theme and tragedy of Mrs. Gaskell's *Ruth?* Can anyone believe that a love affair at fifteen could be regarded as the just cause of a life of secrecy, humiliation, and repentance? Can one suppose that a girl of that age would ever be branded as damned, a 'fallen woman'?

We can believe it if we have the imagination to go back into an England that was very much alive before we or our present freedoms were ever dreamed of. It is not, after all, so very long ago. Mrs. Gaskell wrote *Ruth* in 1853, and the hypocrisy and intolerance that she fought against still flourish, in some degree, in our own time. Her decision to plead the cause of the fallen woman (or child, as we should call her) took considerable courage. She was made to suffer for it, and shed bitter tears over the novel's reception; but the effect of *Ruth*, even in the eighteen fifties, was to diminish by a perceptible margin one of society's meanest injustices to women. In her quiet way she was a pioneer of that advance towards human understanding which softens some of the aspects of life today.

Elizabeth Cleghorn Gaskell, wife of the Unitarian minister of Cross Street Chapel, Manchester, knew very well what she was writing about. Her own married life was singularly fortunate and happy. William Gaskell was a man of great charm, integrity, and intelligence, and their four daughters completed as tranquil and affection- ate a family as any Victorian couple could desire. But the scene of her married life was the grim north of the Indus- trial Revolution, when starvation and despair, dirt, dis- ease, and juvenile prostitution were a commonplace. Her work as minister's wife in the slums had made her famil- iar with facts and conditions which most women of her class and upbringing feared to glance at. Like Dickens, she had done practical rescue work among the 'lost' and 'fallen,' helping them to emigrate to Australia or to find respectable employment at home in places where their past would not be too mercilessly scrutinized. Her first correspondence with Dickens, indeed, seems to have been on this very subject, asking his help and advice for one of her *protégées*, who, like Little Em'ly in *David Copper- field*, was to expiate her sin on the other side of the world.

Emigration, death, or prostitution—these were the three classic courses open to a seduced and abandoned girl of the 'respectable' classes, and popular feeling, reflected with pious horror in Victorian fiction, found death by far the most satisfactory solution. (The poorest class, as al- ways, was perforce less hypocritical and more tolerant, and accidents in high society were desperately concealed. Though even here it is worth remembering that Lady Dedlock, whose whole story hinges on the dreadful secret of having had a lover and an illegitimate daughter before marriage, makes her moral apology towards the end of *Bleak House* by dying at the gates of the cemetery where her lover is buried.) The cruelty of this attitude, the suffering and waste of life that it entailed, weighed on Mrs. Gaskell's mind because she had seen it at close quarters, and when Dickens invited her to contribute a story to his new popular weekly, *Household Words*, she chose this dangerous theme for *Lizzie Leigh*, to which Dickens gave pride of place in the first number.

Lizzie Leigh today reads more like *The Sunday School Penny Magazine* than a work of serious fiction, but it is worth examining as a trial run for the more outspoken novel of two years later. Lizzie is the daughter of a poor farmer and the secret disgrace of her family, having been dismissed in shame from domestic service and not heard of since. Her mother, now widowed, abandons the farm and goes to Manchester with her two sons, determined to find and rescue her erring child. Her search is as frantic and as apparently hopeless as Mr. Peggotty's for Little Em'ly, and with this complication, that her elder son is in love with a pure young woman and dreads the shameful discovery of his lost sister. 'If she were made acquainted with the dark secret of his sister's shame, which was kept ever present to his mind by his mother's nightly search among the outcast and forsaken, would not Susan shrink away from him with loathing, as if he were tainted by the involuntary relationship? This was his dread. . . . He became angry with his mother for her untiring patience in seeking for one who, he could not help hoping, was dead rather than alive.' But Lizzie is of course alive, though 'old before her time,' even when asleep bearing 'the look of woe and despair which was the prevalent expression of her face by day.' The unknown foundling which the pure young woman cares for is Lizzie's child, the mother finds her lost daughter and . . . but no, we are not to be indulged with a happy ending. This is a mid-Victorian story, and Mrs. Gaskell, intent on her special pleading, is yet aware that there must be no relief without retribution. The child dies (Mrs. Gaskell shared the contemporary fondness for tear-soaked deathbeds), Will marries his Susan and returns to the farm, while Lizzie retires with her mother to a cottage 'in a green hollow of the hills,' where she earns redemption by a life of selfless ministering to the neighbours.

It is a long step from this mawkish story to the clearer and firmer intentions with which Mrs. Gaskell conceived the story of *Ruth*. She was already well known as the author of *Mary Barton*, a bold novel of working-class life in the 'hungry forties,' and now the charms of *Cranford* had made her famous. Her creative powers had considerably developed, she was approaching her maturity as a writer and confronted her task with a mixture of anxiety and confidence. The basic theme of the novel, never explicitly stated but consistently felt under the balanced structure, is two-fold: first, that the so-called 'lost' or 'fallen' woman was, as often as not, a human being of great value and potentiality whom it was folly, as well as wickedness, to waste; and second, that an illegitimate child, far from being the badge of its mother's shame, could be the means of awakening the finest elements in her nature.

Nobody would contradict such views today, but in 1853 they were revolutionary. The first requirement in a novel (I quote from Miss A. B. Hopkins's excellent and too little known biography of Mrs. Gaskell) was that 'it should have an influence for good and be suitable for reading in the family circle.' Even Dickens, most humane and progressive of men, had sent Little Em'ly to Australia, and in *Bleak House*, written in the same year as *Ruth*, reassured his readers about Lady Dedlock by letting her die, as we have seen, on the steps of the cemetery. Six years later, in *Adam Bede*, Hetty Sorrel misses the gal-

lows by a hair's breadth, the sentence being commuted to
one of transportation. (Curious that George Eliot, with
her moral seriousness and her long unwedded union with
G. H. Lewes, never chose to say a word on the subject of
sexual justice. Perhaps she felt too vulnerable, and the
extraordinary feat of becoming a revered moralist as well
as a literary figure, while living with a man to whom she
was not married, no doubt absorbed much of her propa-
gandist energies.)

Mrs. Gaskell, having courageously made up her mind,
nevertheless approached the subject with fear and trembling. She was a minister's wife and a mother of daughters, as well as a novelist who had already been sharply
criticized for unorthodox opinions. She had no desire to
preach (she once described herself as a 'sermon hater')
but she knew she must tread on eggs to make her point.
So she chose as her heroine a girl who is only fifteen at the
time of her seduction, an orphan, gently brought up, but
now with no friend in the world beyond a fellow appren-
tice at the dressmaker's where she lives and works in
comfortless sweatshop conditions. And here we come to
the first stumbling-block in the path of the modern reader.
Ruth is 'innocent and snow-pure'; she knows nothing of
the world or of sex; like Oliver Twist in his thieves'
den she retains all the moral scruples and delicacy of
behaviour of a girl brought up in normal protective surroundings, impervious to harsh experience and coarse
companions.

Well, it may have been so. Fate, we must assume, not
any flaw of character, is against her. She is seduced by a
rich and attractive young man who meets her by chance
and ostensibly befriends her, offering her help when she is
dismissed from work at a moment's notice and has nowhere to go. He whisks her away to the mountains of

Wales, and here, deeply in love and rejoicing in tenderness returned, she has her first and only experience of passionate happiness. Mrs. Gaskell had spent her own honeymoon in the romantic mountain valleys around Festiniog, and Ruth's brief love affair is described with quiet lyricism. We are left in no doubt, however, about the selfish and shallow nature of Mr. Bellingham.

The delusive dream is soon over. Abandoned, pregnant, she is saved from suicide by an impoverished dissenting minister, who takes her home to his sister and housekeeper, both women of strong prejudices and opinions who are finally, touched by her misery, persuaded to accept her. So far so good, but here we encounter another knotty point of Victorian morals. In order to protect Ruth and the child that is to come, the kindly Bensons give it out that she is a widow. A justified lie, one would suppose; but Mrs. Gaskell emphatically does not agree. In a humane society a lie would not have been necessary, but having been resorted to (and by a minister too) it brings its cruel and inevitable retribution.

This, however, is to anticipate. The dreaded exposure is delayed until Leonard, Ruth's son, is twelve years old and she herself for several years has been a loved and respected governess in the family of the pharisaic Mr. Bradshaw, richest and most powerful member of Mr. Benson's modest congregation. She has schooled herself to forget her unhappy love, and for the sake of her child (a priggish boy, alas—Mrs. Gaskell was not good at portraying children) has steadily taught herself as well as her charges, so that at twenty-eight she has matured into an intelligent and beautiful woman. This was the point at which Mrs. Gaskell was aiming: through suffering and through her experience of loving-kindness Ruth has learned the importance of human and moral values, and has arrived at the point where she trusts her instinctive judgement. This judgement is soon subjected to cruel tests. Her lover reappears, now a man of wealth and new-made Member of Parliament, and uses every inducement to persuade her to become his mistress. More, when he finds her firm, in spite of the mutual stirring of old passion, he throws caution and ambition to the winds and offers her marriage. A possibly happy solution? Again Mrs. Gaskell disagrees. Ruth has learned enough of her lover's unprincipled nature to know she can never accept him as the father of her child. In one of the most deeply felt scenes of the novel, alone with him in the evening on Abermouth Sands, she refuses him absolutely.

This is a costly victory, as Mrs. Gaskell intended; but there is worse to come. Inevitably, at last, the Bensons' protective deception is exposed, and Ruth is driven out from the Bradshaws' in public disgrace, while the chapel congregation shrinks in horror from a minister who could not only harbour a fallen woman, but lie about it.

This is the point, perhaps, at which a latter-day novelist (always supposing one could be found who considered a seduction and a lie as being worth worrying about) would be tempted to bring the story to an ironic end. Not so Mrs. Gaskell. Her passionate point was that Ruth, in spite of her sin and her many misfortunes, perhaps because of them, was a noble being, and that to save such a one the angels themselves might wink at a harmless deception.

So Ruth begins again her struggle for a new life, and on a humble, a pitifully humble level achieves it. Further than this Mrs. Gaskell dared not go. The nearer she approached the end, it seems, the more she began to dread the public's reaction. She had saved her heroine from the river, she had not sent her by steerage to Australia, she had redeemed her through love of her child and the humanity of pious and humble people. Ruth was alive and modestly independent, a better and wiser woman. What would all the family reading circles in all the God-fearing parlours of England say to that? It is a pity there was no one at hand to cry, as Mr. Brontë was to do at the beginning of her biography of Charlotte, 'No quailing, Mrs. Gaskell! No drawing back!' Mrs. Gaskell, alas, did quail; she did draw back. She resorted in alarm to the conventional Victorian deathbed, which to the modern reader is a sentimental and unnecessary flaw in the novel. 'Why should she die?' wrote Charlotte Brontë, very reasonably, 'why are we to shut up the book weeping?' Elizabeth Barrett Browning was of the same opinion. But Mrs. Gaskell knew her public, and her fears were justified.

' "An unfit subject for fiction" is the thing to say about it,' she wrote with some bitterness after the book was published. 'I knew all this before, but I determined notwithstanding to speak my mind out about it; only now I shrink with more pain than I can tell you from what people are saying, though I could do every jot of it over again tomorrow. "Deep regret" is what my friends here . . . feel and express. In short the only comparison I can find for myself is to St. Sebastian tied to a tree to be shot at with arrows. . . . Of course,' she added, recollecting herself as a minister's wife and mother of adolescent daughters, 'it is a prohibited book in *this*, as in many other households; not a book for young people. . . . I am in a quiver of pain about it.'

It is hard today to imagine *Ruth* being burned, as it was by fathers of families sitting cheek by jowl with the Gaskells in the same chapel. If it shocks us now it is in precisely the sense that Mrs. Gaskell intended. What revolts us is the implacable cruelty and hypocrisy of an age which in many ways seems so much less terrible, so much more stable and comforting than our own.

Oliver Twist *and* Great Expectations

O LIVER TWIST HAS BEEN CALLED A 'DARK and sinister and murderous' novel. It is certainly that; it is also a great deal more. It is a first glimpse of the dark side of Dickens, and the first of his great protests against human misery. It is a melodrama too, a kind of fairy tale, so bursting with life that it is only at the end that we find we have been under a spell and have scarcely noticed a dozen youthful absurdities.

The creaking plot and the impossible coincidences are flaws, but they hardly matter: the rest of *Oliver Twist* has such power, it paints such a picture of a lost underworld, that the magic works today almost as it did in the year of Queen Victoria's accession. It is a novel, in fact, too famous for its own good. Who has not heard of Fagin? Or of Oliver Twist in the workhouse asking for more? Stage versions, films, radio, and television have in a sense come between us and Dickens's first real novel (since *Pickwick Papers* was begun as a series of sketches and became a novel, so to speak, by accident), and it requires an effort of imagination to come to the theme as though for the first time. The effort, however, is worth making; though it has large faults and is a long way below Dickens's best work,

Oliver Twist is one of the spell-binding experiences of a lifetime.

Dickens was not yet twenty-five when he began it, in a burst of creative vitality like a shower of fireworks. Newly married to Catherine Hogarth, he had left his work as a reporter on the *Morning Chronicle* to devote himself to writing. *Sketches by Boz* had been well received, and *Pickwick Papers*, after a slow start, had set the public laughing and made him famous. *Pickwick* was still appearing in monthly parts, with the printer hard on his heels for the next instalment. At the same time he was editing, with his left hand as it were, a monthly magazine called *Bentley's Miscellany*, and it was to provide a serial for the *Miscellany* that, while still at work on *Pickwick*, he started *Oliver Twist*. His brother-in-law Henry Burnett long afterwards recalled how he would work away on the fringe of the family circle, sitting at a little table with the quill pen moving rapidly over the paper, from time to time joining cheerfully in the conversation. 'It was interesting to watch, upon the sly, the mind and muscles working (or, if you please, *playing*) in company, as new thoughts were being dropped upon the paper. And to note the working brow, the set of mouth, with the tongue tightly pressed against the closed lips, as was his habit.'

Nothing could have been more unlike the hilarious fantasy of *Pickwick* than this new story, and his readers, cheerfully carrying home the first instalment, must have been startled to find the opening scene a harrowing one of death and birth in a workhouse. There was humour here, yes, but it was savage; a bitter sarcastic humour with rage behind it. For the first time Dickens was showing his sterner side; the force driving his pen was indignation.

Young as he was he knew a good deal of the wretched side of life, had learned what it was to be poor and outcast and without friends. As a child he had known the inside of a debtor's prison, the misery of working for shillings in a blacking warehouse. As a young reporter frequenting the police courts he had seen much poverty, degradation, and crime, and he smarted with outrage at authority's heartless treatment of the poor and helpless. He had now chosen as his target the existing Poor Law. Things had been bad enough in the past when each parish had been separately responsible for its own paupers, but the new Poor Law of 1834, which was supposed to mend matters, had made them cruelly worse with the invention of the workhouse, which (though authority did not say so) was largely a device for saving the ratepayers' pockets. Under the new dispensation vagabonds, prostitutes, the sick, the old, children, and infants were herded together in a gloomy barracks to be disciplined and half-starved in a manner that would have disgraced a prison. In making his hero a pauper bastard born in these grim surroundings Dickens set about proving to the comfortable public that to treat a child with such 'charity' was a certain way to bring him to crime and misery.

This theme, once embarked on, developed an immediate impetus, for Dickens's imagination responded at a deep level to crime and violence and his evil characters come alive in a startling way. The 'good' characters in *Oliver Twist* are sentimental failures; Fagin and Bill Sikes have haunted our bad dreams for more than a century. The old Jew indeed, sly fence and ponce, corrupter of youth, thief-maker, so affronted Jewish feelings at the time that Dickens found himself in some difficulty, and tried to make amends in another novel. It was no use; Fagin had come alive and has never since been suppressed. Like all Dickens's best rogues he even seems, in his slimy way, perversely attractive, though Dickens meant to present him as wholly evil, sinister, repulsive. And yet the perverse attraction is a part of Dickens's genius; the merry old criminal, holding a daily class for his young pickpockets, addressing them as 'my dear,' feeding them gin and sausages, seduces us with the same cunning as turned homeless boys into thieves and Nancy and her like into drunken prostitutes. Whatever failures *Oliver Twist* contains, Fagin is a masterpiece.

Oliver himself never develops a character, in spite of the famous episode of asking for more. He is little more than the hero of a fairy tale, the good child who suffers a thousand trials and dangers, but passes unscathed through the ogre's dominion to live happily ever after. It is, after all, improbable that a workhouse boy, brought up in brutal and criminal company, should have remained pure and innocent at heart, and unlike his coarse companions have always spoken 'like a little gentleman.'

Dickens, of course, had a problem here: he was dealing with a squalid underworld, with pimps and thieves and prostitutes, yet the tale was for family consumption. It must shock, it must horrify, but not offend; Sikes must be brutal and vicious, but not foul-mouthed; Nancy, his mistress, must be dominated by him without their sexual relationship being glanced at; her profession and that of her companions, young ladies who 'wore a good deal of hair, not very neatly turned up behind,' could never be stated. Even the murder of Nancy, one of the most sadistic passages in literature, is made horrible without any of the verbal realism which most writers would think obligatory today. Dickens, whose taste was for the macabre, did it obliquely; we see Sikes burning the hairs off the end of his club, and trying to keep his dog's feet out of the blood. Which is the more telling method of evoking horror, only time will say.

Dickens has been praised as a great crusader against social injustice, which he was; blamed, too, by more recent critics for dramatizing abuses which, at the time he wrote, were already sufficiently well known. This criticism, I think, is beside the point. Dickens was a rebel at heart and troubled with a highly sensitive social conscience. Causes which had been dully canvassed for years he brought home with a shock to the public, which was all the more willing to be shocked because he also (this was the conjuring-trick) made them laugh. *Oliver Twist* did more for the workhouse child than any number of protests and petitions and questions in Parliament, but that is not our reason for reading it today. We read it for the murk and violence of that lost Hogarthian London which is now almost wholly buried under City skyscrapers; for Fagin, the 'merry old gentleman' with his gang of young thieves shuttered up in a stinking house near Smithfield Market; for the horrors of the old workhouse and the tyranny of officials; for all the reasons which made it a best-seller in its own time. These things do not vanish; they only change their names. If Dickens were writing today he would hardly know where to begin on the gruesome material. When next he comes to treat of a child confronted by crime and the criminal it is twenty-three years later, and the emphasis has changed. He is now not so much crusading against social abuses as exploring certain weaknesses in society and in himself.

Great Expectations has many claims to be considered Dickens's masterpiece, the richest, most deeply felt of all his novels. It was written at the peak of his fame; he was now in his late forties and to all appearances happy in the enjoyment of riches and success. In fact, though he was still at the height of his powers and more famous than any other living author, he was a tormented and unhappy man with only ten feverish restless years ahead. Hope, happiness, and the exuberance of youth belonged to the past.

The accident which had brought him to this private crisis was an emotional one. After twenty-two years of increasingly unsatisfactory marriage he had fallen in love with a young actress called Ellen Ternan, and the violence of his feelings for her was playing havoc with his life. He could not marry Ellen, who eventually (with some reluctance, it seems) became his mistress, and he could no longer endure the proximity of a wife who had given him ten children and who was now unprepossessing, middle-aged, and fat. He insisted on an official separation, and from this time he and the unhappy Catherine lived apart, she for a time with her eldest son in London, he at Gad's Hill near Rochester with his sister-in-law Georgina Hogarth and the rest of his family. Ellen was installed in a little house in Peckham, and the strain of keeping the affair secret at a time when he was the most famous and most easily recognized of men added to the burden of an already overworked and feverish existence.

It was at this point, when the storm over his broken marriage had begun to subside and he was finding what happiness he could in a private life known only to his intimates, that Dickens began to write *Great Expectations*. It is not, like *David Copperfield*, in some degree an autobiographical novel, but personal themes are woven into it: in a sense it can be read as an exploration of his own heart, a critical self-examination.

Dickens himself had been born in fairly humble circumstances and as a child had acutely felt the shame of his father's imprisonment for debt and, even more woundingly, his own experience of working in the blacking factory. Stated briefly these do not sound like crushing disasters, but their effect on Dickens was traumatic: he concealed the facts even from his own children. As he rose in the world and became rich and famous he knew the temptations of snobbery, which in mid-Victorian England were all but irresistible. Only money had power to weaken the barriers of class: to grow rich, to 'become a gentleman,' for most people meant leaving the shame of working-class origins behind.

Dickens's imagination was too deeply involved with the poor and the oppressed for him ever to fall a prey to middle-class snobbery, but he knew its temptations; he knew that fame and money did something to a man, and that something was not to his liking. A rebel and a radical at heart, he had observed in himself the effects of rising socially; he had also learned that appearances are nearly always delusive and that love, however innocent, can be destructive. These are the themes of *Great Expectations*, sombre enough when plainly stated, but handled with a vitality, a humour, a tenderness of imagination which lure the reader entranced from page to page, so that only at the end does he discover that he has been taking part in a morality.

Pip, the blacksmith's boy who stumbles into the arms of an escaped convict on the Kentish marshes, is in humbler circumstances than Dickens ever knew, but there are elements from his own life to be found in the story. The marshes are those of the Thames Estuary which he had known as a child, when his father was a clerk in the Navy Pay Office at Chatham; the prison ship 'like a wicked Noah's ark' had lain out among others in the river in his boyhood, symbols of crime and misery; the blacksmith's forge and the churchyard were in the village of Cooling, within a few miles of Gad's Hill, and Satis House, home of the mad Miss Havisham who takes a fancy to Pip and whom he believes to be his benefactor, can still be seen, an old brick Elizabethan house in Rochester.

Too much stress should not be laid on these fragmentary links with Dickens's own experience, but one cannot believe he could have written as he did of Pip's hopeless and unrewarding love for the tormenting Estella if it had not been for his sufferings over Ellen Ternan. Pip loves Estella, Miss Havisham's adopted daughter, against hope, against reason and to his own unhappiness; his is the most mature and unsentimental of all Dickens's love stories.

And here we come to the one outstanding flaw in this great novel—its happy ending. A love like Pip's for a girl like Estella must inevitably come to grief, and Dickens intended a mournful and final parting. He was persuaded against his better judgement to soften the ending, yielding to the arguments of the novelist Bulwer-Lytton, who read the novel in proof and could not bear to have it end unhappily. It does not matter. The final sentences are ambiguous, as though Dickens knew that he must not wholly depart from his own instinct, and we can interpret it as we please. Estella is a creature born to arouse passion carelessly and as carelessly destroy it, and Dickens was right in his feeling that she could make no man happy.

Yet for all its dark undertones *Great Expectations* is not a gloomy novel. Laughter sparkles through it like a stream which goes underground from time to time and breaks out in the most unexpected places. Joe Gargery the blacksmith, who shares Pip's sufferings under the rule of his wife, Pip's tyrannical elder sister; Jaggers the formidable lawyer, who administers Pip's mysterious fortune and washes his hands of unsavoury clients with rituals of scented soap; Trabb's boy, the obnoxious urchin who sees the first signs of Pip's gentility and makes him suffer for it publicly; Wemmick the lawyer's clerk, so hard in the office, so tender at home—all these are conceived with that magnifying vision and relish for humanity which are an essential of Dickens's genius.

Constructively it is a closely knit novel, each part fitting logically into the next and bearing its weight of meaning in the tale as a whole: only at the end do we see how sharp a criticism has been made of the middle-class moral values of Dickens's time, which are not, to be honest, so very different from our own. Then as now the 'better class' and the grand company are no worthier than humble people, though possibly more amusing. It is the uncouth convict Magwitch who commands Pip's courage and loyalty at the last; felon though he is he emerges with unexpected moral grandeur. Most of us make Pip's mistakes at some time in our lives, both in snobbery and love. No novelist has ever told a more satisfying tale of a heart seduced by fortune and taught a lesson.

Mrs. Beeton and
Mrs. Dickens

I S IT REALLY MORE THAN A CENTURY THAT Mrs. Beeton has been on the kitchen shelf? Yes, indeed, and still holding her own with a firm, ladylike touch, in spite of the great mass industry of modern cookery-book production, in spite of dieting, luncheon vouchers, frozen food, the price of beef, and the disappearance of those inexhaustible Victorian servants to whom she devoted so many humane if subtly authoritarian paragraphs.

She is only barely recognizable today. Gone are those engraved coloured plates of Gothic blancmanges, the shallow dishes of roasted rabbits like beheaded babies, the towering *épergnes* dripping with muscats and smilax which would have done credit to the Veneerings' dinner-table. Instead we have colour photographs of glistening roasts (painted with glycerine in the studio, I believe) and hundreds of plain photographs of capable hands rolling pastry, larding veal, filleting fish, trussing fowls, dressing crabs, clarifying fat, and performing all the mysteries of the kitchen with a patient lucidity which enables even the feeblest mind to follow them.

The great improvement, indeed, of a hundred years on Mrs. Beeton's original *Household Management* is in the illustrations. The early engravings are charming but inex-

plicit; her fish and meat look like the dolls'-house food
which Tom Thumb and Hunca Munca stuffed into the
kitchen range, and her puddings are one and all like Salisbury Cathedral. Whereas now, turning the pages, they
make one hungry. Isabella Beeton would have approved
of colour photography.

At such a size (the current volume weighs as much as
a picnic ham) the great work has sacrificed the personal
touch. Mrs. Beeton was a young married woman, not
twenty-nine when she died, who had learned housekeeping the hard way, by earnest experience, and dedicated
her energies and those of her publisher husband to
smoothing the path of the Victorian bride and ensuring a
happy home for the Victorian husband. 'No amount of
love, of beauty, or of intelligence,' she wrote, 'will make
home life happy without "right judgement" on the part of
the housewife. A woman must rule her household, or be
ruled by it; she must either hold the reins with a tight,
firm hand, never parting with, but seldom using, the
whip; or . . . the hard-working husband is placed, by his
wife's indolence, under the control of his domestics, and
has to depend upon their honesty and zeal alone.' Her
advice is sometimes intimidating, always sound. The nov-
ice is urged to discipline, yet never to forget for a moment
that she is a lady. She should glide about her house like
Agnes Wickfield, with housekeeping-book and store-room
keys in hand. Mrs. Beeton would have had no patience
with Dora Copperfield.

Life is not necessarily more complicated now than
then; in some ways it is simpler. We eat less; there is not
always a nurserymaid or footman to be managed, and the
present-day editors refrain from giving instructions in
good breeding. Yet here and there, if not in precisely her
self-confident cool tone, the authentic voice of Mrs. Beeton

is still heard: 'Friendships should be developed gradually and not be rushed into. In many ways it is a pity the old habit of formal calls and leaving of cards is less regarded nowadays, as the greater formality of social relationships did allow a testing time for new acquaintances, which is very necessary, and which nowadays may need some tact to engineer.' It may indeed, and leisure as well as tact is noticeably scarce. It is not only our kitchens and our eating habits that have changed.

With the current edition I now possess four *Mrs. Beetons*. The first, undated, was published in her lifetime, and the chapters on servants are cautionary reading. Anyone who is puzzled by the disappearance of the old-fashioned 'general' has only to turn to her Routine for the General Servant and they will clearly understand why. My next is the one my mother married with; it still has the beautiful inedible old colour plates and is a little gravy-stained; we do not use it today. The third is my own bridal volume, still much respected, as sensible and economical as ever (for it is a libel, as Nancy Spain pointed out in her biography of Mrs. Beeton, to accuse her of extravagance; she never said 'First catch your hare' or dreamed of beginning a recipe with 'Take twenty eggs . . .'). But I have long since given up trying to fold table napkins, following its Pythagorean diagrams, into the Flat Sachet, the Mitre, the Pyramid, the Rose and Star, the Cockscomb, Fleur de Lys, the Boar's Head, or the Bishop. The current edition is better printed, better illustrated, and easier to read than any of its predecessors. If there is a criticism to be made, it is that it attempts too much. Nobody wants to know about the whole of life (chilblains, marriage, body lice, furnishing with antiques) from one volume.

Perhaps the most striking fact which emerges from a comparison between the early editions and the new is the change in our eating habits. Mrs. Beeton's was by no means the first of the Victorian cookery-books; it was simply, being so practical and comprehensive, the most successful; and if one looks at some of the works available to her when she married, one can see at once her status as a pioneer.

I sometimes turn over the pages of a little-known volume called *What Shall We Have for Dinner?* It was published when Isabella Beeton was sixteen, written under a pseudonym, Lady Maria Clutterbuck, and was the sole literary production of Mrs. Charles Dickens. (She had played the minor part of Lady Maria in an amateur theatrical production two years before.) It consists almost entirely of dinner menus, designed for two, four, six, and up to twenty-four persons, offers no advice, contains only a handful of recipes, and gives a terrifying picture of Victorian hospitality. It is easier to understand Jane Carlyle's nasty remarks about the vulgarity of Dickens's dinner parties when one has studied these bills of fare. 'Such getting up of the steam is unbecoming to a literary man. . . . The dinner was served up in the new fashion, not placed on the table at all, but handed round—only the dessert on the table and quantities of artificial flowers—but such an overloaded dessert! pyramids of figs, raisins, oranges—ach!'

When entertaining, the Victorian table was expected to groan; the status symbol was a superfluity of dishes, and the menus in Mrs. Dickens's book belong to the period of Dickens's established prosperity, when he was living with his numerous family at 1 Devonshire Terrace and beginning to entertain the comparatively famous. Every course must offer at least an alternative, and nobody shrank from sickening repetition. For a little dinner for eight or ten persons Mrs. Dickens recommends three soups, four fish dishes, eleven separate dishes of meat and game, three different cream puddings and a savoury. When lobsters are in season she offers boiled salmon with lobster sauce *and* filleted lobster for the first course, lobster cutlets in the second, and, after the usual three puddings and a savoury, lobster salad. Mrs. Beeton, a few years later, did much to break down the habits of ostentation at the table, and of overeating. She was an enemy to waste, doing much to pave the way for reasonable catering.

Economies of this sort, however, did not appeal to Dickens, who had known too well what it was to be hungry as a boy, and who seems ever after to have remained strongly emotional in his attitude to food. This, of course, is common to us all; what is unusual and significant in Dickens is the extent to which he uses it in his novels as a means of displaying character or evoking emotion. At Mr. Dombey's Christmas party, on a bitter cold day, there is cold veal, cold calf's head, cold fowls, ham, patties, salad, and lobster. The wine is so cold that it 'forces a little scream from Miss Tox,' and through all this shuddering and unfestive meal 'Mr Dombey alone remained unmoved.' The coy warmth, on the other hand, with which Dickens describes Ruth Pinch's rolling-out of a suet crust makes even a beefsteak pudding seem erotic. Food and drink are so pre-eminently his symbols of cheer and security that in the early novels they are inclined to run away with him. (In *Pickwick Papers* there are twenty-five breakfasts, thirty-two dinners, ten luncheons, ten teas, and eight suppers, while drink is mentioned 249 times.) Nevertheless Dickens himself was a fairly abstemious man, and if his wife's menus make a contradictory impression that is because they aim at the mid-Victorian ideal, to which he whole-heartedly subscribed, of full feeding as the soul of hospitality.

The disgrace of the potato is a modern phenomenon, unthought of a hundred years ago, when nearly everyone, man, wife, and maiden aunt, was stout at forty. In nearly all of Mrs. Dickens's family menus potatoes appear in at least two distinct guises, usually 'mashed and brown'—a practice I have encountered only once in my life, when I dined years ago with a Conservative M.P. in his chambers in the Temple. He had an aged cook who had waited on single gentlemen all her life, and the potatoes came up in the grand Victorian mode, mashed and roast, in covered silver dishes.

Suet and starch are two other modern casualties, figuring largely in Mrs. Beeton's early work, as in Mrs. Dickens's. (The two dishes of potatoes accompanying the Dickens roast will be followed by suet roll, with macaroni as a savoury.) Dickens himself appears not to have had a particularly sweet tooth, or to have satisfied it chiefly with 'milk punch' and other hot, spiced, and sweetened drinks, of which many recipes have survived from the days of Georgina Hogarth's efficient housekeeping. (A raw egg beaten up in a glass of sherry or champagne was the pick-me-up on which he relied during his reading tours.) Mrs. Dickens's menus are singularly repetitive in their puddings, and more meals than one would have thought possible end with bloaters. A Yarmouth bloater, like toasted cheese, was a favourite savoury at Devonshire Terrace, but to find it recommended again and again for a 'dinner for four or five people,' at the end of a substantial meal and following, say, apple fritters or a boiled batter pudding, suggests almost an obsession.

The emphasis on rich and starchy dishes, as well as

the monotony of Mrs. Dickens's collection, makes one wonder whether Dickens's growing distaste for his marriage, which culminated in the famous breach and in prolonged unhappiness for both parties, may not have been—at least partly—due to the fact that while still young she became mountainously fat. Professor A. A. Adrian, in his biography of Catherine Dickens's sister, Georgina Hogarth, scotched the persistent rumour that the trouble was due to her having, like some other Victorian ladies, taken secretly to drink. This, it seems, was not so, but a fondness for some of her own recipes alone would account for the monstrous alteration in her appearance by the end of the Devonshire Terrace period. Her Italian Cream, to take a recurring example, begins—'Whip together for nearly an hour a quart of very thick scalded cream, a quart of raw cream . . . with ten ounces of white powdered sugar, then add half-a-pint of sweet wine and continue to whisk until it is quite solid. . . .'

Poor lady, she would have done better to follow the advice of Mrs. Beeton, but alas, she was born too soon; the cookery-books of her time thought nothing of gallons of cream and quantities of beaten yolks and powdered sugar, accepting these things in the lavish dairy-and-stillroom tradition of the eighteenth century. Her late husband, she wrote in her Preface, addressing her readers in the character of Sir Jonas Clutterbuck's widow, had been a man of very good appetite and excellent digestion, 'and I am consoled in believing that my attention to the requirements of his appetite secured me the possession of his esteem until the last.' There is a sad irony, as one turns the page of this muddled, inept and unhelpful little book, in calculating the short space of time between its appearance and the harsh withdrawal of Dickens's esteem for ever. A few years after the book's appearance the door was walled up between his room and hers, and the following year saw the separation agreement. The 'matutinal meal' was no longer 'a time to dread, only exceeded in its terrors by the more awful hour of dinner.' Dickens was remote and indifferent at Gad's Hill, and there was no longer anyone but herself to cater for.

The Boyhood of Fabre

ENIUS SEEMS RARELY TO BREAK OUT SPONTA-
neously, with nothing to account for it. There
is generally some predilection, however
slight, in family or environment, some traceable influence or happy chance to breathe on the spark and
feed the first smouldering mental ardour which will blaze
in maturity. The great composer is born in a family of
musicians, or one that at least has had some contact with
music; the poet, even Burns at the plough, is touched, as
by the tip of a finger, by education; and there is a tradition
of scientific inquiry in most of the families which have produced great scientists.

Yet once in a while the miracle seems to occur; an effect
of great splendour is produced without visible cause.
There will be a sort of immaculate conception, and a mind
of great power and originality will develop where heredity
and environment would lead one least to expect it, engen-
dering in itself, apparently without any fertilizing contact,
a violent impulse towards some science, some art, which it
pursues with unaccountable love.

This seems indeed to have been the case with Fabre,
who all his life was puzzled by the contrast between what
he was born and what he had become. The question appears and reappears in varying forms all through his *Sou-*

venirs Entomologiques, massive and beautiful harvest of his scientific life. How did it start? Where did it come from, this passionate interest in the grasshopper, the wasp? He was never able to find the clue, and neither can we. The fascinating puzzle remains: a child of ancient poverty, ignorance, prejudice, superstition, forcing himself, unaided, and as though beckoned by a vision, into the clear exhilarating light of scientific discovery, to become the observer, the interpreter, the poet of a hidden world.

Jean-Henri Fabre died in 1915. It is with a start that one realizes he was born in 1823, the year when Dickens was pasting labels in the blacking warehouse; the year Byron sailed for Greece.

He was the child of illiterate and poverty-stricken peasants who were always trying, and always failing, to scrape a living off the barren stony uplands of the Cévennes. ('One of the most beggarly countries in the world,' said Stevenson, when half a century later he travelled it with a donkey, 'like the worst of the Scottish Highlands, only worse.') Snow, wind, and wolves were their enemies in winter, and in summer the limestone plateau dried and bleached like a skeleton. Almost nothing would grow.

To be rid of one hungry mouth, Fabre *père* sent the boy in infancy to live with his grandparents, and it is with another inward start that one grasps his description of these survivors from the eighteenth century. Both were totally illiterate, and knew of the world beyond their own granite plateau only by hearsay. His grandmother still wore the huge eccentric headdress of the Rouergue; his grandfather was a typical sour and silent peasant of the *ancien régime*.

I always remember his serious look; his unshorn locks, often thrust with a fist behind one ear and spreading their antique Gallic mane over his shoulders. I see his small three-cornered hat, his short breeches buckled at the knee, his resounding wooden sabots crammed with straw.

To them, cattle were interesting as a means of livelihood, and the wolf as a dangerous neighbour; but beyond these the brute creation was ignored. An insect, lower still, was something to be washed out of a cabbage with a grunt of disgust or cracked under a thumb-nail. Yet it was from the hearth of these grandparents that Fabre, a barefoot urchin, wandered out into the heather to satisfy his first absorbing curiosities—the beginnings of that passion for personal knowledge of phenomena which was soon to develop his genius for exact, intimate, and yet imaginative observation. He has left us a curiously touching account of his first scientific experiment, conducted when he was five or six years old:

There, in solitude, among geese and calves and sheep, I awoke to the first glimmerings of intellect. Behold me one day, hands behind my back, a dreamy urchin, gazing at the sun. This dazzling splendour fascinates me. I am a moth, drawn to the light of the lamp. Is it with my mouth or with my eyes that I apprehend this glory? Such is the question posed by my dawning scientific curiosity. Reader, do not smile: the future observer is already practising, experimenting. I open my mouth as wide as possible and close my eyes. The glory vanishes. I open my eyes and close my mouth. The glory reappears. I begin again. The same result. Now it is done— I know for a fact that I see the sun with my eyes.

The special marks which so richly distinguish Fabre from other naturalists were already perceptible in the boy, if anyone had been interested. He was by temperament and imagination a poet, and it was from nature and especially from the beautiful, grotesque, unknown, and almost inscrutable world of the insect that he received his most intense aesthetic experience. He saw, with an imaginative grasp rare indeed in that peasant environment, that the world was by no means only man's. The insect creation—blind and indifferent to man as man to the insect—was more varied, complicated, bizarre, following patterns of marvellous ingenuity and skill which were all the more startling because, clearly, instinct and not intelligence was at work. It was, in some ways, a nightmare world; yet it had a compelling beauty. In it the female was entirely dominant and terrible—huntress, devourer, mighty mother, allowing the inoffensive drone, the small and anxious male spider to exist only to perform his necessary but despised function. Sometimes his necessity, even, was all but ignored: among the mantises the male was often carelessly devoured during copulation, while among certain pond and plant flies whole generations were produced and reared without sexual contact. (Were these strange formulae of reproduction, Fabre came to wonder, relics of earlier experiments on the part of the Almighty, before, in the higher creation, He hit on the reproductive plan which apparently satisfied Him?)

To the ragged child, now going daily to sit on a back bench in the schoolmaster's earth-floored cottage, the beauties of the despised insect world spoke with the force of revelation. He finds a beetle, 'smaller than a cherry-stone, but of an unutterable blue,' and carries home his 'living jewel' in an empty snail-shell, plugged with a green leaf. The image of a pigeon, roughly printed on the cover of the ABC, invites him more kindly than the letters which no one can be bothered to explain.

His round eye, ringed with a coronet of dots, seems to smile at me. His wing, of which I count the feathers one by one, speaks to me of soaring flight among the lovely clouds; it transports me to beech woods, their smooth trunks rising from a carpet of moss where snowy mushrooms peep, like eggs deposited there by some wandering fowl; it carries me to snowy summits where my bird leaves the starry imprint of his rosy feet.

Later, through the miserable boredoms of a squalid school, he consoles himself under the shelter of his desk, examining a snapdragon berry, a wasp's sting, the wing-case of a beetle, an oleander fruit.

Fabre himself, though in the *Souvenirs* he returns again and again to the fringe of the question, was never able to determine at what point in his dreaming boyhood it became clear to him that what he wanted was *knowledge*. From that unidentified moment, however, it was the sole end to which he struggled, against what difficulties, hardships, discouragements, he alone fully knew. His parents, worn down and embittered by poverty, saw no necessity, once he could read and write, for further schooling. Only by the hard way of scholarships and self-support could he prove his claim to a grudging continuance of education, and even this was interrupted for long periods as his parents, who had failed first as farmers, and then as keepers of a succession of sordid little village cafés, claimed his labour, and he was sent to work as a stone-breaker on the railway, or the roads, or to stand selling a handful of lemons on the corner of the street.

Yet through these discouragements, marvellously, his resolution hardened, and from his letters to his younger brother, whom he dragged after him up the steep path of education, we feel something of the almost mystic experience which the unfolding of the intellect, and the apprehension of his own faculties, had become.

Today is Thursday; nothing beckons you out of doors; you choose a quiet corner where only a soft light penetrates. There you are, elbows on table, a fist behind each ear and a book before you. Intelligence awakens, will-power takes control, the external world dissolves, the ear no longer hears nor does the eye see, the body is no more present; it is the soul that studies; she remembers, she summons up her learning, and light is born. Then the hours fly away, quickly, quickly, so quickly, there is no counting the time. Is it already evening? . . . But a flock of truths is ranged together in the memory, diffi-culties that delayed you yesterday have melted on re-flection, whole volumes have been devoured, and you are content with your day.

Perhaps it was as well, for posterity, that he had no very clear idea of where this learning was leading him. Faith and reason both told him that it would lead to independence, to that path of science towards which his imagination ardently pointed, to freedom to work his own rich vein of scientific ore. And so, for his last thirty years, from the time Fabre was sixty until he was close on ninety, it certainly did. But the preceding forty years, the whole prime of his life, were to be worn away by poverty and the struggle for existence; by ceaseless striving to support a growing family on a primary-school teacher's pittance; by hack-work, producing countless little school textbooks—jewels of lucidity indeed, but very far from being the life's work to which he now knew himself com-mitted. If he could have foreseen those forty years of frustration, ever working to earn the means to buy leisure to work, never quite achieving it, he might have re-nounced the struggle, and we should have been without the *Souvenirs*, marvellous fruit of his last years of obser-vation and reflection, haunted by memories of his boyhood as by a recurring dream.

One thinks of Darwin (with whom, in old age, he

corresponded eagerly to disagree) and his long life of research made possible by domestic peace and private means. 'I have had ample leisure,' Darwin wrote in his autobiography, 'from not having to earn my own bread.' One remembers the moneyed and cultured background, Shrewsbury, Cambridge, the heaven-sent opportunity of the five-year voyage in the *Beagle* . . . and the great evolutionist, the charming and lovable recluse of Down, is not difficult to explain.

What a contrast to the hopeless beginnings, the discouragements, the lack of recognition, the bitter poverty of Fabre! There is something exquisitely painful in the thought that he was sixty years old, and white-haired, before he had scraped together sufficient savings to retire behind his garden wall at Sérignan and embrace the work of his life.

The contrast between the recluse of Down and the recluse of Sérignan is painfully clear; but peace descends on liberated genius at last, and behind the high Provençal wall, for thirty years, the great work is being written. Letters are passing, too, between the two old men, mutually arguing, contradicting, acknowledging one another. The fact that Fabre, in old age, learned English the more freely to communicate with Darwin (with whom he disagreed) seems to gather up, as into the palm of one's hand, all that is most touchingly patient, noble, even religious, in the scientific spirit.

The Disappearing Ghost-Story

Some Reflections on Ghost-Stories, in Particular Henry James's *The Turn of the Screw*

A MINOR DIFFERENCE WHICH HAS COME OVER the English winter is the disappearance, as though by change of climate, of the ghost-story. Not long ago no Christmas Eve, at least, was complete without one, and an occasional ghost-story was as much a part of the long evenings as coal fires and candlelight. Why is it so no longer? The supernatural shiver is enjoyable, even though it makes us unwilling to go to bed. The 'dear old sacred terror,' as Henry James called it, has pleasure in it, or we should never have been so eager for the stories. Whereas now, if a ghost so much as ventures to appear in the Christmas number of a magazine, it does so with a whimsical air, conscious of being only seasonable trimming.

One of those slow alterations has taken place, one of those 'weather changes of the human intellect' which, as Dr. Dover Wilson pointed out, has robbed the ghost in *Hamlet* of all his terror and given the play's producer a fresh problem. We do not believe in ghosts, and would never dream of entertaining children, as I remember my mother doing once before I was seven years old, by advancing unexpectedly from a dark passage, robed in a sheet, with whitened face, carrying in her hands a dish in which some sort of greenish phosphorescence flickered.

This sharp decline in belief in the supernatural is largely due, no doubt, to electric light. Scepticism, even in religious matters, would never have gone so far if we had been obliged to keep to the lighting arrangements of our ancestors. Gas ushered in the age of unbelief, and with instant electricity the last ghost vanished. If such a survey could be carried out, I am sure we should find that belief in the supernatural increases as we get beyond the reach of company's electricity, and that psychic experience in any district bears an exact relation to the number of lamps and candles.

If anyone doubts this let him remember, if he can, the days when candles were the only light by which we went to bed. They flickered; they threw curious shadows; they blew out in draughts. They never showed us quite enough, and the flame shone always dazzlingly in the eyes, so that one could never be sure what was going on in the shadows. Old houses were capable of the most extraordinary transformations, suggestive changes of atmosphere quite impossible today, when artificial daylight precedes us on stairs and landing at the touch of a finger. You can strike a match in the dark and light a candle, but it takes time: elemental terrors can take shape in that delay.

In one respect, but one only, this new freedom from supernatural terrors is a pity. It has spoiled our enjoyment of even the best ghost-story; it has turned such an insidious essay in horror as Henry James's *The Turn of the Screw* into a curiously unmoving, though still beautiful, period-piece. It is fascinating now chiefly because, at each turn of the screw of terror, we do not wince; we are not pinched at all; yet we can see how Victorian flesh was made to shudder. (Whether in fact it is a ghost-story at all, or an elaborately ambiguous study of paranoia, we shall consider presently.)

We are so different from James's contemporaries that there is not a page on which we do not stand convicted of lack of sympathy. It is not only that we are released from supernatural possibilities; there is a difference, too, in our judgement as to what can, or cannot, be said. In polite company today there are no unmentionables. There is nothing, really, that cannot be discussed, privately at least; and this has deprived us of many a prurient thrill. What is a nameless sin, a nameless vice? They all have names; often the same as they had in the Middle Ages, when they were so appreciatively catalogued by the Church. So we remain disappointingly frigid to Henry James's hints and understatements. His delicate evasions, his exquisite advancing and retreating and side-stepping (and where would Henry James have been without the comma?) here have nothing to do with social nuances or with the range of emotions taken for granted today. His art is expended on what are now sterile and worked-out areas—the fear of ghosts, the belief in absolute evil.

The story opens, very properly as you will remember, on Christmas Eve. There is a house party, and the guests are lingering late round the fire in the hall, shivering agreeably over the ghost-stories that have been told. One guest throws it out that he has in his possession a story which is beyond everything they have yet heard—'For dreadful—dreadfulness. . . . For general uncanny ugliness and horror and pain . . .'

Having said so much, he is reluctant to say more, and his hearers' and the reader's curiosity is skilfully sharpened. It is not his story to tell; he must send to town for a manuscript; he is not sure that the story ought to be told at all. And it is on this tantalizing note, of reluctance because of some peculiar dreadfulness, that the party finally breaks up, and 'handshook and "candlestuck," as somebody said, and went to bed.'

When the manuscript arrives a few days later it proves to have been written many years ago by a young governess of twenty in her first post. The post was a lonely one. She had been sent to the country to take charge of a pair of orphans, a boy of ten and a girl of eight, whose guardian, benevolent though he seemed in a worldly way, had made the singular condition that she should never trouble him—'but never, never; neither appeal nor complain nor write about anything; only meet all questions herself, receive all moneys from his solicitor, take the whole thing over and let him alone.' The governess is thus neatly sealed off from appeal, from any reference to her employer such as good sense would suggest; and the stage—a pleasant country house presided over by a motherly housekeeper and inhabited by discreet servants and the loveliest little girl the new governess has ever seen—is pregnantly set.

The boy, Miles, is due to come home from school. It is the end of his first term, and it is here that Henry James drops the first covert hint of mysterious evil. The governess receives a letter from the headmaster indicating in ambiguous terms that Miles is expelled. ' "They go into no particulars. They simply express their regret that it should be impossible to keep him. That can have but one meaning." ' Are we allowed to know what the governess guesses? No, it is better nameless. The 'one meaning,' she conjectures, can be only ' "that he's an injury to the others." '

There is this dark hint, then, about little Miles, who, when he arrives, is even more lovely and endearing than his sister. So indignant now is the governess at the sinister suggestion contained in that 'horrible letter' that she decides never to refer to it, never even to appear to question him. The nature of the foundations on which this supremely skilful story is laid is thus made clear: nothing must ever be given a name, and the reader must never be quite sure what it is that he is afraid of.

This was Henry James's solution of an extremely difficult problem. How could he present 'portentous evil' without being driven to anticlimax by specifying the 'limited deplorable presentable instance'? The only way, as he afterwards explained, was to put it all on the reader. 'Make him *think* the evil, make him think it for himself, and you are released from weak specifications.'

Acting on this principle, he next presents us with something else which cannot be pinned down. The governess's predecessor, it appears, a Miss Jessel, had gone away for a holiday and never returned; and later on it had leaked out that she was dead. What had she died of? Nobody seems to know. Mrs. Grose, the housekeeper, is reticent, and we and the governess together are left with the feeling that we have once more been offered a mysteriously sinister suggestion.

It is at this point, the ground being well mined with possibilities, that the solitary governess encounters her first apparition. It is no conventional transparent ghost, and it does not come at night, but at twilight; so that her first thought, as she approaches the house at the end of an evening stroll, is one of displeased surprise that the house should contain a visitor of whom she knows nothing. At some distance, and through the dusk, they exchange a long and mutually questioning stare. 'We were too far apart to call to each other, but there was a moment at which, at shorter range, some challenge between us, breaking the hush, would have been the right result of our straight mutual stare. . . . Yes, it was intense to me that during this transit he never took his eyes from me, and I can see at this moment the way his hand, as he went, moved from one of the crenellations to the next. He stopped at the other corner, but less long, and even as he turned away still markedly fixed me. He turned away; that was all I knew.'

Again—and we are not precisely told why—'for a reason that I couldn't then have phrased'—the governess says nothing, not even to Mrs. Grose; and it is not until one chill wet Sunday a little later, when she catches sight of the same mysterious stranger looking in at her through a window, that she decides to confide in the housekeeper. She does so because, seeing his gaze fixing her, and also roaming intently about the room, 'On the spot there came to me the added shock of a certitude that it was not for me that he had come. He had come for someone else.'

Her story produces something extraordinary from Mrs. Grose. From her vivid description the man is clearly none other than Peter Quint, who had been valet to the children's guardian and who in the previous year had been continually about the place and for long periods left in charge. The only oddity about his being seen around the house at this time is that he is no longer in his master's service, and is moreover dead.

Gradually, in breathless question and answer between governess and housekeeper, the impression of Quint is built up which is all the richer in suggestion for being nowhere explicit. We are made to feel that he was a sinister, unprincipled character; he drank; he was 'much too free' with little Miles, whom he liked to play with and spoil; the boy had been completely under his spell. All this is disagreeable enough, especially when it seems now suf-

ficiently clear that it is little Miles whom Quint has come
back to seek: but there is always the suggestion that there
is far more that is horrible about Quint than can ever be
stated. There is a shadow hovering about him which it is
better not to examine; and it is this nameless something,
this hint of a detail too scabrous to be put into words, that
sharpens our suspense as we follow the story, and seems
with every page to be more imminently on the point of
breaking the surface.

We are now, in company with the governess, further
unnerved and threatened by a second apparition, this time
of a woman; and her identity is not long left in doubt. It is
Miss Jessel. The governess sees her when she is sitting
alone with little Flora by the lake; and it becomes horribly
clear to her that, just as Quint is looking for the boy, so is
Miss Jessel stalking Flora. More, she becomes convinced
that these innocent children, these pretty angels of loving
manners and exquisite tractability, are in the habit of
seeing Quint and Miss Jessel as clearly as she does, and
are concealing the fact. They are looking for Quint and
Miss Jessel (whom they never mention) as earnestly as
Quint and Miss Jessel are looking for them. They secretly
leave their beds at night, to watch; and Miles is even on
one occasion found in the garden by moonlight, ambig-
uously waiting. What does it all portend? Having stated
his situation, and by hint and counter-hint considerably
worked on our nerves and our curiosity, Henry James is
compelled, at least to some degree, to clarify it. His hold
on his present-day reader is here far less certain than on
his contemporaries, for the prosaic reason that we cannot
believe in his ghosts. But he is offering us something
more; he is making persistent, serious suggestions about
absolute evil; and it is only when he is obliged, not to
state—good heavens, what vulgarity!—but to glance at,

hint, and turn discreetly away from a possible statement as to what that evil might be, that we see at last how utterly we are bound to fail him. 'No, no—there are depths, depths! The more I go over it the more I see in it, and the more I see in it the more I fear. I don't know what I *don't* see—what I *don't* fear!'

Let us look, then, let us indelicately remove the veils of discretion so flawlessly woven, and see what it is that is unmentionably dreadful about Quint and Miss Jessel, and discover how far we can share their author's horror.

The main fact emerges without much difficulty: Quint and Miss Jessel had been lovers. Further, it becomes clear (though only, of course, if one quite dreadfully and inordinately probes) that Miss Jessel had failed to come back after her holiday because she was pregnant, and her death had been a direct or indirect consequence of that pregnancy. She had died by suicide or in childbirth.

It is sordid, but comprehensible. We feel sorry for the woman rather than appalled; and as though he had sensed this weakness, and had been prepared for it, Henry James uncovers a circumstance which is clearly intended to sterilize all pity. Quint had been a servant, and Miss Jessel, handsome, 'infamous' Miss Jessel, had been a lady. The governess and the housekeeper bring it tremblingly out.

'Of what did she die? Come, there was something between them.'

'There was everything.'

'In spite of the difference—?'

'Oh, of their rank, their condition'—she brought it woefully out. '*She* was a lady.'

I turned it over; I again saw. 'Yes—she was a lady.'

'And he so dreadfully below,' said Mrs. Grose.

A love, then, which crosses the barriers of class becomes unnatural, corrupt. (But only, we are bound to observe, if it is the woman who stoops; reversed, the situation is romantic.)

This is for us a difficulty; but nothing in comparison with the harsh assumption which follows. Because of their infamy Quint and Miss Jessel are damned, and it is their damnation which makes them so dangerous and so unequivocally evil. For it emerges, or so the governess has gradually come to believe, that they are striving to maintain over the children the influence which they undoubtedly had in life; that they are in a measure succeeding, since the children are aware of them; and that their object is the total depravity and then the death of the children, so that they can possess them as some sort of comfort in their eternal misery.

Henry James must here, even in his own time, have confronted a special difficulty, for in order to achieve the full horror of his tale the corruption of the children must first be feared, then suspected, and finally made absolute. How, even in 1898, to make two particularly charming children of ten and eight so convincingly depraved that the reader sorrowfully accepts their inevitable damnation? Henry James did his best, and no doubt struck a note of particular horror for contemporary readers; but the strokes fall harmlessly on a generation which, were it ever faced with a suspicion of utter depravity (now in any case meaningless) concealed under perfect childish lovableness and good manners, would turn with anxious optimism to the psychiatrist. All that Henry James can do is to suggest the unspeakable. Stripped of its unspeakableness, it is not very nice, but hardly worthy of damnation. The children, intimate with Quint and Miss Jessel as they had been, were apparently aware of their intimacy and had witnessed 'infamies.' So far, then, they had been touched by 'wickedness,' and the apparitions were drawing them steadily in. Flora's depravity is demonstrated by her desperate secretiveness. She sees Miss Jessel as clearly, the narrator suspects, as she does herself, and conceals this 'inconceivable communion' from her distracted governess, who, being a Henry James heroine, naturally finds it out of her power to say anything plainly or, save in the last extremity, to ask a question. 'To gaze into the depths of blue of the child's eyes and pronounce their loveliness a trick of premature cunning was to be guilty of a cynicism in preference to which I naturally preferred to abjure my judgment.'

Dissimulation and lying, however, in however infamous a connection, being not enough to warrant a little girl of eight being described as 'lost,' there is something more; and it is almost touching to see Henry James casting about in his sensitive and well-bred imagination for something which shall be—oh, beyond everything. After a dramatic interlude, in which Flora is apparently tempted into mortal danger on the lake by the evil enticements of Miss Jessel, he produces the final, the inconceivable spiritual horror. It turns out to be bad language.

Flora has been missed, pursued, and found. The governess discovers and confronts her in the sedges by the lake, within view of the distant but recognizable apparition of Miss Jessel; and for the first and only time, in so many words, accuses her of being in some sort of communion with the dead woman. The child does not admit it, and takes refuge in implacable hostility against her governess. She falls into a fever, is removed to Mrs. Grose's room, and there in her delirium convinces even the faithful housekeeper of her corruption.

> She shook her head with dignity. 'I've heard—!'
> 'Heard?'
> 'From that child—horrors! There!' she sighed with

tragic relief. 'On my honour, miss, she says things—!'
But at this evocation she broke down; she dropped with
a sudden cry upon my sofa and, as I had seen her do
before, gave way to all the anguish of it. . . .

I couldn't have desired more emphasis, but I just
waited. 'She's so horrible?'

I saw my colleague scarce knew how to put it.
'Really shocking.'

'And about me?'

'About you, miss—since you must have it. It's beyond everything, for a young lady; and I can't think
wherever she must have picked up. . . .'

The depravity of Miles remains still to be established.
It is built up without delay. The letter which the desperate
governess at last nerves herself to write to their guardian
is secretly taken, by Miles, from the hall table. This produces the appalling, the thrilling suspicion that ' "he
stole—*letters!*" ' But it was not that, though he admits,
with the most engaging candour in the world, that he has
taken the governess's letter. The crime at school had nothing to do with stealing.

'What then did you do?'

He looked in vague pain all round the top of the
room and drew his breath, two or three times over, as if
with difficulty. He might have been standing at the bottom of the sea and raising his eyes to some green twilight. 'Well—I said things.'

'Only that?'

'They thought it was enough!'

It is out at last, then; or as out as Henry James can
decently allow. He has talked about the 'infamies' to 'those
I liked.' And they, of course, had repeated them. He has
been expelled, the poor little boy, for smut.

It is the unspeakableness of this revelation which measures the gulf between our prosaicism, the 'infamy,' as he might possibly have called it, of our conversation, and Henry James's butterfly-wing, insinuating delicacy. And the gulf is even wider than that, for it is the unspeakable and invisible which brings on the tragic climax. Just as the governess nerves herself for the final, the all but unphraseable question—'What were those things?'—she sees once more the image of Quint at the window, and clasps the child in her arms and turns on the apparition with shrieked defiance. She has a flash of triumph as it comes to her that though she sees 'the white face of damnation,' the boy does not, and rejoices—'it may be imagined with what a passion'—that the spell is broken. 'But at the end of a minute I began to feel what it truly was that I held. We were alone with the quiet day, and his little heart, dispossessed, had stopped.'

We must now turn to the neo-Freudian interpretation of the story, first propounded by Miss Edna Kenton in 1924 and analyzed at length by Mr. Edmund Wilson in his essay *The Ambiguity of Henry James*. The theory is that 'the young governess who tells the story is a neurotic case of sex repression, and the ghosts are not real ghosts at all but merely the hallucinations of the governess.' Since Edmund Wilson in his celebrated essay went minutely through the story, testing the theory at every point and finding it completely watertight, we need not follow that trail again, but must agree that 'When one has once been given this clue to *The Turn of the Screw* one wonders how one could ever have missed it.' It is perfectly true that nowhere in the story does James offer any 'proof' that the children, or indeed anybody else beside the governess, have seen the apparitions. At every turn he is careful to leave the matter open; the reader can assume

ghosts or he can assume hallucinations. Almost everything in the story can be read in these two senses.

So is this elaborate and beautiful construction not concerned with the supernatural at all? Is it simply a horrid
account of a governess's delusions? Is this why, though
fascinated, we have not been chilled, and the 'infamy' and
'corruption' have not touched us? One can argue it either
way, but even after many rereadings it is impossible not to
believe that Henry James's *intention* was to evoke, with
the subtlest of touches, a supernatural chill, not simply to
show the results of a neurotic obsession. It could not have
escaped his notice that, if there were in truth no ghosts, if
Quint were never on the tower or Miss Jessel by the lake,
if the children were innocent and there were no corrupting
spirits prowling at Bly, the story, as an essay in horror,
simply collapses.

But it is also true that at every turn, with the utmost
care, he has provided himself with an escape-clause, deliberately leaving a loophole in every argument. This
equivocation belongs to the Jamesian technique of giving
a *frisson* with every hint by walking elaborately round it
and never stating it. Ambiguity, with James, had started
as a literary device, and had gradually grown in importance until now, as here, it was practised for its own sake.
In this story he carries it, as Edmund Wilson admits, 'to a
point where it seems almost as if he did not want the
reader to get through to the hidden meaning.' And is there
a hidden meaning, after all? Is it not true to say that often
the beautifully built up clouds of words conceal a vacuum
which the reader, for better effect, is invited to fill, and
that if he is unequal to the task it remains empty?

My view of the Kenton-Wilson theory is that it has
grown out of that very change in our responses which has
neutralized our reaction to the ghost-story. *Because* the

apparitions were no longer terrifying a more critically acceptable horror had to be invented. And since we are no longer asked to believe in the apparitions we are offered instead the conclusion that the governess's odd behaviour literally frightened the little boy to death.

It is impossible to read *The Turn of the Screw* and believe that this prosaic interpretation was really all that Henry James intended. His skill in evasions, his providing every clause as it were with loopholes, until the texture of the prose is like a net, is prodigious, but in *The Turn of the Screw* it has done him a disservice. Or rather it is we who have done it, with our fondness for illumination and our lack of reticence. Henry James's contemporaries went to bed with candles and could be trusted not to come out with indelicate questions; whereas we have light-switches everywhere and cannot be trusted. That, in the last analysis, is the difference.

Dr. R. W. Chapman

SCHOLARSHIP IS A PLANT OF SLOW GROWTH; it rarely flowers before middle age, its fruits ripen late. Other writers may succeed early, and find themselves enjoying a fame their talents can support: the scholar toils in private, with small hope that his work will ever be generally known. Only a few, and those mostly in old age, know the pleasure of being famous.

Dr. R. W. Chapman, who spent a great part of his life in bringing Dr. Johnson and Jane Austen before the public, reached that enviable point in his late sixties, and at seventy-two, when I first met him, still had not lost the sense of pleased surprise that came to him first in 1949, when he became aware that he was regarded as an authority—'not just on Johnson and Jane Austen' (I quote from a private letter), 'but on scholarship in general. People took to saying, "This will carry weight, coming from you." ' Three years later, in the winter of 1952, his *magnum opus* was published, the great three-volume edition of Johnson's letters, begun in 1919 and acclaimed as a splendid monument, not only to Johnson, but to his editor as well. In the same winter appeared a second edition of his *Jane Austen's Letters*, long out of print and greatly sought, and a book of *Johnsonian and Other Essays and*

Reviews, which established him as a remarkable essayist. Such tact and persuasiveness has his style, even in an index or a footnote (some would say more especially in these marginal preserves, where he feels most at home), that his admirers have sometimes deplored his concentration on textual criticism and wished he had written more, so to speak, under his own steam. But in the face of this complaint Dr. Chapman remained firm. The scholar's reply, he once wrote, is that 'if he has not "known genius familiarly," he has known dozens of people who could write, say, readable essays, and some who could write very good ones. He has known few whom he could trust to make the best use of the delicate tools of editorial scholarship.' Those are the tools he long ago chose to make his own, and he was fortunate in living a life all of one piece, a continuous exploration of the field that first attracted him in youth. Without that undisturbed continuity nothing much, in the world of scholarship, can be done: Dr. Chapman's life was as closely fitted to his purpose as though he had been invented by a novelist (Trollope rather than George Eliot) to exemplify the urbane and happy scholar.

Robert William Chapman was born on October 5, 1881, at Eskbank, near Dalkeith, the youngest of six children of an Anglican clergyman. He was not infrequently accused of being a Scot, a circumstance which, if true, would imply considerable detachment in one of Dr. Johnson's greatest living champions; but the fact is, both his parents were English. His father, soon after taking his degree, had been attracted to Dundee by a scholastic advertisement, and had there taught for some years before he came under the influence of Bishop Forbes, and took orders in the Episcopal Church of Scotland. His mother was a

Dr. R. W. Chapman

Yorkshirewoman whose family, following the jute trade, had migrated to Dundee in the mid-nineteenth century. His father died when he was three years old, and the widow with six children settled at Carnoustie, in what Dr. Chapman remembered as 'surely the dullest piece of country in these islands.' They were, as one would imagine, far from rich. The children attended Dundee High School, and here the precocious youngest carried off whatever prizes were to be had; 'intellectual, not athletic,' he was always scrupulous to add, for though tall and rangy, and something of a walker and climber in the academic tradition (to say nothing of his more eccentric repute in Oxford as a cyclist), he was too delicate as a boy to shine at games, and in unguarded moments would admit that he had never learned to swim.

From Dundee he won the first bursary to St. Andrews, and there spent 'four rather idle years,' learning Greek under a great teacher, Professor Burnet. These four years cannot have been so very idle, for he left St. Andrews with the Guthrie Scholarship, and the Adam de Brome Scholarship to Oriel, and went up to Oxford in 1902 at the age of twenty-one. Here his chief intimates were George Gordon, who became President of Magdalen, and Wilfrid Normand, later Lord President of the Court of Session, who retired from the House of Lords in 1953. His scholarships brought him £80 apiece, and he eked this out by coaching in the vacations; except for an occasional weekend spent reading novels, playing bridge and drinking wine he would recall that he 'did nothing expensive.' He shared lodgings with Normand in his final year, and claimed that it was Normand who chiefly kept their noses to the grindstone. Both achieved a First in Greats, and Chapman won further glory with the Gaisford Prize for Greek prose. He was now, by taste and destiny, committed to Oxford, and as soon as his viva was over was appointed assistant to Charles Cannan, Secretary to the Delegates of the Oxford University Press, where he was to remain for the next thirty-six years.

His chief concern at the Press, apart from administrative duties, was with editions and lexicography, both Greek and English. The great *Oxford English Dictionary* was then under way, and his touch can be distinguished in its examples. (His Hon.D.Litt.Oxon was an honour conferred on the completion of the *Dictionary*, as his Magdalen Fellowship was in part a recognition of his Johnson studies.) He also had much to do with the planning of the revised *Liddell and Scott* and of several English dictionaries, including the still unfinished 'unconcise' *Dictionary of Modern English* planned by H. W. Fowler.

He lived during these years first in St. John Street, then in Oriel as a member of the Common Room, amusing his bachelor leisure with Early English punctuation and the Greek Particles, for all the world as though he were a character in a novel which set out to be mildly funny at the scholar's expense. But this calm and sheltered existence was not to last. His work at the Press brought him into contact with Miss Katharine Metcalfe, a young tutor at Somerville who had recently taken a First in English, and who had been encouraged by Sir Walter Raleigh to undertake a new, textually accurate, edition of *Pride and Prejudice;* and deeper sympathies were discovered than even a common interest in textual criticism. There are still old students of Somerville who recall the ribald verses composed in dismay at the rapid progress of this courtship, for Miss Metcalfe's career as a don was now briskly cut short, as was Mr. Chapman's bachelor peace in Oriel. They were married a few months after the publication of

Dr. R. W. Chapman

Pride and Prejudice, and translated to the sphere of married dons, North Oxford.

This was Robert Chapman's real introduction to Jane Austen. He had read the novels as a boy, in random copies borrowed by his sisters in the days when there was no money to buy books; and he now felt the 'bite' of a marvellously fresh and entirely congenial subject. Together the Chapmans planned a complete edition of Jane Austen's novels; but the births of children, and the three flights of stairs which their North Oxford house so typically encased, left Mrs. Chapman little time or strength for editorial labours, and the 1914 war put an effectual end, for the time being, to that project. Robert Chapman enlisted in Godley's Own, a volunteer regiment which already had Bridges and Raleigh among its recruits; then transferred to the O.T.C., and in 1915 obtained a commission in the Royal Garrison Artillery. He was soon afterwards sent to Salonika.

Here he had what he described, after forty years, as 'a reasonably comfortable war.' There was a good deal of boredom, great heat, and worse discomfort; but there was at least this amelioration, that both sides were tacitly agreed to have no hostilities during the hours of daylight: it was just too hot. Battles were fought in the evening or round about dawn, so for the rest of the time the officers sat or lay gasping in their dugout, under a scorching roof of boulders and corrugated iron. To some it was a purgatory of boredom, but Robert Chapman had taken a box of books, and sat upright and absorbed in his stifling burrow. The box contained the Clarendon Press Catalogue, Lamb's letters, *The Hundred Best Latin Poems*, and Boswell's *Johnson*. The Boswell, now closely read for the first time, 'took.' He sent to Oxford for Johnson's *Journey to the Western Islands of Scotland*, and for all three editions of the *Tour to the Hebrides*, which he collated during his months in Macedonia.

He also, on an impulse which he found difficult to explain, occupied himself in camps and troop trains by writing essays. IIis first was on a notable Oxford figure, the Regius Professor of Greek Ingram Bywater, whom he had known and loved and who had died in 1915. He called it 'The Portrait of a Scholar,' and it is still as witty, as pointed (though never acerb), as pleasurable to read as on the day it was written, when many people well remembered Bywater and could judge the delicate shrewdness of its touch.

The wit, spontaneous and unemphatic as the ghost of a smile, which makes even the least of Dr. Chapman's footnotes unsafe to ignore, lest one should miss its glance, is as characteristic in this first essay as in anything written later; the smiles are faint, the merest reflections of a private pleasure; but they are haunting, and glimmer in the mind long after the book is finished and laid aside. Here, for example, is Professor Bywater: 'a spare figure, much swamped and muffled in greatcoats and a soft hat, stepping delicately down the High Street of Oxford, and pausing to regard the windows of booksellers and antiquarians with a chill glance of recognition and dispraise.' Who else would have lit so unerringly on that final, nice, discriminating word; or have recalled, in the lightest, least obtrusive of parentheses, that 'his copious memory was stored with the lapses of lesser scholars'; or have observed in passing, when considering the urbanities of the Regius Professor's London house, that 'the habitations of professors are in general, perhaps, too apt to emphasize the dignity of labour'?

The essays written during this period were collected together and published in 1919, a small volume highly characteristic of its author, a man then standing at the beginning of a long, arduous slope of scholarly labour, and delighted to be there. What, he asks in an essay on 'The Textual Criticism of English Classics,' are the present rewards of scholarship? 'Most of the obscurities that admit of enlightenment, and most of the corruptions that admit of correction, have been explained or mended. There is still room for labour, but not much room for fame.' The editor's task, to which he rejoiced to be committed, involved long and tedious labour, much of it obscure. 'It is often his misfortune that he cannot but seem to come between his author and the reader's enjoyment, by labouring on "evanescent atoms." ' No man has ever suffered from this misfortune less; his happy genius was always in the way of inviting, and making possible, greater intimacy. The lucidity and apparent ease of his own style smoothed the reader's path through many a critical thicket: I say 'apparent ease' because nobody knew better than Dr. Chapman that simplicity is difficult, since

> it is always easier to say in twenty words what should be said in ten. . . . Every man who understands the art of writing, and has tried to write well, is aware that the process of composition is commonly not the simple transference of thought into language, but the laborious attempt to work into coherent shape ideas which have been in his mind but which have still to be clarified and arranged; and the temptation to gloss over weak places by deliberate ambiguity is unmistakable.

This temptation, if he ever felt, he totally resisted; it is impossible, even in the densest undergrowth of footnotes, to feel a moment's hesitation as to sense. One has occasionally, in these early essays, a faint hallucination that Johnson is lurking somewhere near at hand; not the easy, colloquial Johnson of the letters, but a more ponderous personality; but this naturally has nothing to do with ambiguity. It merely, in the first intoxication of his Johnsonian enthusiasm, leads him to say when writing, for instance, of spoons, that an embossed bowl is 'repugnant to convenience,' whereas later he might say it is unpractical.

Back at the Oxford University Press after the war, and now Secretary to the Delegates following the death of Charles Cannan in 1919, Mr. Chapman (as he still was) began to devote his leisure to Jane Austen and Johnson. The complete Oxford edition of the novels, based on a minute collation of all the lifetime editions, appeared in 1923. The *Minor Works*, published in 1954 as Volume VI of the series, had appeared separately as *Volume the First*, *Volume the Third*, *The Watsons*, *Sanditon*, and *Lady Susan*, all edited from the original manuscripts.

'In the roaring twenties I made a small hit with my type-facsimiles of eighteenth-century poems.' This typical little piece of self-mockery (for Dr. Chapman was tenacious of even the smallest contribution to the most esoteric periodical, and probably from force of habit collated and indexed himself) is to be found in some notes of his work which he made in his latter years at the request of a friend. In fact, the twenties were a decade of tremendous work both in England and America, for his official duties took him several times to the New York branch of the Press, and he improved these opportunities by pursuing Austen and Johnson letters through libraries, universities, and private collections. In 1925, in mid-Atlantic, he accosted Pierpont Morgan in the smoking-room and asked to be allowed to collate the Austen letters, which at that time Morgan still privately possessed. The meeting was mutually fruitful: the Chapman edition of the letters grew apace, and Morgan begged for any leavings there might be from the surviving manuscripts which Mr. Chapman was seeking for the British Museum. 'I am a modest man,' Pierpont Morgan told him; 'all I ask are the crumbs from the rich man's table'—an understatement still delightedly remembered. *Jane Austen's Letters* were published in 1932—a marvel of depth and lucidity in notes and index and a rich mine for all future students of Jane Austen. The way was now clear for Johnson.

Dr. Chapman's edition of Johnson's letters was received with full scholarly acclaim, and I shall not try to cover that ground again. The scope of the edition, which aimed at nothing less than completeness and accuracy (and how ambitious that aim is only other workers in the same field really know), and the depth and perspective it achieves by means of its index and notes, brought it a proper fame, both here and in America. In giving life to his author Dr. Chapman performed a service second only to Boswell's, and this, perhaps, is a clue to his special quality as commentator and elucidator: he possessed the life-giving as opposed to the deadening touch. One reads his indexes with enjoyment: they have been compiled through no mechanical system of card-indexing or cross-reference, but have been made on hundreds and hundreds of large sheets of paper covered in the course of years with Dr. Chapman's not easily legible hand: they are, in the least obtrusive way in the world, creative and personal. Ingenious typographical devices of his own invention make them clear as well as entertaining to the reader; they are nowhere pedantic, but shed light and indicate paths which might otherwise be missed; copious and elaborate as they are, they are never in the least repugnant to convenience.

It must be a rare and curious experience to come as

fully into possession of another life as Dr. Chapman did of
Dr. Johnson's. He not only came into possession of it, he
displayed it, so that others enjoy the fruits without the
labour—a labour of which few, indeed, are capable. Yet
he made no claim to a complete understanding of his
author's mind; Johnson remains perennially fascinating
because he is at once so humanly and intellectually vast,
and because he is also an enigma. 'It is only by familiarity
with the mass of his recorded wisdom, and by testing its
application to life, that we come to perceive the breadth of
knowledge and depth of insight that give his judgments
their weight and force.'

Recognition of this crowning achievement came at a
time when Dr. Chapman was still young enough to enjoy
it. He seemed, indeed, in his seventies, quite young
enough for anything; his vitality had long been the despair of his contemporaries. The only concession that he
made to age was to give up his lifelong habit of bicycling
inordinately about Oxford; since moving to Old Heading-
ton even he would admit that the distance, and the hill,
were a little much. He continued to wake at half past five
each morning, to make his own tea, and with books,
paper, ink, and cigarettes to put in a lesser man's working
day before breakfast. His correspondence was prodigious
and eccentric; new writing-paper and envelopes were
rarely used, but any scrap of paper lying at hand—old
galley-proofs, publishers' slips, the backs of envelopes
—was snatched up to convey the day's reflections or
second thoughts, bestow praise, rebuke an error, or
carry a congenial argument a stage further: he must
have spent a good deal of money on postage stamps. He
was an earnest gardener, of the single-handed, vegetable
sort; rolled his own cigarettes; was an amateur ornitholo-
gist; took no part in politics, although, like Johnson, he

Dr. R. W. Chapman

was temperamentally a Tory. The best time of the day for work he always found to be the hours before breakfast; the second best, those between tea and dinner. He liked to go to bed early, but if a subject really 'bit' he was sometimes moved to go on and on, incapable of sleep.

So many subjects 'bit' him in the course of his long life, all ancillary to the main design yet all different, that it is hardly possible here to mention them all. Even Dr. Chapman himself, faced with the scrupulous bibliography which he (naturally) compiled of his own writings, had an uneasy feeling that the thing was incomplete. Yet his final volume of *Johnsonian and Other Essays and Reviews* covers the ground sufficiently well for the main body of his readers, who are unlikely to try to follow him into the more learned by-ways of his single-minded yet multifarious life. Aspects of Johnson are there, and of Jane Austen; also textual criticism and lexicography, and a fine funeral oration on the death of the Society for Pure English, of which he was a pillar so long as it lasted, producing pamphlets of just that elusive yet stimulating flavour of amusement in the application of scholarship which is the unobtrusive signature of his style. These essays barely glance at classical literature; one would not deduce from them that he was an amateur of Greek poetry. Nor do they betray his more convivial side; he was always an intensely clubbable man; though with this qualification, that his drinking and dining out were always (since he loved to live much at home) for the sake of something more than sociability: good conversation, the gossip of scholars, the give-and-take of learned and civilized minds. It would be hard to name a man who better succeeded in what he set out to do, whose life was more of a piece, or even happier. He enjoyed as well as extended the pleasures of literature.

The Wandering Albatross

W E HAVE ALL BEEN BROUGHT UP ON *The Ancient Mariner*. Its haunting measure sinks early into the subconscious memory, and in spite of all the vicissitudes of familiarity it remains one of the most powerfully incantatory poems in the language. That albatross! I believed as a child that it was a magical bird; a sort of spirit, which was no doubt the feeling Coleridge intended to evoke. But it is not the albatross which is supernatural; it is the daemon, 'one of the invisible inhabitants of this planet,' which avenges the slaying of the bird and leads the crew into such disasters and visions.

Nevertheless, the poem has laid a spell on the albatross which still universally and imaginatively persists, in spite of John Livingston Lowes's demonstrating forty years ago, in *The Road to Xanadu*, that the legend of its being ill-luck to kill one was not a sailor's superstition at all, but something which Wordsworth thought of and suggested to Coleridge. It is worthwhile to turn back to Wordsworth's recollection of the incident:

In the autumn of 1797, he [Coleridge], my sister, and myself, started from Alfoxden pretty late in the afternoon, with a view to visit Linton, and the Valley of Stones near to it; and as our united funds were very small, we agreed to defray the expense of the tour by writing a poem. . . . Accordingly we set off, and proceeded, along the Quantock Hills, towards Watchet; and in the course of this walk was planned the poem of *The Ancient Mariner*, founded on a dream, as Mr. Coleridge said, of his friend Mr. Cruikshank. Much the greatest part of the story was Mr. Coleridge's invention; but certain parts I suggested; for example, some crime was to be committed which should bring upon the Old Navigator, as Coleridge afterwards delighted to call him, the spectral persecution, as a consequence of that crime and his own wanderings. I had been reading in Shelvocke's Voyages, a day or two before, that, while doubling Cape Horn, they frequently saw albatrosses in that latitude, the largest sort of sea-fowl, some extending their wings twelve or thirteen feet. 'Suppose,' said I, 'you represent him as having killed one of these birds on entering the South Sea, and that the tutelary spirits of these regions take upon them to avenge the crime.' The incident was thought fit for the purpose, and adopted accordingly.

Before Coleridge wrote the poem it had never, it seems, occurred to seafaring men that it was unwise to shoot an albatross. There are many accounts of voyages, from Captain Cook onwards, in which these noble birds are shot for food, or sport, or only for wantonness, and nowhere is there any suggestion of retribution. Now, however, it is another matter; the poet has actually given birth to the legend, and the superstition is established. Quite recently there was even a strike in a west of England port because a crew refused to handle some crated albatrosses, shipped for zoological purposes.

I never supposed that I should see an albatross, and

several years ago, when setting out on a sea voyage to the Cape, I had been so often told that it was a tedious trip, nothing but empty sea after Las Palmas, that I never dreamed anything so extraordinary could happen. But in fact I was wrong, for south of the Equator there was a broad river like blood which ran through the ocean, which the ship followed for more than a hundred miles, and in the Southern Ocean, after days of gale, when we were so far south as to feel the wind blow cold, there were indeed albatrosses.

The river of blood was first seen by two boys with whom I had spent much time in the bow of the ship, looking for sharks and whales; for flying-fish, which from time to time sprayed out of the bow-wave like sequins; and for the schools of dolphins which accompanied us in play for hours at a time, disappearing without warning and then joyously overtaking the ship at more than twenty knots. The sharks had been niggardly, not choosing to show more than a slippery triangle cutting a slit like a knife down the breast of a wave; but the whales had been generous, rolling like black discs in the distance and fountaining up their delicate jets of spray. Now came this mysterious blood-red phenomenon, a mile wide, suspended like crimson dust in the water and creaming redly along the sides of the ship.

We watched it in fascination, propounding theories. The boys were all for a wounded whale, and we strained our eyes for a glimpse of this vast monster, who could the multitudinous seas incarnadine, yet keep so far ahead. One of the officers, when questioned, replied that some dirty tanker had been scraping her tanks, and that what we saw was rust. We did not wish it to be rust, and we did not believe him.

Only the Captain was able to satisfy us, being, unlike

his officers, as much interested in what went on in the sea as in what happened in his ship. He said it was red plankton, which sometimes appeared in tropical seas at this season. The whales would be following the plankton, not the ship, and when the plankton came to an end we should see no more whales. The plankton came to an end the following day; the sea was blue again, and the whales, true to his prophecy, were seen no more.

Now there were head winds, which became gales, and the ship plunged majestically on through seas which grew daily greyer, a heaving expanse in which for days we saw nothing—no flying-fish, no sharks, no racing dolphins—but only, once, a little gleaming object like a pearl or bubble of ice, which appeared on a wave and turned out to be a jettisoned electric-light bulb, one of the millions that travel about the oceans of the world, useless and indestructible, living for ever.

The first albatross, which we had hardly dared to hope for, appeared at the significant moment, out of nowhere, when we had climbed into the crow's-nest. This exposed pocket, constructed round the upper part of the mast and joined to the foredeck by a vibrating perpendicular iron ladder, was nothing like so good a place for scanning the ocean as the rounded and glass-protected bridge of the ship; but it was the place from which a watch, at the appropriate season, was kept for icebergs; it was cramped, cold, and difficult of access, and passengers were not allowed in it; all these circumstances naturally made it desirable. We were given permission to go up, provided we were accompanied by a junior officer, provided we did not talk about it, provided we went up early in the morning before anyone was about. We were now only two days out from Cape Town, and the wind, which had been blowing a gale for nearly a week, had turned very cold.

The Wandering Albatross

We had been hoping for an albatross, but none had appeared, and we were beginning to think we had been misled by the Captain in being told that one or more appeared on nearly every voyage. But the albatross, it seemed, had been waiting for this; for no sooner had we all four crept up that shaking ladder, keeping our eyes away from the deck where two seamen with buckets and brooms had grown horribly small, and had reached the tiny platform and closed the trap, than he materialized at once out of the vacant air, and sailed slowly past, across, and again past us. When he came close, his 'inexpressible strange eye,' as Melville called it, meeting our own, his size appeared prodigious, suspended on wings of improbable length and narrowness; but when he sailed away again, making one of his endless circular sweeps, the sense of proportion was lost in the grey expanse, and it might have been a solitary herring-gull planing and gyrating. He kept us company for several minutes, as much interested in us, it seemed, as we in him, and then vanished as mysteriously as he came.

We looked at one another with amazement, no longer caring that our teeth chattered and that our hands gripping the rail were blue with cold. It is hard to explain why the apparition was so moving, but it felt in that moment as though the Ancient Mariner had laid his hand on all of us. We remembered the poem, and it was not the wind alone that made us shiver. Was there, as well, a Spirit accompanying us, watchful and invisible, protector and avenger of albatrosses, as the Mariner had said?

> Under the keel nine fathom deep,
> From the land of mist and snow,
> The spirit slid; and it was he
> That made the ship to go.

We had no cross-bow; not even a catapult; but if we had, I do not believe even the boys would have dared use it. And yet one saw how easy and tempting it might have been. The great bird had sailed so close that we had caught the impersonal gaze of his yellow eye, had seen the webbed feet folded back under the tail-feathers, had measured the incredible wing-span at a guess—a good twelve feet across, we agreed; possibly more. If we *had* shot him, one of the boys said, he would have dropped like a bomb down to the distant deck.

An hour later he reappeared, this time with a companion, and the pair followed steadily in the wake of the ship. We watched them from the afterdeck, unable to believe in their size when they were at a distance, astonished afresh each time they overtook and passed us, almost within reach, and we saw the dazzlingly white body, the butter-coloured beak and legs, the exquisitely folded feet. The wings were a dark brownish-grey, with elegant long black tips which seemed barely to miss sweeping the surface of the sea; they were decorated at the shoulder with a startling lozenge of white which gave a highly formalized air to the top design, and led the eye to the breast and underside of the wings, which were as white as snow.

It is no wonder the albatross is mythical, a creature of legend and poetry. He comes apparently from nowhere, he follows ships like a ghost, sometimes for days on end, so that sailors believe he habitually sleeps on the wing. He can outdistance the fastest ship without effort, seems never to rest, and except for his short summer breeding season in remote islands of the Antarctic, where each pair of albatrosses produces one magical egg, spends the rest of the year and the long dark winter at sea.

To approach this mythical being so close, to pass through the rim of the circle of his sea life—we, land creatures far out of our element, and he, half-bird, half-spirit, a creature of sea and air—was a thing to remember for ever.

It seems there are several varieties of these great birds, but the Wandering Albatross, *Diomedea exulans*, the one so fatefully shot with a cross-bow, the one that appeared beside us in the crow's-nest, is the most impressive, though less solitary than the Ancient Mariner would have us believe. By the afternoon of the day on which we had sighted our first from the mast there were no fewer than sixteen of them flying powerfully in our wake, circling and passing, dipping at floating refuse, and occasionally coming to rest on the waves, like gulls.

I am afraid it is not for mystical reasons that they follow ships, but for trash from the galley; they eat the food they 'ne'er have eat,' and come back for more; I imagine they know the routes as well as anybody. And it appears they do not really sleep on the wing either, as sailors believe; though one may seem to accompany a ship for days and nights, it is not the same bird. They come down on the sea and are quickly lost to sight in the trough of a wave, for the Southern Ocean is full of hills and valleys. What is mysterious is that they seem to keep up a perpetual patrol; when you look for the one you have been watching he may have gone, but another has taken his place.

Unlike the souls of drowned sailors, which they were long supposed to be, they are large eaters; when gorged they sometimes find they cannot take off again, even with that great wing-span, and beating the sea with their feet; and have to float till digestion lightens the load. Also, more humiliating still, when an albatross has come down on a ship by mistake, and is captured, it seems to suffer inexplicably from sea-sickness. Sailors are always pleased when this happens, for although they no longer shoot them with cross-bows, or indeed take any action against them in the air, they regard a captive albatross as a trophy. They make stems for tobacco-pipes out of the long hollow wing-bones, and from the powerful feet, which have no hind toe and seem to be made of ribbed and yellow leather, make little clawed pouches to keep their money in.

But the sea-sickness is an illusion, as I learned from Rear-Admiral Sir William Jameson, who profited by many Antarctic months in the *Ark Royal* during the Second World War by becoming an authority on albatrosses. The albatross brings up the contents of its stomach to 'lighten ship' in the hope of an imminent take-off. If harassed it will even disgorge quantities of oil, which, it was quite recently believed, it ejected to calm the waters in stormy weather; but this, too, is a part of the lightening process when the bird is in difficulty. This and much more, including details of flight and courtship as beautiful as anything ever recorded in ornithology, is to be found in the Admiral's book, *The Wandering Albatross*, which, exact and scientific as it is, is yet touched with a strange poetry, and should be kept, with *The Road to Xanadu*, conveniently near Coleridge.

The Ghost of Beatrix Potter

OST OF THE HALLOWED BOOKS OF CHILD-
hood lose something of their magic as
we grow older. Beatrix Potter's never.
She even, to the mature eye, reveals fe-
licities and depths of irony which pass the childish reader
by; the dewy freshness of her landscape recalls Constable;
her animals, for all the anthropomorphism of their dress
and behaviour, show an imaginative fidelity to nature, a
microscopic truth that one finds in the hedgerow woodcuts
of Thomas Bewick.

It would be unwise to say any of this if she were still
alive. She died in 1943, her brief creative period (thirteen
years in all) having come to a close some thirty years
before, since when she had evolved into a rather crusty
and intimidating person, interested mainly in acquiring
land and breeding Herdwick sheep, and whom nothing
annoyed more than to have her books appraised on a
critical level.

Graham Greene was sharply rebuked when he wrote
an essay (a more or less serious one, though Miss Potter
took umbrage at what she interpreted as mockery) in
which he discussed the period of the 'great comedies'
—*Tom Kitten*, *The Pie and the Patty-Pan*, *Tiggy-Winkle*—and the subsequent 'dark period' of *The Roly-Poly*

Pudding and *Mr. Tod*, the 'near-tragedies,' using the tone of a sober scholar discussing Shakespeare. 'At some time between 1907 and 1909,' he wrote, 'Miss Potter must have passed through an emotional ordeal which changed the character of her genius. It would be impertinent to inquire into the nature of the ordeal. Her case is curiously similar to that of Henry James. Something happened which shook their faith in appearances.'

Miss Potter was affronted. Nothing, she told him in a 'somewhat acid letter,' had disturbed her at the time of writing *Mr. Tod* save the after-effects of 'flu, which had not altered her so-called genius in any way. She sharply deprecated any examination of her work by the 'Freudian school' of criticism. Yet the essay, despite its Gioconda smile, was a flattering one, and anybody but the author of *Peter Rabbit* would have been pleased. She had become, indeed, curiously ambivalent about the whole of her *oeuvre*. On the one hand, though she enjoyed the matter-of-fact acceptance of children, she was irritated to fury by any considered appraisal of her work; yet at the same time she could not have enough of the adulation which came to her in her latter years from America. Though she would see no others she would welcome reverent strangers from America, and the two or three poor-quality children's books of her late middle age all went to American publishers and were not in her lifetime allowed to be printed in England. The reason for this, I believe, was that she was privately aware that they showed a sad falling-off, and while she was fairly confident of praise from the professional priestesses of 'kid lit.' in America she was unwilling to expose herself at home. Though she was impatient of serious attention from her compatriots, any hint of criticism exasperated her still more.

The Ghost of Beatrix Potter

Miss Janet Adam Smith fell into this thorny trap in 1942 with an article in *The Listener*. 'Great rubbish, absolute bosh!' Beatrix Potter wrote to her publishers, who had thoughtfully sent her a copy, thinking she would be pleased to see herself placed, within her limits, in the 'same company as . . . Palmer, Calvert, Bewick and a host of earlier English artists.' To Miss Adam Smith she also wrote that she had read the article with 'stupefaction.' Her wrath was increased by a humourless misconception, since she plainly thought she was being accused of copying these artists. Much taken aback, Miss Adam Smith hastened to reassure her, explaining that 'your illustrations often give the reader the same kind of pleasure as the pictures of these earlier artists,' and quoting a relevant passage from one of Constable's letters. Worse and worse. Miss Potter (or Mrs. Heelis as she was in private life) now thought she was accused of copying Constable, and replied with a long expostulatory letter, ending with the tart postscript, 'When a person has been nearly thirty years married it is not ingratiating to get an envelope addressed to "Miss." ' (An observation which would pass without comment in any of the several books about Tabitha Twitchet.)

I could, if asked, have warned anybody that it was unwise to meddle at all with Beatrix Potter, having nearly done so myself in 1939, when I was very sharply sent about my business. Like most people who have been wholly entranced by her little books in infancy, I had long believed that Beatrix Potter was dead. The occasional new production that one came across in bookshops (*A Fierce Bad Rabbit*, for example) was so egregiously bad compared with the early masterpieces as to strengthen the suspicion that they were written by somebody else. The bookshops denied this, and were not believed. It was no good asking questions about Beatrix Potter, because at that time nobody knew anything about her.

It was in the early days of the war that I first discovered that she was still alive, and living in the Lake District. My stepdaughter was at school near Windermere, and brought home tempting scraps of some local legends that were current about her. She was very old. She was very rich. She was a recluse. She was a little mad. She drove round the lake on Sundays in an open carriage, wearing black lace and sitting very stiffly behind the coachman. (This, it turned out, was a memory of her mother, Mrs. Rupert Potter, who had done exactly that.) Or alternatively, and this was the most popular legend of all, she did labourer's work in the fields, wearing sacks and rags.

It was very puzzling, but at least it seemed undeniable that she was still alive, and I fell, like Graham Greene and Miss Adam Smith soon after, into the innocent folly of wishing to write about her. Clearly, if she were as reclusive as people said, one must approach with care, and since it seemed desirable to go to the fountain-head as a precaution against inaccuracy or offence, I decided to write to her.

The sensible approach, indeed the only one, since I did not know where she lived, was through her publishers, and I wrote to Frederick Warne and Co. for her address. They replied with ill-concealed horror that on no account, in no possible circumstances, could her address be given. She lived in close retirement, she never saw anybody, they had her express instructions that nobody must ever be allowed to write her a letter.

This could have been final, but it was also rather a challenge to ingenuity, and since my intentions were of the most serious and respectful description I could not see why they should refuse to forward a letter. They did not refuse, though they clearly shrank from the impertinence, and in due course an extremely polite missive was forwarded to Sawrey. I told her of my lifelong pleasure in her books (addressing her, I am thankful to remember, as Mrs. Heelis), expressed my admiration and my wish to write an essay on her work, and asked if I might one day call on her to check some facts and submit what I should write for her approval.

Back came, in a few days, the rudest letter I have ever received in my life. Certainly not, she said; nothing would induce her to see me. 'My books have always sold without advertisement, and I do not propose to go in for that sort of thing now.' Her reply could hardly have been more offensively worded if I had asked her to sponsor a deodorant advertisement.

Well, that was that, I thought. It would be impossible to write anything in the face of such hostility, a snub so out of proportion to the occasion. I tore up the letter in indignation, not knowing that I was only one of innumerable people who had had the breath knocked out of them by her acerbity.

And then, in 1943, she died; and Raymond Mortimer, at that time literary editor of *The New Statesman*, asked if I could write him an article on Beatrix Potter. I did my best, but it was a poor best, for nobody seemed to know anything about her and the crumbs of fact I could gather were contemptible. I knew only that she had lived and farmed for years in the Lake District and was the wife of a country solicitor. I had to confine myself to an appreciation of her work, and even this contained some sad inaccuracies.

It soon became apparent, from the meagre obituary

notices which followed, that I was not the only one who had failed to find out anything. The tone, everywhere, was one of surprise that she had been so recently alive, and it was suddenly borne in on me that what I wanted to do was to write her biography. Alas for such optimism! Here was a life so innocent, so uneventful that one would have supposed the only difficulty would be in finding something to say. Yet, when I approached her widower, the gentlest of men, who received me with a trembling blend of terror and courtesy, it appeared that he considered himself under oath to conceal the very few facts that he had in his possession. He knew remarkably little about her life before their marriage, which had taken place when she was approaching fifty, and what he did know he was unwilling to divulge. He impressed me as a man who for thirty years had lived under the rule of a fairly dominant feminine authority, and whenever, reluctantly, he imparted a scrap of information or a date, he would glance apprehensively over his shoulder, as though every moment expecting the door to open.

The house was indeed palpably haunted by her. She had not long been dead, and the imprint of her personality, clearly the more dynamic one in that marriage, was on every chair and table. Her clothes still hung behind the door, her geraniums trailed and bloomed along the window-sill, her muddles lay unsorted at one end of the table while he took his meals at the other, even a half-eaten bar of chocolate with her teeth-marks in it lay whitened and stale among the litter of letters on her writing-table.

Yet he had expressed himself willing, after much patient argument, that a biography should be written, and as a man of honour truly believed that he was doing his best. He had been, it is true, quite implacable at first, and had been at pains to explain, with the most considerate politeness, why such a project was impossible. She would not have wished it, he said; what was more, she would never have allowed it; and here he looked over his shoulder again and blew his nose in a large and dubious handkerchief. The argument which finally convinced him, in spite of his obvious misgiving that agreement was treachery, was that sooner or later, either in England or America, a biography would be written, and it was perhaps better to have it written while he was still alive and could presumably exercise some control over the biographer. He seemed relieved to think that by this means he might escape the attentions of some frantic American, but I had to promise that every word of every line should be subject to his inspection, and left the cottage after that first interview with my point gained, in the deepest possible dejection.

I knew exactly what he had in mind; the sort of biography he had at last brought himself, after the most scrupulous searching of conscience, to consider. It would be about a quarter of an inch thick, bound in navy blue boards with gilt lettering, and would be called *A Memoir of the late Mrs. William Heelis*. We did not discuss the point, but I am sure he took it for granted that it would be for private circulation.

Then began a series of evenings which we spent together and which I look back on with misery. Every question, however innocuous, was met with the frightened response, 'Oh, you can't mention *that!*' Any detail of her parents, the date of her birth, even the fact of her marriage to himself fell under this extraordinary prohibition. Night after night I stretched my tact and ingenuity to breaking-point, feverishly changing from subject to subject, retreating at once when I saw his poor eyes watering in alarm, creeping back each night to my cold bedroom at the Sawrey Inn to sleepless hours of knowing the whole thing to be impossible.

And then, after many evenings and by the merest accident, I changed my tune. Some tremulous negative, some futile protest over a harmless question, produced that sudden trembling which I have experienced only two or three times in my life and associate with the crisis known as losing one's temper. I found myself banging the table with clenched fist and crying 'Mr. Heelis, you *must not obstruct me in this way!*' The moment it had happened, in the petrified silence, I was overcome with embarrassment. But the effect was magical. He jumped, looked over his shoulder again as towards a voice he knew, pulled himself together, blew his nose, apologized, and suddenly seemed to feel remarkably better. I had never meant to do it, but the inference was plain. Tact, compliance, the yielding deviousness that had cost me so much effort were things he was unaccustomed to and could not deal with. With decision, with firm opinion, he felt at home, and responded in the most eager and obliging manner. Pleased at last to be able to express his pride in his wife's fame he brought out his boxes of letters, rummaged in the bottoms of wardrobes and at the backs of drawers for photographs, produced such addresses and names as from time to time crossed his uncertain memory. The thing was started; I breathed a sigh of relief; though not without foreboding that my difficulties were only begun.

They were indeed, for over his eager compliance, which even extended to giving me two of her water-colours, hung the cloud of that final inspection of the manuscript which I knew would mar all. Left to himself, with typescript before him, I knew how his trembling hand would score it through, how little, how very little would come back unscathed, how in despair I would fling that little into the wastepaper basket.

Outside the precincts of Castle Cottage there was no such reticence; there were many people living who had known her well, Potter cousins, the niece of her last governess, Miss Hammond, innumerable farm and cottage neighbours who thought of her only as the eccentric little figure that the Lake District remembers—the odd bundle of country clothing, clad in innumerable petticoats, full of good humour, of authority, of sudden acerbities which could flash out quite brutally and inflict hurts where she probably never intended them. 'I began to assert myself at seventy,' she wrote to one of her cousins a few months before she died, but this was an understatement. She had been asserting herself for thirty years, and the Lake District had come to respect her as a person it was dangerous to oppose, but very safe to love.

Those who spoke of her with the most feeling were the shepherds and farmers with whom she was most akin in temperament, and to the poetry of whose lives she had always responded, almost with the nostalgia of an exile. On her deathbed she had scribbled a note of indecipherable farewell to her old Scottish shepherd, the 'lambing-time man' who had come to her every spring for nearly twenty years, and with whom she had kept up a long and affectionate correspondence. He had preserved all her letters, dated and wrapped up in little parcels in the recesses of his cottage, and he sent them to me as an act of piety, for love of her memory.

I took innumerable journeys, sometimes with Mr. Heelis, more often (and more fruitfully) alone, over the fells and along the valleys, to cottages and farmhouses that she owned, talking to the people who had known her. She had been a workmanlike landlord, most practically interested in fences and gates, the felling and planting of timber, the repairing of walls. As a sheep-breeder she was knowledgeable and shrewd, and the farmers round about thought of her principally as a dangerous rival at sheep fairs and ram shows, an enigmatic and authoritative presence in the Keswick tavern where the Herdwick Sheep Breeders' Association held its meetings.

At the same time I embarked on a sea of correspondence, which ebbed and flowed for more than a year. Beatrix Potter, for all the crowded busy-ness of her later years, when she was managing a number of farms and doing important work for the National Trust in the Lake District, possessed that last-century sense of leisure which permitted her to write long and frequent letters to a great many people—sometimes even to people she had never met, but whose personalities, when they wrote to her, had taken her fancy. Now, these letters began to flow into my hands, not only from English senders, but from places as far afield as America and New Zealand; and the task of deciphering and sifting them for their shreds of biographical interest was for a time quite heavy.

To me, the series of letters which Warne's, her publishers for more than forty years, had kept without a gap since the day when they first accepted *Peter Rabbit*, was the most interesting of all, for they reflected her slow and painstaking development as an artist, her emotional growth from girl to woman, her emergence from unhappy and respectable nonentity into the kind of personality about whom biographies are written. The Warne family had played an important, and more than professional, part in her life, and without their help and confidence the book could never have been written.

But however much help I had from her publishers,

relations, and other friends, there was still to be faced the final confrontation with Mr. Heelis, when, as I privately guessed, he would bring up reinforcements of prohibition and his mandate would fall on everything I had written.

I remember that on my last evening in Sawrey, returning from a walk with which I had tried in vain to recruit my spirits, I found a penny lying at the foot of a stile and decided to toss for it; whether I should give it up there and then or write the book as I saw it and be prepared to forget it for years in a locked drawer. The penny said heads, and I put it in my pocket as a charm. The drawer was the thing. I did not know how old Mr. Heelis was, nor how I should explain my curious delay; but I was resolved I would not expose myself, or him, to the long-drawn agony of his excisions.

As it turned out, the penny proved a true oracle, for the poor widower, left alone and at a loss without the mainstay on which his thoughts and decisions had so long depended, died a few months after, before the book was finished, and I never paid that final visit to Sawrey. I do not believe he turns in his grave, honest man, nor that the stout little ghost which haunts the place would still, after all this time, find it necessary to be angry.

Beatrix Potter: The Missing Years

WRITING *The Tale of Beatrix Potter* twenty years ago, the story of a life so quiet and outwardly uneventful that it was difficult to unravel, I came upon a period of sixteen years or so of which almost nothing was known.

It had been possible to trace out the early years in considerable detail. There were still two first cousins and other, less close, relations still alive, to say nothing of Beatrix Potter's widower, Mr. William Heelis; but none of these could offer anything to fill the long extraordinary gap between the year she was seventeen and her early thirties. 'Nothing happened, that's why,' said the more communicative of the cousins, 'she just went on living in Bolton Gardens with those dreadful parents and going for long boring holidays with them three or four times a year. Nothing else happened at all.'

> She continued to move [I eventually wrote], a captive planet, through the Potter phases; through Bolton Gardens, holidays, visits to relations, changing her position according to the time of year. Somewhere in this decade she fell ill with rheumatic fever, an interruption of the regular progress which left her with a very slight, though permanent, weakness of the heart. At some

point in it she took up, and at another abandoned, the study of fungus. During some part of it she spent much time in drawing fossils in the South Kensington Museum. . . . But apart from these tiny milestones, these fragments of incident no bigger than pebbles, the most assiduous scraping away the mould uncovers nothing.

Beatrix Potter was born on July 28, 1866, and today, a hundred years later, anyone who is interested may know how the missing sixteen years were spent. Beatrix Potter's own secret journal of the period has come to light and has been transcribed by Mr. Leslie Linder.[1] The story of that discovery, and of the breaking of the code, is an extraordinary little biographical drama.

Mr. Linder is an engineer, specially concerned with the component parts of lifting tackle. He was given one or two Beatrix Potter books as a child, but had (so he says) more or less forgotten them when he picked up her biography and idly began it. The effect it had on him was unexpected. He became fired with a passion for her works, which he began to collect in every available edition, progressing rapidly to drawings, holograph letters, and every scrap of information concerning her that single-minded and assiduous search could conceivably uncover. His Beatrix Potter collection is now an extremely handsome thing, fit for a museum, and it is splendidly fitting that this self-dedicated champion of Pottereana should be the man to interpret an entirely unknown work, a diary 200,000 words long, and to break the code in time for her centenary.

I must go back a little to explain about this journal written in code. While I was gathering material for the biography several loose sheets of this same journal were

[1] *The Journal of Beatrix Potter 1881–1897*, transcribed from her code writings by Leslie Linder (London: Frederick Warne, 1966).

put into my hands, some by Mr. Heelis and some by Mrs. William Clark of Ulva, who had been Caroline Hutton, Beatrix Potter's favourite cousin. The sheets were not the original code writing, but transcripts made by Miss Potter herself quite late in life. She had evidently made the transcriptions for amusement, scribbling on torn-out pages of exercise-books, and since they dealt with her childhood, and with reminiscences of her dearly loved Potter grandmother, Mrs. Edmund Potter, they provided valuable biographical matter. I saw several scraps of the original cipher, and described it as 'a self-invented script-writing which was partly a kind of infantile shorthand, partly a script so small that (like the Brontës' childhood manuscripts) no inquisitive grown-up, unless prepared to go to the length of using a magnifying-glass, could decipher it.' These fragments were in due course returned to their owners, now both dead, and have not been seen since.

In 1952, however, Mrs. Stephanie Duke (whose mother was Beatrix Potter's first cousin, and to whom, as a child, *The Tale of Mr. Jeremy Fisher* had been dedicated) came upon a bundle of old papers at Castle Cottage, Sawrey, which had been Beatrix Potter's married home for thirty years. (I well remember the comfortable muddle of that interior, with Mr. Heelis gingerly exploring wardrobes and shoe-boxes for letters and watercolours, and am not surprised that even ten years after his wife's death there were considerable untouched deposits.) These papers, in a meticulous hand, were all in code, and since Mrs. Duke could make nothing of them she gave them to the National Trust, which stored them in Beatrix Potter's farmhouse, Hill Top, Sawrey.

Here Mr. Linder, hot in pursuit of his great subject, first examined them, and later borrowed a number of sheets in the hope of deciphering them. He worked on them for four years without success and, finally, on the last evening before returning the papers, picked up a sheet to try his luck once more. 'On the evening of Easter Monday, 1958,' he recalls, 'I remember thinking to myself, I will have one *last* attempt at solving this code-writing, more to pass the time than with any anticipation of success. I selected a sheet at random, and then, quite by chance, noticed a line near the bottom of the page which contained the Roman numerals XVI and the year 1793. Was this a clue—could something of consequence have happened to a Pope bearing the numerals XVI, or to King Louis XVI in the year 1793? I consulted a Dictionary of Dates without success, and then . . . the index to the *Children's Encyclopedia*, where I read, "Louis XVI, French King; born Versailles 1754; guillotined Paris 1793." Here at last was a possible clue!'

The clue was valid. The word which followed the date began with an x, and he made the obvious guess that it might be 'executed.' Again he was lucky, and 'with the help of these assumed symbols, other words were deciphered, and by midnight on that memorable Easter Monday practically the whole of Beatrix Potter's code alphabet had been solved.'

The complete deciphering of the journal took him another five years, for apart from the difficulties of the code, the script-writings themselves, like the stitches in the Tailor of Gloucester's buttonholes, were 'so small—*so* small—they looked as if they had been made by little mice.' But at last the gigantic task was finished—more than 200,000 words of a private record which Beatrix Potter never dreamed anyone but herself would read—and the missing gap in her known life, those fifteen years or so between her late teens and her thirties, from the time when she first put up her hair and wore a gold watch and chain on Sundays, to the day when she published *Peter Rabbit*, was filled at last.

I sit with the heavy volume on my knee, turning the close-packed pages with a mixed feeling of wonder and suffocation. For the answer to that question, *What had happened?* is still, broadly speaking, 'Almost nothing.' The book is a monument to talents and energies repressed, to youth and life frustrated, to the dead hand of convention and respectability. The marvel is that Beatrix Potter emerged at all. Without genius she could never have done it. In her thirties she discovered the form in which her originality, both as artist and writer, could perfectly flower, and for more than a decade her life was centred in her score of incomparable little books for children. The books earned money, and with money she bought freedom. But before the discovery and the escape, the hidden years of the journal were slowly lived through, in a period and in a social class which of all others have perhaps been the dullest and most disheartening for women.

Turning the pages of the journal one can almost smell the boredom of the Potter household. I suppose no other unmarried girl's diary has been so discreet and impersonal as this, yet even in her long factual accounts of this or that, in a tart aside or occasional murmur of anguish, the awful Potter atmosphere seeps through. We hear of 'odious fits of low spirits,' of headaches and neuralgia, of being always tired, the syndrome so common among Victorian young women of the moneyed middle class, with no prospect before them and nothing whatever to do.

The Potter parents do not at all improve on close acquaintance. Mama, indeed, is scarcely mentioned, save for the rather awful communication that her hair 'takes off,' but Papa's presence reverberates like a gong. Mr.

Potter had been called to the Bar, but had never practised, having too much money to need to earn any more; his life-work, if such it can be called, was amateur photography, in which he became expert. For the rest, he attended Royal Academy exhibitions—'a great resource,' Beatrix observes, 'for people of our station'—black-balled prospective members at the Reform Club and Athenaeum, got into furies with Mr. Gladstone and the newspapers and worried himself sick over the Stock Exchange. 'My father says the country is going to the deuce, and his spirits get worse and worse.' He is 'hot and huffed,' 'most standoffish and unsociable,' 'constantly on the lookout for matters of complaint.' 'I should have enjoyed it more,' she records after a pony-and-trap outing, 'without Papa and the flies,' and on another occasion, 'Must confess to crying after I got home, my father being as usual deplorable.' He seems to have kept her penuriously short of pocket-money, even after she was grown up; the journal abounds in sighs for a few shillings, and she mentions only one instance of his giving her a present: 'May 6. My father gave me rather an extraordinary present, viz. certain Bonds of the North Pacific Railway which have paid no interest since April, '93, the company being in the hands of the receivers.'

What is extraordinary about this endless secret self-communication is that after all it is so very impersonal. Thousands of words describe the pictures in innumerable exhibitions, thousands more the holiday places and seaside resorts in which the Potters, accompanied by their London servants and with carriage and horses following by train, spent an average of four months a year. There are no confessions or revelations, or if there are, they are so discreetly veiled as to be almost invisible. (One thinks with amazement of Marie Bashkirtseff, at the same period and at the same age, writing her dynamic self-centred

journal far into the night, and the contrast is curiously
touching as well as laughable.)

Why did she write in code? Originally, we know, out
of a youthful admiration for Pepys, but also for the sake
of creating a world of her own, away from supervision and
interference. She had possessed that private world in
childhood, when she lived in a fantasy of fairy tales and
the lives of her pet animals, and the end of childhood had
come as a frightening shock. 'I have begun the dark journey of life,' she wrote at seventeen. 'Will it go on as darkly
as it has begun?'

But it is not all gloom and foreboding—quite the
reverse. Personal emotion is vigorously repressed and she
turns a brisk attention to newspapers and current politics
and to everything else that she sees in her small world.
(Its smallness is startling when we learn that although
she was born and had spent her life within two miles of
Piccadilly, she could record in her nineteenth year, after a
carriage drive, 'It was the first time in my life that I had
been past the Horse Guards, Admiralty and Whitehall, or
seen the Strand and the Monument.' And at nearly thirty
she suddenly reflects, 'I wonder why I never seem to know
people? It makes one wonder whether one is presentable.')

Her political views, imbibed from Papa, are fiercely
and innocently reactionary. After the unemployed riots of
1886, the ring-leaders, she considers, 'ought to be hung at
once like dogs,' and as for 'old Gladstone,' that cowardly
mismanager of Empire, 'The old lunatic will soon stand
alone.' But little by little, notably under the influence of
her Socialist-minded cousin, Caroline Hutton, she begins
to perceive, though warily, that the labouring classes do
actually suffer from 'miserable wages of eleven shillings a
week, their insanitary cottages, their appalling families

and improvidence'—disabilities quite unknown to 'people of our station.' In another thirty years she will have become that formidably capable farmer and landowner, Mrs. Heelis of Sawrey, repairing walls, shoring-up cottages, looking after her farms and tenants with a jealous eye.

Where is the Beatrix Potter of so many people's imagination, the creator of prose-and-water-colour masterpieces about mice, squirrels, frogs, hedgehogs, rabbits? She is here to be found, sure enough, laboriously learning her trade, but still a long way from recognizing it. The instincts of artist and naturalist are equally strong. 'I cannot rest, I *must* draw, however poor the result.' 'I can't settle to anything but my painting, I lose my patience over everything else . . . I *will* do something sooner or later.' And at the same time, in the silent third-floor room that had once been the nursery, she is classifying fossils and studying funguses and moulds as though her life depended on it. The long summer holidays are her periods of field-work, London the place where she plies between home and museum, growing specimens of slimes and moulds, preparing slides, drawing mysterious phenomena under the microscope. Her researches even carried her so far as to bring her to new ideas on the propagation of the spores of algae, and to writing a paper, 'On the Germination of the spores of Agaricineae,' for the Linnaean Society.

But this is at the very end of the sixteen years' journal, when we have already come across the significant words: 'Wrote picture letters to the little Moores . . .' and know that those hand-written stories with pictures, the forerunners of Peter Rabbit and Squirrel Nutkin, of Pigling Bland, Mrs. Tiggy-Winkle, and Samuel Whiskers, have already begun their career through the penny post. From now on, for another thirteen years, there will be the creative flow, and after that, the escape from Papa and Mama to independence, to farming, to middle-aged marriage, the final thirty years of hard work and happiness.

Mrs. Heelis of Sawrey, experienced, shrewd, on occasion formidably opinionated and crusty, is difficult to reconcile with the shy and silent child who was Beatrix Potter. But she is here in the larval stage in this secret journal, half-buried, it is true, under drifts of detail and alluvial deposits of words, but still there—observant, absorbed in the natural word and her interpretation of it, poetical, practical, wholly unsentimental. 'I forgot,' she writes towards the end, 'to set down on Sun. April 12th a few minutes after eight I saw a fine meteor. . . . I was much impressed by it, a strange visitor from the outside of the world. I do not often consider the stars. . . . It is more than enough that there should be more than forty thousand named and classified funguses.'

The Wolf Men

OST OF US HAVE SOME READING EXPERI-
ence in childhood of which, when we are
old enough to judge, we feel we should be
ashamed. It is usually impossible to re-
capture the old pleasure, but it is a mistake to apologize.
These first responses to bad literature are fresh and genuine, and often, by contrast, prepare the way for more
rewarding tastes when the time comes.

When I was eight or nine years old, attending a modest day-school in Gordon Square (next door to a theolog-
ical library, the imposing Gothic façade of which appeared on the cover of the school syllabus with no hint
that the school's was the obscure little door on the extreme
right, like a tradesman's entrance), I stumbled on an
absurd boys' adventure story which coloured my imagination for years and left who knows what unexpected traces
in the deeper layers of an undisciplined imagination.

When I say 'stumbled' I mean that I did just that: no
one lent it to me, no one recommended it. I was ferreting
alone among shoes and galoshes in the cloakroom when
my hand, probing a pile of coats in search of my slippers,
came upon the hard corners of a book, and drew out the
volume which was to become an Influence.

The cover was a shock; nothing on my father's shelves

had prepared me for this surprise attack on my most primitive emotions. The title of the book was *The Wolf Men*, and the cover design was of a skinny and repellent savage—not quite a man, I could see that at a glance, ears too long, brow too low, teeth too fang-like—falling backwards among flying boulders from the edge of a cliff. That such things could be was an unnerving and at the same time obscurely pleasurable shock. I had to know more, and opened the book with caution at a coloured picture. But this really frightened me; I shut the book with a gasp and put it back urgently under the pile of coats. My nerves would stand no more. For this had been a picture of the Wolf Men in attack, and the traumatic effect (at an age when to be pursued in the dark and eaten by something is an anxious and recurrent expectation) was such that I went home in a nervous condition and could by no means be prevailed upon to say what ailed me. The odd thing was that, in spite of the apprehensions and the night-fears induced by this first glance at an unknown book, I knew with mystic certainty that this was something to which I was committed. I brooded for some weeks, eventually consulting the sole confidante of this period of my life, a girl cousin, with the result that we both asked our parents, without explanation, whether we might have *The Wolf Men* (author Frank Powell, publisher Cassell, price, I think, three-and-six) for Christmas.

I recall that when Christmas came we were both so much dismayed by the cover that it was some weeks before we dared even look at the outside corners of the pictures. But we could see, from the edges of the pages, where the pictures were, and little by little, opening an inch with our thumbs and peering in to see if our nerves would stand it, we gradually worked through the illustrations and arrived at the stage where we could dare to read. The story exceeded our most terrified expectations, and for a time our parents believed that it did us harm. We became afraid of the dark, screamed at the slightest noise, and were sometimes hauled trembling from under the piano with our faces bathed in tears of voluptuous terror. Looking back, I am convinced that it did us nothing but good, and am glad that our parents were neither Freudian nor squeamish; for the experience, drawn out over several years and in spite of all our symptoms of distress, was an experience of pleasure. I have a theory that it is wholesome, at some time in one's life, to know the taste of terror; that it enlarges the mind and leaves a valuably tender spot in the imagination; that in conditions of real safety (warm dark house, parents downstairs, far-off murmur of voices) it causes the adrenalin to flow, exercises the emotions, induces catharsis, discovers one's inner nature, and teaches one all those profound sensations of relief and sanctuary which animals know when at last they reach the asylum of the burrow. For of course we always fell asleep at last, exhausted and perfectly happy, waiting only for another day when we could renew our pursuits, alarms, and supernormal terrors. For years the Wolf Men game was our favourite recreation, to be started at any moment by a glance, a sign, an ominous scratching sound with the finger-nails. We were never at a loss, could reduce each other to tears at a moment's notice, and were a puzzle and annoyance to nearly everybody.

In time of course the excitement died down, and eventually both our precious volumes disappeared and were never seen again. They were always being borrowed by little boys of our acquaintance, and when in the end they failed to return and nobody could remember who had last had them, we were not greatly concerned. We knew *The*

Wolf Men almost by heart, its fearful characters had passed into our mythology, the harm or the benefit, whichever it was, had been done, and Frank Powell's masterpiece had left its ambiguous mark on both our characters. It was not until I had long been grown up that I began to yearn once more for its preposterous pages, and searched in desultory fashion for a second-hand copy. None, alas, has ever come to light. Nobody that I know possesses a copy, professional book-finders have failed to locate one, the publisher's file copy was destroyed in the blitz on Paternoster Row, and the only way I know of reviving the old pleasure (I have done this more than once) is by spending the day in the Reading Room of the British Museum. There, the sole copy of *The Wolf Men* is shabby with use and some of the pictures fall out. I read it behind a barrier of more sober-looking volumes, because really, sitting between an American research Fellow and an African divine, in that stuffy hush which incubates so many theses, one does feel a little foolish with *The Wolf Men*. And I must confess its effect on me is not what it once was. It is as ill written and ridiculous a work as ever I laid eyes on.

And yet it has something . . . If I ever found a second-hand copy that I could keep I believe it would bring tears to my eyes, even now. Goodness knows I have suffered enough emotion in my time at the hands of Mr. Frank Powell.

I do not know who Frank Powell was or is, nor whether he ever wrote another work. *The Wolf Men*, I learned during my orgies in the Reading Room, was published in 1906, so that it was far from new when I discovered it. It was on Cassells' list of Books for Boys for that period, and is about an accidental journey into the interior of the earth where, in a dark world lit by forests of luminous fungus, a degenerate race of savage men exists amid the relics of a marvellous civilization, together with all the notable prehistoric animals that a well-informed boy of ten might know about after a few Saturday afternoons spent in the Natural History Museum.

I have been told, by several people to whom I have described it, that this is a hackneyed theme and *The Wolf Men* an obvious crib from some other work. (They usually cite Conan Doyle's *The Lost World* or Joseph O'Neill's *Land Under England*.) But it is earlier in date than anything else of the kind that I know, and I like to think that the cribbing was the other way round. It appears to me now as an early and naïve example of science fiction, distinguished by its Edwardian flavour and by absurdities which were certainly not apparent to me when I first read it. If anything, these now give it an additional charm, so that I enjoy it on several levels at once, as one savours the later novels of Henry James.

The first thing to be understood is that it is a book purely for boys; the sort of boys who, in stiff collars and Norfolk suits, were ten years old round about 1906. (I dare say both Oswald and Noel Bastable were fond of it.) There are not only no women in it, there is not even a breath of suggestion that more than one sex exists, either on this planet or inside it, which is exactly as it should be and shows Powell's psychological sympathy with his audience.

The hero-adventurers of the tale are five, three mature, two young. They have not a vestige of character between them, but there are serviceable descriptive devices for telling them apart. Professor Mervyn is the Scientist (grey-haired, addicted to specimens) whose ambition is to penetrate by submarine beneath the great ice barrier of the North Pole and 'reach the open sea which

we know exists beyond.' (Make allowances: this is
1906.) He is supported by Sir William Seymour, Baronet, 'a man in the prime of life, over six feet in height and
broad in proportion, his bearded face tanned by many a
year of travel under a tropical sun.' And with them goes,
for no good reason that I can see now, except perhaps
comic dialogue, an American millionaire, Silas K. Haverly, 'one of the railway kings of America,' an explorer in
his spare time, a great one for laconic comment and biting
off the ends of cigars.

The two young men are Garth Hilton, an inventor
('You remember what a fellow Garth always was for
making model boats?') and his 'old school chum,' Tom
Wilson, an engineer and presumably a fairly precocious
one, since he is only eighteen. Between them, it is surprising to learn from the Professor, 'they have managed to
construct a submarine, which, if it but answers their expectations, will prove the very thing I have been waiting
for.' This do-it-yourself craft is 350 feet long, beam 50
feet, capable of 45 knots on the surface and 30 sub-
merged, the engines 'drawing their own supplies from the
air as they work,' which disposes of the fuel problem.

The saga starts with some fairly routine mishaps, including an attempt by foreign spies to steal the submarine, shooting one of the baronet's footmen and chloro-
forming the American on a train, which need not detain us
here, since they are only part of the warming-up process
as Powell gets into his stride. Haverly escapes from the
train in time, encounters a friend driving a powerful Pan-
hard, and makes a hair-raising dash for the dock where
the Seal (our trusty submarine) is waiting with steam up,
straining to start on her quest of the Great Unknown.

'What speed have you got on?' . . .

'Forty,' returned Oswyn.

'I guess she'll do better than that. Chuck the lever over.'

'It's risky in the dark,' returned Oswyn, yet he obeyed. . . . Beneath the added power the car leapt forward like a thing of life. . . . Her every bolt and rivet quivered and sang with the throbbing of the mighty cylinders. She was a veritable projectile.

Presently Haverly consulted his watch.

'Is she doing all she knows?' he asked.

'Every inch,' was the reply. 'Great Scott! You surely don't want her to do any more? We're doing over 50 now. What would happen if we struck an obstruction?'

What, indeed!

Two months later, we are facing the Great Ice Barrier; we submerge, nose along the sea bed, enter a dark tunnel in the ice and finally surface to find ourselves in 'the mighty waters of the Polar Sea.' This is what the Professor had in mind all along, but it is only the beginning of our heroes' troubles. They are sucked into a dark canyon by the magnetic attraction of the Pole, survive a volcanic eruption and plunge into a subterranean river, 'each instant deeper and deeper into the bowels of the globe'! The Professor consults his instruments and the truth of their predicament dawns on them all. Yet, magnificently, 'they retired, to forget for a while the dangers of their novel position in the pleasures of the table.'

This is one of the reassuring features of *The Wolf Men*. After a thousand adventures, when the submarine has been disabled by the attacks of a giant squid, dashed against cliffs by a tidal wave, hurled over a cataract, captured and overrun by Wolf Men, and our heroes have all been in turn left for dead in their blood, the reader's nerves are calmed by the assurance that at least they could all tuck in to a good meal. The decks are awash with blood, but 'their first meal aboard the recovered vessel was one they never forgot. Wilson, ever an adept at the culinary art, had surpassed himself. The saloon table literally groaned beneath the weight of good things: it sparkled with cut-glass and silver.' These meals restore our emotional balance, performing the same function as the Porter in *Macbeth*.

We certainly need some relief, for no sooner do we step ashore in the subterranean world than the real horrors begin. It is a twilight world, lit only by the phosphorescence of the fungus forest. Giant squids and 'loathsome forms' inhabit its waters, megalosaurus and triceratops roam its jungles (to say nothing of ichthyosaurus, megatherium, and vampires) and our heroes are puzzled by prints of an ape-like foot and by wolfish howls. This is the nub of the story, the horror to which even the giant vampire bat, membranous wings, hyena-like teeth and all, is a mere nothing. The underworld is inhabited by creatures straight from the subconscious. 'Their long, fearfully distorted limbs, their hideous feet and hands, armed with talon-like nails, their lean, emaciated bodies, covered with coarse brown hair; their low, receding foreheads, flat noses and immense protruding wolf-like fangs—all this, crowned with a mass of thickly matted hair, which hung almost to the loins, seen in the dim, ghostly twilight of the underworld, made up a picture of diabolical horror such as would be difficult, if not impossible, to beat.'

These are the very creatures that have always lurked on dark landings and on the tops of wardrobes, known to every child long before he opens the pages of *The Wolf Men*, or comes on their modern counterpart in the horror-strip. I still find them frightening, and am not surprised. What does seem rather a puzzle, one which perhaps only an analyst could solve, is how once, as a normal and reasonably well-behaved little girl, I responded with such satisfaction to descriptions aimed at the fantasies and primitive instincts of little boys. 'Letting the murder lust within him have full sway, the lad beat his enemy's head to a shapeless pulp against the stones of the beach,' etc., etc. Perhaps we are all much the same at that age: but I think it was chiefly the terror that held me in thrall, the primitive instinct of flight which was so stimulated and fed, leaving me for life a skilled and resourceful evader.

I had hoped to give a short account of our heroes' adventures in the haunts of the Wolf Men, but I find this impossible: there are too many: there is a crisis on nearly every page, very often in italics, so that I suspect the story to have been originally written as a boys' serial, the rhythm of crisis dictated by a long series of rather tight instalments. From among so many nightmarish episodes I would specially mention the Professor's duel with Rahee the Terrible, the hairy giant spider as big as a pony, to which all the Wolf Men's prisoners are ritually sacrificed. It took me years to get over Rahee, and I am not quite free of him yet, privately maintaining that my amateur's interest in spiders and other arachnids (this sometimes surprises my friends) is a form of compensation, a love-hate relationship due to the night-sweats of long ago, when any creak was the sound of the bars of Rahee's cage being sl-o-w-ly lifted.

A word must be said about Powell's style, which repays study. He is a true master of the *cliché*, though this I failed to appreciate when I first read him, since all *clichés* are new and striking the first time. Even as early as 1906 he had the classic phrase for every situation. 'For an hour the *duel raged*, the creatures' efforts growing feebler as the time went on, while the *crimson rain* which sprinkled down over the engineer *bore grim testimony* to the *sanguinary nature* of the struggle.' I forgot to say that this scene takes place in the bone-strewn feeding-ground of the giant vampires ('a veritable harvest of death'), where two of the creatures are fighting over Tom Wilson, who has been picked off the deck of the submarine by one of them while his chum goes below for a moment, tired out after a fight to the death with an ichthyosaurus; but the style so perfectly reflects the matter that one hardly needs to explain.

There are some fine prototypes in the story, whom I remember with affection. There is Nordhu, High Priest of Ramouni, Ruler of the Underworld, a once superior being who controls and directs the beastly population of five million Wolf Men; he is a figure of sinister power and still crops up with undiminished vigour in the more juvenile grades of space-fiction. 'Tall he was, and lean as a greyhound . . . His face . . . must have been pleasing once . . . but passion had left its mark upon the features, and the eyes, cold and merciless in their glitter, betrayed the hideous cruelty of their owner's nature.' Then there is Chenobi, gigantic sole survivor of the noble race of the Ayuti (connected, I need hardly tell you, with Atlantis), who befriends our heroes, destroys Nordhu and Rahee, and, assisted by the opportune birth of a volcanic island from the depths where they happen to be, returns with them in the end to the upper world. He is Superman in person, noble, invincible, and pure, a bearded Galahad riding on a giant elk, throwing in his lot with the explorers for the best and nicest reason, because 'I long for a friend.' I never cared for him quite as much as for Rahee or the Wolf Men, but in a tight corner he was a great comfort.

Whenever the question arises of protecting the young

from deliberately frightening reading, I remember the bliss of *The Wolf Men* and am silent. I can say nothing in its defence except that I *feel* it did me more good than harm. Were my aggressive and delinquent tendencies purged and calmed by its delicious terrors? I should like to think so. But even if this is unlikely and my theory worthless, the mere memory of that foolish book is a fond pleasure.

Amitié Amoureuse

O NE OF THE PERQUISITES OF MIDDLE AGE IS
being allowed, with little or no disapproval,
to enjoy the pleasures of romantic friendship. By romantic friendship I mean exactly
what I say. Not a love affair. Not the sort of businesslike
camaraderie which depends on an occasional luncheon
with something to discuss. Neither of these, but something in between, with some of the advantages of both.

There must be an implicit sexual attraction, an atmosphere of 'Ah, if we were younger . . .' to give the thing its
special and delightful flavour. There must be exchange of
confidences, a liking to be seen together, a sense of mutual
support and appreciation. Given the right ingredients,
amitié amoureuse can add such charm to life that I am
surprised it is not more generally cultivated.

It is a pleasure, of course, quite impossible for the
young. In the days when men were expected to have hon-
ourable intentions a romantic friendship was the last
thing to be thought of. A young man was a scoundrel if he
tried it, a young woman compromised if she permitted it.
Raising expectations and toying with affections were
among the unspeakable activities of bounders, while 'leading him on,' which was what unscrupulous females and
adventuresses did, was only comparatively less reprehen-

sible. Nineteenth-century fiction is full of narrow escapes, with heroes on the brink of unhappy marriages through sympathy misunderstood or obligations imposed by watchful parents. (Look what a narrow squeak Edward Ferrars had: it would have served him right to have got stuck with Lucy Steele.)

In our own time, with the new sexual freedom we are always hearing about, it is just as impossible, though for the opposite reason. Sex is so fashionable among the young that no other form of intimacy gets a chance. Indeed, it is easy to see why. Once the old barriers are down the boys will be out to get their money's worth, and the girls, poor things, will be walking a perilous edge in a state of anxiety. I never open the Sunday papers without being harrowed afresh by teenage problems, and confess I wouldn't know what to advise, though I am truly sorry for them.

But in middle age, as Hamlet so impertinently reminded his mother, the problem is supposed to be over. Most of us are married, or have arrived at some alternative to suit our requirements, and are no longer instantly suspected if we show a little affectionate civility. Girls in my day were often *farouche* with young men, or anyway much less charming than they became later, because of the fear of being considered predatory. Never having a brother, I was myself inclined to think young men much cleverer and more alarming than they probably were, and in my anxiety not to pursue was often over-cool, when I would much rather have been welcoming—if only I had dared. What a comfort it is, devoted as I am to my own generation of both sexes, to be on easy and affectionate terms with the men I am fond of, never pausing to think whether I shall be either pounced on or suspected.

One cannot, of course, have many concurrent *amitiés*,

but it is better for discreet reasons to have more than one. The ideal number is either two or three, for then the thing is seen for what it is, not as a possible cover for something else. Spouses (hateful word) are usually reasonably tolerant of a syndicate, but hostile to a single system, which so often looks like a love affair; and so often is.

What, I can imagine myself being asked by the incredulous, are the advantages of the kind of thing you have in mind? Well, they are many, and I will deal with the negatives first. An *amitié* has most of the charms and none of the risks of a mild love affair, which makes it specially suitable both to the middle-aged and the happily married. Adultery even in these days is a tricky enterprise; fewer people than you would suppose are willing to undertake it. There is the nuisance of secrecy, obligatory if good manners are to be observed, but dreadful for the nerves. There is the problem of where to go—a formidable one, except in novels, where everyone is so passionate, and where at least one of the lovers always has a flat, and there are no children, resident relations, servants, or office hours to be contended with. Theatres and restaurants are out of bounds, for there is always somebody one knows, and it is death to be seen together. Oh dear me, no, it is a full-time occupation, fraught with anxiety and upsetting to the nourishing calm of middle-aged life. Nobody should embark on it who hasn't got nerves of steel and a secret willingness to face all possible consequences.

Whereas this other pastime, which for want of a better word I am calling *amitié*, has all the comforts of openness because there is nothing, or should be nothing, to conceal. The most devoted husband and wife are the better for an occasional outing with somebody else, and in midde age it is usually assumed safe for them to have one. There is nothing like it for morale, for *amour propre*, for all those things that are better expressed in French. Men as well as women are sensitive on the subject of growing old, and few things are more reassuring than a leisurely luncheon, a flatteringly confidential talk, a theatre, a dinner, an occasional exchange of letters with an attractive but safely independent contemporary. It is a marginal form of love, to be sure, which blesses these quiet intimacies, but not to be despised. Once one was too young for it: soon one will be too old: the happiest people are those who are grateful for the interval.

It takes a special sort of man to be adept in this relation. He must *like* women, and I suppose it is a sad truth that only a few of them do. He must feel cherished in their company and able to enjoy a friendship in which sex plays only a symbolic and implicit part. He must also be good company himself, a pleasing talker, agreeable to look at, discreet as well as amusing, if possible a man one has known for a very long time. Such men are rare: their price is above rubies. It is also an asset, I must confess, if they are comfortably off, able to afford a taxi and used to the best restaurants. I do not think they should be *too* distinguished, for then people stare, and one is obliged to feel uncomfortably grateful. Nor should they be *too* popular, for that can be tiresome too; it is no fun lunching with a fascinator who is constantly being signalled from other tables.

The same requirements apply to the woman, though in a different order. (She need not have money, though if the man is hard-up this is to be recommended.) She should look nice, be cheerful and not stupid, a good listener, a sympathetic talker, never woebegone, never bowed down by domestic or (God forbid) medical problems. She should also be quite free from the illusion that she is being taken out to lunch because the man is in love with her. It is an advantage for her to be happily married, but a tactful woman will not talk about her husband. (Or if she does, not much; enthusiasm should be taken for granted, not stated.) Adepts understand these rules, and conversation is the better for them.

Everyone knows that falling in love, in the initial stages before the hells begin, acts as a tonic. Does it cause the adrenalin to flow, I wonder, or some other magical elixir of transformation? Looks improve, the weather brightens, wits sparkle, the sound of the telephone is interesting, a delicious buoyancy sets in. At the onset of an *amitié amoureuse* the symptoms are milder, of course, but they do one good. It is a homeopathic dose, small, but beneficial. There are no shattering reactions, no tears, no sleepless nights; nothing, in fact, but a subtle gilding of all the edges of life, comforting the heart, the spirits, and the digestion.

It would be a mistake to think of the *amitié amoureuse* as a purely latter-day pleasure, due to common sense and sexual tolerance. I sometimes think the Victorians were better at it than we are. Look at Dickens's many emotional levitations. (I am not thinking of Ellen Ternan, but of several well-behaved ladies before her time.) Look at Carlyle and Lady Ashburnham. Browning, I believe, was both vulnerable and respectable, and even Mrs. Gaskell in middle life enjoyed a blameless *tendresse* for Charles Eliot Norton. And to go still further back, what friendship of the heart is more justly celebrated than that of Dr. Johnson and Mrs. Thrale? It is true poor Dr. Johnson behaved badly when Mrs. Thrale was a widow and in love with Piozzi, but his anger at her second marriage, his unforgivable letter, are simply the measure of his emotional outrage. He had for years enjoyed her patient friendship, her flattering attentions, her lively and intelligent company, and the cruelty of her finally preferring a musician's company to his own was what his heart failed under.

The continued ability to fall slightly in love from time to time, cherishing the sensation for its own sake without rushing to the fray, is really the gift that makes the whole thing possible. Falling slightly in love is no problem, even when youth is past. It is tasting the marzipan and leaving the plum-cake alone which is the discipline essential for survival.

AFTERTHOUGHT

IT OCCURS to me that some readers may like to pursue the subjects of these essays on their own, but may be at a loss to know where to find further information about, say, Flora Thompson, the Countess of Huntingdon, Lord Ferrers, or even Jean Henri Fabre. (All the others are easily found in any good library.) There is no biography of Flora Thompson, but her trilogy of novels is published as one volume, *Lark Rise to Candleford*, in The World's Classics (Oxford University Press), and O.U.P. have also recently republished a later work, *Still Glides the Stream*. The fullest account of Lady Huntingdon's life is an obsequiously pious work in two volumes, *The Life and Times of Selina Countess of Huntingdon*, by 'A Member of the Houses of Shirley and Hastings,' published in 1840. There is also *Lady Huntingdon and her Friends* by H. C. Knight (1853), *The Countess of Huntingdon and her Circle* by Sarah Tytler (1907), and a chapter in Ronald Knox's book on the eighteenth-century religious revival, *Enthusiasm* (Oxford: Clarendon Press; 1950).

The best account of Lord Ferrers is to be found in Howell's *State Trials*, Vol. XIX (1813). Fabre's great work, *Souvenirs Entomologiques*, is in most good libraries, and there are excellent translations of parts of this work by A. Teixeira de Mattos and others. Dr. R. W. Chapman's editions of the letters of Samuel Johnson and of Jane

Austen are easily available; they are great masterpieces of scholarship and sources of pleasure. His own essays are harder to come by, and of these *The Portrait of a Scholar and Other Essays Written in Macedonia* (1920) is worth searching for.

M. L.

A Note About the Author

Margaret Lane, daughter of a newspaper editor, was born in Cheshire, England. An Oxford graduate, she started her writing career on Fleet Street and spent some time in America as a free-lance journalist. Her first novel, *Faith, Hope, No Charity*, was published in 1935 after she returned to England and was awarded the Prix Iémina Vie Heureuse. It was followed by several other books of fiction, and later of nonfiction, among which her book on the Brontës is considered an outstanding literary biography. After many years she again wrote a novel, *A Night at Sea*, which was a success on both sides of the Atlantic, and the next year, 1966, its sequel, *A Smell of Burning*, appeared. Margaret Lane is married to the Earl of Huntingdon and they live in London and in the New Forest.

A Note on the Type

The text of this book is set in Monticello, a Linotype revival of the original Binny & Ronaldson Roman No. 1, cut by Archibald Binny and cast in 1796 by that Philadelphia type foundry. The face was named Monticello in honor of its use in the monumental fifty-volume *Papers of Thomas Jefferson*, published by Princeton University Press. Monticello is a transitional type design, embodying certain features of Bulmer and Baskerville, but is a distinguished face in its own right.

This book was composed, printed, and bound by Kingsport Press, Inc., Kingsport, Tenn. Typography and binding design by Guy Fleming.